16.99

South East Essex College
of Arts & Technology

THE EUROPEAN BUSINESS ENVIRONMENT

THE EUROPEAN BUSINESS ENVIRONMENT

Edited by

Neill Nugent and Rory O'Donnell

MACMILLAN

First published 1994 by
THE MACMILLAN PRESS LTD
Houndmills, Basingstoke, Hampshire RG21 2XS
and London
Companies and representatives
throughout the world

ISBN 0–333–56642–4 hardcover
ISBN 0–333–56643–2 paperback

A catalogue record for this book is available
from the British Library.

Printed in Great Britain by
Mackays of Chatham PLC
Chatham, Kent

Contents

List of contributors

Walter Cairns is Senior Lecturer in Law and Languages at Manchester Metropolitan University.

John Fahy is Lecturer in Strategic Marketing at Trinity College, Dublin.

David Jacobson is Senior Lecturer in Economics at Dublin City University.

John A. Murray is Professor of Business Studies at Trinity College, Dublin.

Neill Nugent is Professor of Politics at Manchester Metropolitan University.

Rory O'Donnell is Director of the National Economic and Social Council, Dublin.

Martin Rhodes is Lecturer in Government at Manchester University.

Peter A. Vipond is Principal Lecturer in Financial Services at London Guildhall University.

List of abbreviations and acronyms

ACP   African, Caribbean and Pacific countries
BRITE   Basic Research in Industrial Technologies of Europe
BTG   British Technology Group
CAP   Common Agricultural Policy
CCP   Common Commercial Policy
CCITT   International Telephone and Telegraph Consultative Committee
CCT   Common Customs Tariff
CEA   European Insurance Committee
CEA   Energy Commission (France)
CEEP   European Centre of Public Enterprises
CEFIC   European Chemical Industry Federation
CEN   European Committee for Standardisation
CENELEC   European Committee for Electrotechnical Standardisation
CET   Common External Tariff
CNES   National Centre for Space Studies (France)
CNET   National Centre for the Study of Telecommunications (France)
CNRS   (French) National Centre for Scientific Research
COREPER   Committee of Permanent Representatives
DGA   Delegation Genérale a l'Armament
DSU   Deficit Spending Unit
EAGGF   European Agricultural Guidance and Guarantee Fund
EBRD   European Bank for Reconstruction and Development
EC   European Community
ECJ   European Court of Justice
ECU   European Currency Unit
EEA   European Economic Area
EEC   European Economic Community
EFA   European Financial Area
EFE   European Financial Environment
EFPIA   European Federation of Pharmaceutical Industry Associations
EFTA   European Free Trade Association
EIB   European Investment Bank
EMS   European Monetary System

EMU	Economic and Monetary Union
EP	European Parliament
ERDF	European Regional Development Fund
ERM	Exchange Rate Mechanism
ESF	European Social Fund
ESPRIT	European Strategic Programme for Research in Information Technology
ETUC	European Trade Union Confederation
EU	European Union
EUREKA	European Programme for High Technology Research and Development
FAST	Forecasting and Assessment in Science and Technology
FDI	Foreign Direct Investment
FRS	Financial Reporting Statement
GAAP	Generally Agreed Accounting Principles
GATT	General Agreement on Tariffs and Trade
GDP	Gross Domestic Product
GERD	Gross Domestic Expenditure on Research and Development
GNP	Gross National Product
GSM	Groupe Speciale Mobile
IAS	International Accounting Standards
IASC	International Accounting Standards Committee
ICT	Information and Communication Technologies
IEPG	Independent European Programme Group
IMF	International Monetary Fund
IOSCO	International Organisation of Securities Commission
ISDN	Integrated Services Digital Network
JV	Joint Venture
MAAs	Mergers, Acquisitions and Strategic Alliances
MEP	Member of the European Parliament
MFA	Multifibre Arrangement
MNC	Multinational Company
NAFTA	North American Free Trade Area
NATO	North Atlantic Treaty Organisation
NEB	National Enterprise Board (UK)
NSI	National System of Innovation
NTB	Non-Tariff Barrier
ONERA	National Office of Aeronautical Studies and Research (France)
OECD	Organisation for Economic Cooperation and Development
PTO	Public Telecommunications Operators
RACE	Research in Advanced Communications for Europe
R & D	Research and Development
S & T	Science and Technology
SEA	Single European Act
SEC	Securities and Exchange Commission

SEM	Single European Market
SME	Small and medium-sized Enterprise
SSAP	Statement of Standard Accounting Practice
SSU	Surplus Spending Unit
STAR	Special Telecommunications Actions for Regions
TBP	Technology Balance of Payments
TEU	Treaty on European Union
UK	United Kingdom
UNICE	Union of Industries of the European Community
USA	United States of America
VAT	Value Added Tax
VER	Voluntary Export Restraint

Introduction

Neill Nugent and Rory O'Donnell

A EUROPEAN BUSINESS ENVIRONMENT?

The context, or the environment, in which business is conducted is subject to rapid change in modern industrial societies. However, the nature and the depth of the change which has occurred in Europe in recent years has been particularly dramatic, with political, economic, legal, social, technological and other forms of change combining to bring about what amounts to a transformation of the business environment.

A central feature, arguably *the* central feature, of this transformation is its *Europeanisation*. Europe, and more particularly Western Europe, is rapidly strengthening its identity in many different respects, and as it does so it is becoming ever more important as a framework for, and as a focus of, business activity. The implications of 'the European dimension' for the structure, for the conduct, and for the scope of business activity are now very considerable indeed.

At the heart of this emerging European business environment is a fledgling European economy, in which national economies are increasingly interconnected and interdependent, in which national economic policies and policy approaches are increasingly coordinated, and in which the regulatory regime to which business is subject is increasingly European-wide. Key features of this developing European economy, and associated European business environment, include the following:

• Amongst the member states of the European Union (EU)[1] there has been, since the mid-1980s, a vigorous push to create a Single European Market (SEM). The SEM, which incorporates the economies of all the member states of the EU, and which also extends most of its provisions to the member states of the European Free Trade Association (EFTA),[2] has created, in effect, an economic zone covering virtually the whole of Western Europe, in which there is

1

(apart from some restrictions which apply to the EFTA states) virtual free movement of goods, services, capital and labour.
• Many of the laws, rules and policies which govern and shape economic and business activity in Western Europe are now determined at European rather than national level. This is most obviously the case in the EU, where a wide variety of microeconomic decisions are already taken by EU authorities, and where macroeconomic decisions will increasingly be so too if the projected plans for the creation of Economic and Monetary Union (EMU) are ever realised. But European economic and business decision-making does not occur just within the framework of the EU, as is demonstrated, for example, by the wide variety of matters which are covered in the context of EU-EFTA deliberations (in what is known as the European Economic Area), and by the laying down of European specifications on goods and products in European standards bodies.
• West European trade has a very strong regional character, with intra-EU trade accounting for just over 60 per cent of total EU trade – a figure which rises to just over 70 per cent if EFTA countries are added. All EU member states conduct over 50 per cent of their trade with other member states – with Denmark, Germany and the UK being the lowest (each being in the region of 55 per cent) and Belgium/Luxembourg (for whom figures are jointly collected), Ireland and Portugal being the highest (each being in the region of 74 per cent). Intra-European trade has been the fastest growing element of trade for both EU and EFTA countries for some years.
• The EU presents a common front to the outside world on trading matters. That is to say, the member states of the EU, protected by a Common External Tarrif (CET) and on the basis of a Common Commercial Policy (CCP), act as one in international trading negotiations. Pursuing a policy that is, in most respects, liberal, and not of the 'Fortress Europe' kind which some non-EU states claim to have detected, the EU is a very powerful international trading bloc.
• If attention is moved beyond Western Europe to the former republics and satellite states of the Soviet Union, the transformation towards capitalism that is occurring there, coupled with the trading agreements which have been contracted between the EU and Central and Eastern European countries, opens up the possibility of, in time, a European-wide economy and business environment.

A strong case can thus be made out for suggesting that a European – or, more accurately, a West European – economy and business environment are rapidly emerging and, in some respects, already exist. They are being driven and shaped by a wide variety of forces, not least the increasing European orientation of much of business itself, much of which consciously sees itself as not only *responding* to Europeanisation but also *creating* a Europeanisation of markets and of companies.

Recognition of the existence of a European economy and of a European business environment must, however, be placed in the context of a recognition of other economies and other environments. Business is also profoundly affected by what happens at the national and global levels.

Regarding the national level, many very important differences continue to exist between the countries of Europe in respect of such key variables for business as patterns of training, skills, industrial relations, financing, innovation, attitudes, and behaviour. Although there has been a gradual 'flattening out' of variations in the policies pursued by national governments, differences still exist over wide areas of economic and market-related policies. As for business companies themselves, many of the most powerful firms in Europe, though extensively involved in global and European activities, retain a 'home base' to which they are, in many respects, tied.

Regarding the global level, economic and business life in Europe is clearly strongly shaped by a range of international factors. Amongst the most important of these are: the multilateral liberalism of trade which has characterised the post World War II period; the dramatic internationalisation of money and capital markets which, since the 1970s, has led to a phenomenal growth in global capital flows; and the emergence of powerful industrial competitors in hitherto inward-looking or underdeveloped parts of the world.

In so far as a European business environment can be said to exist, it must thus be understood within the context of the other environments, national and global, which provide the framework for the conduct and operation of business activity.

THE FOCUS ON THE EUROPEAN UNION

In terms of its geographical 'scope', the main focus of this book is on the European Union and its member states. In focusing on the EU, attention is directed at one of the world's major economic zones. The economies of the EU countries are, when taken together, comparable in size to the world's largest national economy – the USA – and are much larger than Japan. A few figures may be cited to illustrate the economic importance and strength of the EU:

• The member states of the EU have a combined population of over 340 million people, as compared with a US population of 252 million and a Japanese population of 124 million.

• The combined Gross Domestic Product (GDP) of the EU countries accounts for around 24.8 per cent of world GDP. This places it very slightly ahead of the USA, which accounts for around 24.1 per cent, and well ahead of Japan which accounts for 16.1 per cent.

• EU exports to the rest of the world account for about 20 per cent of world exports, whilst imports account for about 16 per cent of world imports. The comparable figures for the USA are 12 per cent and 15 per cent, and for Japan

9 per cent and 7 per cent. The EU is, thus, the world's largest external trading bloc.

As well as identifying the key features of the European business environment at both EU and national levels – and, where appropriate, at global and regional levels too – it is also a central concern of this book to assess the relative importance of the levels and of the interrelationships between them. A recurring theme of all the chapters is that whilst many business-related matters are now best understood and analysed at the EU, rather than the national, level, the extent to which Europeanisation is occurring is both partial and uneven.

THE DIVERSITY OF BUSINESS AND OF BUSINESS ACTIVITY

There are, approximately, 16 million enterprises in the EU. These vary widely in many respects – size, sector, market-focus, public-private ownership, internal structure, financial base, etc. To give just three examples of variations:

1. *Size*: Large enterprises (500 or more employees) account for almost 30 per cent of jobs in the EU, small and medium-sized enterprises (10–99 employees) account for 41 per cent, and microenterprises (1–9 employees) account for 29 per cent. On average, there are about 45 enterprises per 1000 people in the EU, with the ratio ranging from about 30 in The Netherlands, Germany and Denmark to more than 60 in Portugal and Greece. (These figures mean, of course, that there are many more larger firms in the former three countries than there are in the latter two.)
2. *Sector*: At EU level the service sector accounts for about 63 per cent of GDP and 60 per cent of employment, the industrial sector for about 34 per cent and 33 per cent, and agriculture for about 3 per cent and 7 per cent. At the national level there are variations within these total EU figures, most notably with respect to agriculture which is more important in the southern countries and in Ireland than it is in the northern countries.
3. *Private-public ownership*: In all EU member states business is conducted primarily by private sector firms, but in all states public sector firms are also to be found – most commonly in connection with public utilities and natural monopolies. The forms and the extent of public ownership vary enormously, but, in general terms, it can be said that state-run companies account for around 12 per cent of economic activity in the EU.

Given such heterogeneity in the nature of businesses and of business activity, it is clearly not possible to provide in one book a detailed analysis of all the aspects of the business environment which apply to all forms of business. Attention is therefore focused in the chapters which follow on the principal features of the overall business environment and on the characteristics which have implications across the business spectrum.

THE STRUCTURE OF THE BOOK

In most situations the conduct of business involves three elements or stages: (1) the *acquisition* of resources, such as labour, capital equipment, materials, and property rights; (2) the *production* of a good or service; and (3) *distribution* and *sale*. This book examines the different environments which shape these elements of the business process.

In Chapter 1 Neill Nugent considers the political environment. This involves examining the wide range of EU and national policies and decision-making processes which impact on business. Amongst the themes to emerge from the analysis are: the increasing extent to which business-related policies are determined at the EU level; the increasing convergence of national policies since the early 1980s, but the continuance of some significant differences between EU countries; and the persistence of variations in national policy processes, not least in regard to the way in which business interacts with policy-makers.

Rory O'Donnell examines the overall economic environment in Chapter 2. Stress is laid on the fact that economic activity is conducted at several levels – the local and regional, the national, the European, and the global. Particular concerns of the chapter are: the principal structural features of EU national economies; the grand economic designs of the EU – notably the building of the SEM and of EMU; and the place and priorities of the EU in the global trading system.

The legal dimension of the European business environment is examined by Walter Cairns in Chapter 3. He begins with an introduction to the different legal traditions of the EU member states and then proceeds to an examination of the major similarities and differences in the business law of those states. The development and nature of EU law is then traced – from its origins in the Founding Treaties of the European Community in the 1950s to the complex mixture of treaty, legislative and judicial processes that are now interwoven together in the EU's legal make-up. The chapter concludes with an explanation of the substantive content of EU business law, with particular attention given to how it applies to the SEM.

Labour is a key resource in business activity and, consequently, the labour market and labour relations are a highly significant element of the European business environment. In Chapter 4, Martin Rhodes shows that developments on this front must be seen in the context of changes in the nature of employment and unemployment in Europe. He identifies three patterns of labour market regulation – 'Northern', 'Mediterranean' and 'Anglo-Saxon' – and shows that each of these embodies different dimensions of flexibility. The existence of these different traditions is important in explaining why there has been only

limited EU-level action as regards the regulation of labour markets, and why
there has been stiff opposition to the creation of EU-level labour relations.
Instead of, as many would like, pursuing the Europeanisation or internationalisation *of* labour market regulation and labour relations, the EU has tended to
concern itself more with what might be seen as the unavoidable implications
of Europeanisation and internationalisation *for* labour market regulation and
labour relations – namely, deregulation and reductions of workers' rights.

In Chapter 5, Peter Vipond examines the financing, reporting and taxation
of business activity. The movement towards the creation of a European Financial Area (EFA) is outlined and is set in the context of the wider internationalisation of financial markets. Attention is also drawn to some of the important
traditional differences between EU countries in terms of the nature of their
financial systems and how these relate to business. Whilst recognising the
continued relevance of both national and global financial environments, Vipond
argues that achievement of European goals requires some regulation of financial markets and financial institutions at European level.

Those aspects of the business environment which affect the ability of business
to develop and manage successful transactions with their target customers are
analysed by John Murray and John Fahy in Chapter 6 on the marketing
environment. Features of what they regard as an emerging European-wide
marketing environment, and ways of understanding this environment, are
explored. The authors suggest that factors such as firm rivalry, entry threats,
substitution possibilities, and the changing bargaining powers of buyers and
sellers, all point to a European market that is, and increasingly will be, characterised by intensified competition, increased uncertainty in some sectors, and
widespread restructuring. It is also stressed in the chapter that the debate about
the extent to which a pan-European market is becoming established is a variant
of a wider debate on the globalisation of markets. Murray and Fahy suggest
that each of these debates is badly framed and they offer an alternative framework which transcends the polarised conception of markets as being *either*
international, European, national, or local.

The business environment in which European firms operate is strongly
shaped by the technology and infrastructure that is available to them. These
aspects of the business environment are examined by David Jacobson in Chapter 7. As regards technology, the larger EU states are compared in terms of the
strengths and weaknesses of their national systems of innovation (NSIs), the EU
as a whole is compared with its main trading competitors, and the question is
asked whether a European system of innovation is emerging. The point
is emphasised that whilst the EU has sought to Europeanise aspects of innovation – most notably by promoting Research and Development (R & D) – its
outputs have been modest when set alongside the impact of NSIs and the
forces of global technological change. As regards infrastructure, attention is
focused on transport and telecommunications, with the point being made that
whilst Europeanisation and globalisation are most certainly having a decided

impact, especially on telecommunications, national structures and preferences continue to be important – with significant consequences for business.

THE RATIONALE OF THE BOOK

This is not a book which directly concerns itself with business skills. Nor is it a manual or a catalogue which is focused on listing and detailing the 'hard facts' on matters such as market sizes, market shares and market opportunities. Rather it is a book which examines, in an analytical and discursive manner, the key aspects of the different environments in which business in Europe, and more particularly business in the European Union, is conducted.

Each of the contributors has written to the same general brief: namely, to identify, and consider the implications of, the principal features of their subject areas at national and EU levels and, where necessary, to note the importance of other levels too. This they have done, although the very different nature of much of their subject material has naturally resulted in some differences in approach.

It is our hope that the book will be of use and of interest to both students and practitioners of business in Europe.

Notes

1. The European Union (EU) was constituted by the 1992 Treaty on European Union ('The Maastricht Treaty') which came into force on 1 November 1993. The EU developed out of the European Community (EC) and contains the EC within its ambit. At the time of writing (early 1994), the member states of the EU are: Belgium, Denmark, France, Germany, Greece, Ireland, Italy, Luxembourg, The Netherlands, Portugal, Spain and the United Kingdom. The nature of the EU, and its relationships to the EC, are explained in Chapter 1.
2. The European Free Trade Association was founded in 1960. At the time of writing, its member states are: Austria, Finland, Iceland, Liechtenstein, Norway, Sweden and Switzerland. The membership of EFTA is likely to diminish in the mid–1990s, with some of its members leaving to join the EU.

CHAPTER 1

The political environment

Neill Nugent

WHAT IS THE POLITICAL ENVIRONMENT?

The political environment of business in Europe varies between countries and within countries varies over time. There are, in broad terms, two main aspects of this environment.

The first aspect is the policies and the decisions of politicians and public officials which affect business. At a general level, the importance of this aspect of the political environment is seen most obviously in differences between countries regarding the balance between market forces and public intervention in the functioning of their economies. At more specific levels, the importance is seen in the many different ways in which public decision-makers – including those who place great faith in the merits of markets – intervene to guide, shape, control, regulate, stimulate and offset market activities and consequences.

The nature of what might be thought of as 'business policies' has changed somewhat in recent times. Until the 1970s the policies of many West European governments were based in no small part on management of domestic economic demand and – in some countries much more than others – relied heavily on state support for what were seen as important sectors and industries. When, however, from around the early 1970s, it became evident that European business was losing much of its competitive power in such traditional strongholds as steel, textiles, cars and electrical equipment, and that it was also finding it extremely difficult to compete in the new high-tech industries, the attention of governments turned increasingly to supply side policies. These policies were in many respects more specifically focused than the rather blunt policy instruments associated with traditional demand management, and they also embraced a greater focus on the efficiency and competitiveness of business.

The second main aspect of the political environment is the processes and mechanisms by which business-related policies and decisions are made. The most obvious focus of analysis in this regard is national governments. They, after all, are ultimately accountable for the functioning of national economies. However, it must be recognised that whilst nation states are very important economic units, and whilst many important decisions affecting economic and business activity are taken at the national level – and in some countries at subnational levels too – it is increasingly the case that many key matters are now decided at levels 'above' the nation state. At the global level, forums in which important decisions are taken include the General Agreement on Tariffs and Trade (GATT), the International Monetary Fund (IMF), and Western Economic Summits. At the international regional level the most important forum in Europe is, by far, the European Union (EU). This movement 'upwards' – from the national to the transnational level – marks a fundamental change in the political environment of business and is a reflection of the increasing internationalisation of markets, trade and finance.

Having established that the political environment of business consists of public policies and decisions which affect business, and the processes and mechanisms by which these policies and decisions are made, the question arises as to what areas of policy do affect business. The short answer is that a great many do. There are policies for different business processes: for extraction, for manufacturing, for construction. There are policies for different stages of the productive cycle: for development, for production, for distribution. And there are policies for expanding/contracting sectors, for labour intensive/capital intensive sectors, for large firms/small firms, etc.

In terms of the ways in which governments make divisions between policy areas, some policies have very clear and direct implications for business, others have less direct, but still very important implications, and only a very few have limited implications. So, taxation policy, monetary policy and competition policy are amongst the policies which clearly fall into the first of these categories. Policies falling into the second category include environmental policy (pollution laws can dictate production processes and can significantly affect production costs), education policy (technically advanced economies require well-educated and trained workforces), and transport policy (transport infrastructure can influence business location and can affect both production and distribution costs). Public order policy and health policy are examples of policy areas which fall into the third category, but even their implications for business are not without significance.

Clearly then a very great range of policies may be said to be business related and, therefore, of interest to us here. This chapter does not attempt to examine all these policies in detail, but focuses rather on their general nature and on the decision-making processes associated with them. The examination is organised into four sections, with policies and decision-making processes each examined at both national and EU levels.

NATIONAL POLICIES

All European governments want businesses which are based and conducted within their countries to be successful. They do so because business success is the essential condition of a successful economy and a successful economy is a central aim of governments. It is a central aim for several reasons: a growing economy facilitates the furtherance of many specific policy goals – increasing the prosperity of citizens, improving education and health services, extending social welfare provision, etc.; perceptions by electorates of governmental economic performance and future economic prospects are usually crucial in determining the outcomes of elections; a strong economy can enhance a country's influence and negotiating power in international economic and political forums; and a government which is seen to be presiding over a vigorous and healthy economy is usually well judged and admired by other governments.

Governments are, therefore, normally anxious to do all they can to ensure that business and national economies perform as well as possible. However, governments often disagree about what 'performing well' means – is, for example, the first priority high economic growth, low inflation, or low unemployment? Furthermore, those governments that do share broadly similar objectives often disagree over the best means of achieving their goals – the disagreements being explained either by the existence of objectively different situations or by subscriptions to different analyses of what are, and what is the relative importance of, the key economic mechanisms. As a result, significant differences are apparent between countries, and within countries between governments of different party political compositions, regarding the policies that are followed.

There are many ways in which the governments of the EU member states intervene in economies which have implications for, or are specifically directed at, business. These can be grouped under five – in practice interconnected and overlapping – headings: macroeconomic and financial policies; policies designed specifically for business; governments as regulators; the role and importance of public ownership; and governments as customers.

Macroeconomic and financial policies

Macroeconomic policies affect not only business but society as a whole. In determining their nature governments are, therefore, obliged to take on board many considerations in addition to their implications for business.

Examples of macroeconomic and financial policies, with illustrations of some of their particular implications for business, include the following: exchange rate policy – an overvalued currency undermines the competitiveness of exports and makes imports cheaper, whilst an undervalued currency does the reverse; interest rate policy – high interest rates discourage, and low interest rates encourage, business investment; fiscal policy – corporation tax levels affect company profitability, personal income tax levels affect disposable incomes and therefore consumer demand, and indirect tax levels on goods and services affect the price of goods and services and therefore also affect the level and pattern of consumer demand; public expenditure policy – levels of public expenditure, and policy priorities therein, affect, amongst other things, the amount and nature of economic activity in state-owned firms and determine the extent to which public services such as health, education, defence, road construction and sewerage can give contracts to, and can make purchases from, private business firms.

One of the most important economic developments in the EU in recent years has been the way in which some of the macroeconomic policy instruments just mentioned, in particular exchange rate and interest rate adjustments, can no longer be so easily used by governments as in the past. A key reason for this is the establishment of the European Monetary System (EMS) and its associated Exchange Rate Mechanism (ERM), and, more broadly, the movement towards Economic and Monetary Union (EMU). The ERM of the EMS has as its purpose the creation of exchange rate stability which, in turn, places restraints on national economic and monetary policies. (Hence the pleasure expressed in some circles in the UK when sterling was obliged to withdraw from the ERM in the autumn of 1992.) EMU implies a convergence of key aspects of national economic and monetary policies and performances. (See below and Chapter 2 for a fuller explanation of the nature of, and problems associated with, the EMS and EMU.)

Policies designed specifically for business

Sitting alongside macroeconomic policies are numerous policies which are specifically designed for business. Some of these are medium-range policies which have implications for many spheres and aspects of business activity, whilst others are more narrowly focused and are directed at particular business activities, sectors, and even individual firms.

Such is the number and variety of these policies that it is not possible to identify them all here. The most important of them, however, constitute part of three broad policy areas:

• *Competition policies*: Since around the early 1980s, competition policies in most West European countries have become more fully developed and vigorous. In some cases predating, in others following, the movement towards strong competition policies at EU level, the purpose of such policies is to give a greater emphasis to the role of the market as an enhancer of business efficiency and competitiveness. Some EU countries have been more enthusiastic about competition policies than others – the UK has been to the fore and Italy to the rear – but all have become at least a little less sympathetic than they used to be to state subsidies, to anti-competitive mergers and to cartels between companies.

• *Industrial policies*: The increasing emphasis at both national and EU levels on the role of the market has obliged governments to reconsider the nature of their industrial policies. Industrial policy used to be as much about managing decline as stimulating expansion, but since about the mid–1980s the balance has tilted so that industrial policy in most countries is now focused more towards promoting potential growth industries, especially in the advanced technology sectors. A problem with industrial policy is that it frequently involves dispensing state aid of some kind – usually in the form of investment grants, loan assistance or cash subsidies – which means that it does not always sit easily alongside national and EU competition policies. The car industry, for example, has seen many such tensions, with the pivotal role of the industry leading to frequent government intervention in several states and a reluctance to stand aside and let market underperformance take its natural course.

• *Policies for services and for small- and medium-sized enterprises (SMEs)*: The decline of much traditional large-scale manufacturing industry, coupled with the high capital and low labour intensities of many of the new high-tech industries, has forced governments to think much more than they did formerly about policies which can assist both the services sector and SMEs. Regarding services, policies range from attempts to provide favourable conditions for the expanding financial services sector to infrastructure projects designed to promote tourism. Regarding SMEs, the preferred policy has been to use public authorities and agencies as facilitators – through, for example, the establishment of advice and information agencies, and the provision of loan guarantee and loan subsidy schemes to assist business 'start-ups'.

Governments as regulators

Governments, or government approved bodies, lay down laws and standards for the conduct of business activity. They do so for two main reasons. First, they wish to improve the functioning of the market. This they attempt to do by, for example, prohibiting restrictive practices (and thereby hopefully stimulating competition), and specifying what constitutes a commercial contract (and thereby hopefully enhancing business confidence). Second, they wish to provide protection to those who are active in, or are affected by, the market. This is attempted by such measures as specifying health and safety standards on marketed products, laying down entry requirements for those who wish to practise a trade or profession, and controlling the emission of pollutants into the environment.

The extent to which business is subject to regulation varies both between countries and between sectors. Regarding countries, business has traditionally been subject to greater regulation in the more advanced and industrialised countries of Northern Europe than in the poorer and less industrialised countries of Southern Europe. This is still just about so, but – following economic advancement in the South, and a certain amount of deregulation in the North – not as much as previously. Regarding sectors, there are considerable variations, but in general terms regulation tends to be at its most encompassing and strongest where at least one of the following three sets of circumstances applies: (1) important public health and safety issues arise – such as they do in respect of many aspects of the chemicals and pharmaceuticals industries, transport services, and public utilities such as gas, electricity and water; (2) asymmetric information is available to buyers and sellers – as in the insurance industry; (3) the effects of business failure would have consequences far beyond the firms immediately involved – as in banking.

In addition to variations in the amount of regulatory activity to which business is subject, there are also variations in the processes and mechanisms by which regulation is effected. These processes and mechanisms can be thought of as being spread along a spectrum on which, at one end, business is self-regulatory, at the other end, government is the regulator, and in between there is a variety of mixed and shared systems. Where a business activity or sector is placed on the spectrum depends on many factors. These include: the extent to which important vested interests have lobbied for self-regulatory powers; the existence of appropriate and representative business associations able to undertake the task of self-regulation; the extent to which only business itself has the knowledge and expertise necessary for regulation to be possible; and the cost to government of employing sufficient numbers of inspectors for effective regulation. Chemicals, financial services, and leisure/tourism are examples of very different business sectors where a considerable measure of self-regulation is permitted by governments.

Irrespective, however, of the extent and form that regulation takes in European countries, deregulation has been increasingly in vogue since the late 1970s/early 1980s. This has stemmed from a growing belief that excessive regulation – of productive processes, of retailing, of labour markets, etc. – undermines competitiveness. The extent of deregulation has varied between countries, but the spirit has been widely shared, driven forward in no small part by the Single European Market (SEM) programme, which has obliged all EU member states to dismantle many of the national standards and specifications which are deemed to have protectionist consequences.

The role and importance of public ownership

There is widespread public ownership of business activity throughout Western Europe. It comes in four main forms: nationalisations – as, for example, with most national railway companies; controlling shareholdings – these are common in France where they are found in industries as diverse as steel, pharmaceuticals, and computing; use of state banks – in Greece, for example, state banks own many large companies; and use of state holding companies – these are especially important in Italy and, to a lesser extent, in Spain.

Much of the business activity which is located in the public sector takes the form of natural monopolies and/or was largely pioneered and developed by states themselves when national economies were taking their modern form. In consequence, utilities, transport, energy, postal services, telecommunications, and exploitation of national resources are the areas of economic activity where public enterprise is most commonly found, although it does also exist to some extent in 'mainstream' business sectors, including manufacturing. Where there is particularly extensive public ownership – as in France, Italy and Greece – it is usually a consequence of one or more of the following three factors: ideological legacy (France has experienced three major nationalisation waves – the 1936–7 Popular Front, the post-war Liberation, and the 1981–3 Mitterrand 'socialist period'); political resistance to change (Italy's public sector is highly politicised and very closely tied in with national decision-makers); and a desire on the part of governments either to protect declining industries (such as steel and shipbuilding) or to promote expanding high-tech industries (such as computers and electronics). The last of these factors has created considerable difficulties in the context of those EU laws and policies which lay down restrictions on state aid to business, since governments are usually more tempted to make available, and if necessary find it easier to conceal, aids of various kinds to enterprises in the public sector than to enterprises in the private sector.

Since the early to mid–1980s most governments have responded to the increasing emphasis on competition in Western Europe by making their public enterprises, or at least aspects of their activities, more sensitive to market forces. There has also been some movement in the direction of privatisation: in the UK around 40 per cent of what had been in public ownership in 1980 had been sold into private hands by the end of the decade; in France the 1986–8 conservative government sold off FFr120 billion of public sector companies in twenty-nine flotations, whilst the conservative government which assumed office in 1993 announced plans for another twenty-one companies – including some of France's largest and best known – to be sold; in Greece, the removal from power of the socialists in the 1990 elections saw the introduction of a major privatisation plan, though in the event a mixture of political and practical problems resulted in it being only very partially implemented before the social-ists returned to office in 1993; and in 1991–2 the Belgian, Italian and German governments all announced plans for sell-offs or partial sell-offs of state-owned companies.

Governments as customers

Governments and other public authorities are extremely important purchasers of products produced by business. This is especially so in industries such as defence equipment, roads and buildings construction, and – in those countries where hospitals are state owned – pharmaceuticals. Traditionally, public authorities have been guided not only by market forces but also by a range of other considerations in using their very considerable purchasing power. In particular, they have sought to use their power to help generate national and local economic growth, to stimulate or maintain economic activity in particular areas and locations, and to assist business sectors and firms that are in trouble. The use of public purchasing for such purposes is, however, now becoming more difficult: partly because of reduced levels of public expenditure in some countries – especially on defence equipment as a result of the post-Cold War 'peace dividend'; partly because many public authorities are becoming more sensitive to market pressures and are feeling obliged to accept the most competitive bids for contracts, rather than the bids which are most politically and socially acceptable; and partly because EU public procurement legislation now obliges public authorities in the member states to open up many types of tenders to non-domestic bidders.

All governments make some use of the full range of policies and policy instruments that have just been outlined. The particular mix they utilise, however, varies considerably, as may be illustrated by briefly contrasting Germany and France, the two largest West European economies.

German post-war policy has been designed primarily to ensure that the social market economy, which was created in the early post-war years, functions effectively. There are, as Horn has pointed out (1987, p. 43), three main aims of the social market economy:

1. The highest possible economic welfare through competition, steady economic growth, full employment and free international economic relations.
2. An efficient monetary framework – and in particular a stable average price level achieved through an independent central bank, stable budgets and balanced foreign accounts.
3. Social progress through maximisation of the national product, social security, and adequate redistribution of income and wealth.

As originally conceived, free enterprise was to be at the heart of the German social market system and the role of the government was to support the market rather than to be interventionist in it. In practice, however, there was never a completely hands-off approach, and over the years governments have been quite prepared to intervene so as to affect or to stimulate economic developments when they have judged it to be necessary. This has led many to wonder whether, particularly since the 1970s when intervention increased considerably, Germany can be said still to have a 'real' social market economy. Examples of governmental intervention include: contracting sectors (such as steel, shipbuilding and textiles) and growth sectors (such as aerospace, electronics and computers) have both long benefited from national and regional tax advantages and investment subsidies; the government has been very active – both as an employer itself and through financial assistance to the private sector – in encouraging and assisting technological innovation and the development of new processes and products; vocational education and job training and retraining have been generously funded; and various financial incentives designed to encourage industry to be 'environmentally friendly' have been made available. Additionally, in the special circumstances obtaining since German unification, massive sums of money have been injected into the territory of the former German Democratic Republic to help rebuild its economy.

French post-war policy has displayed less faith than German policy in the benefits of markets and has put more emphasis on the advantages which can accrue from government direction and management. This direction and management has taken four main forms. First, national economic plans have been used to try to shape and channel the development of economic activity. Having been quite influential in the 1940s and 1950s, the plans lost much of their significance in the 1960s and 1970s, but in the 1980s their role was partly reasserted when they were put on a much more decentralised basis and were allocated resources for purposes such as vocational training, industrial aid, and research and technological development. Second, there has been an almost continual commitment on the part of governments to direct state control of a substantial segment of French business and industry. (The extent of this control peaked in the mid–1980s when the state owned thirteen of the twenty largest firms in France and had a controlling share in many others.) Third, the heavy reliance of the French system of finance on credit, coupled with the strong influence of the government on the cost and allocation of that credit, have been used to try to boost particular business sectors (especially in high-tech industries) and to assist particular firms (especially those which are seen as being, or as potentially being, 'national champions'). Fourth, considerable amounts of state aid – in various guises – have been dispensed to both declining and expanding sectors and firms. Prominent amongst the beneficiaries of state aid have been the steel, computing, electronics, aerospace and motor industries.

But just as the German social market approach has far from excluded public intervention in the economic life of the nation, so has the more interventionist French approach not excluded an extremely important role for market forces. It is a role which has increased in recent years as governments of both left and right have sought to loosen the regulatory framework, have opened up financial markets, have directed state aid much more towards research and development, and have privatised some major companies.

The German social market and the French *dirigiste* traditions sit towards opposite ends of the spectrum of policy approaches that are available to the governments of Western, and increasingly too Central and Eastern, Europe. They are not, however, quite at the ends, for the social market approach is outflanked by the economic liberalism that has been characteristic of the UK since the Conservative Party assumed office in 1979, while *dirigisme* is outflanked by the economic autarchism that is still such a feature of many of the former satellite countries and former republics of the Soviet Union. In practice, virtually all West European governments are located somewhere in the centre of the spectrum, leaning perhaps in a social market or a *dirigiste* direction but – like the Germans and the French themselves – being far from pure illustrations of either approach. Few governments have attempted to veer sharply away from 'centrist' positions and those that have made the attempt – such as the French Socialists between 1981 and 1983 and the British Conservatives after 1979 – have not achieved as much as their supporters initially hoped. (President Mitterrand's socialist 'experiment' was brought to an end after only eighteen months, amidst severe balance of payments difficulties, a huge budgetary deficit, and a massive loss of confidence in the franc. The much vaunted, and extensive, British privatisation programme has not produced a comparable increase in market competition: many monopolistic positions have been maintained, business has continued to receive state assistance of various kinds although at reduced levels, and most privatisations have been accompanied by close state supervision.)

A number of factors combine to explain why national 'policies for business' do tend to be similar in key respects. First, the very logic of capitalism imposes limitations on the policy options available to governments in that, amongst other things, it obliges them always to be sensitive to the desire of business to make profits. Second, business firms and associations exercise considerable influence on the governments of most West European states and they usually use this influence to press the case for similar sorts of policies – prioritisation of anti-inflationary measures, low corporate taxes, state subsidies and grants for specified purposes, etc. Third, governments in democratic states must be sensitive to the desires of their electorates. One such desire is invariably for economic well-being. Sometimes more specific desires and attitudes are also important – in recent years, for example, there have been few votes to be won in most West European states by promising major nationalisation programmes. Fourth, and a factor which merits particular attention, is the increasing internationalisation of economic life. Modern European states, especially those which are members of the EU, are subject to many different international restraints on what, in policy terms, they can do. Four aspects of this internationalisation are especially important.

1. The increasing economic and financial interdependence of states – which arises from the internationalisation of capital markets, of trade, of manufacturing, of consumption, etc. – means that it can be potentially extremely risky and hazardous to attempt to buck prevailing trends in terms of macroeconomic policy. This was nowhere more clearly illustrated than with the failure of the French Socialist government's attempt between 1981 and 1983 to seek growth via domestic expansion at a time when France's major trading partners were deflating and their economies were slowing down.

2. The mobility of companies and of capital makes it difficult for states to impose more burdensome regulatory environments than neighbouring states because business and investment may be directed elsewhere. A major reason why the EU has become increasingly involved in regulatory activities is to try to prevent standards being driven down to unacceptably low levels.

3. Many of the traditional tools used by governments to protect and control their economies are no longer so useful, or in some cases are no longer even available. For example, trade tariffs – a traditional protective tool – have been abolished between the member states of the EU, whilst the tariffs imposed on non-EU products entering EU countries are not now determined by national governments but are jointly set, by majority vote if necessary, at EU level. Similarly, exchange rates, which in the past could be relatively easily adjusted to maintain competitiveness, are now, for those countries which are members of the ERM of the EMS, subject to controls and restrictions. (Though, as is shown in Chapter 2, turbulence in the ERM in 1992–3 weakened the tightness of the controls and restrictions on most currencies.) Another example of the declining force of national control mechanisms is seen in the opening up of financial markets: with business no longer confined to approaching domestic financial institutions for credit, it is much more difficult for governments to use national credit regulations to control and direct business activity.

4. The policies and laws of the EU are increasingly promoting a convergence in the economic and business policies of the member states. Based, for the most part, on open and free market principles, these policies and laws both prevent and require member governments to adopt particular policies and to engage in particular courses of action. For example, many of the measures which are designed to create the SEM prohibit attempts by governments to seek to protect their domestic firms and businesses behind non-tariff barriers. Similarly, the ever advancing EU competition policy prohibits, amongst other things, state aid to industry except under specified circumstances.

It is to be emphasised that, of course, not all policy differences between countries have been, or are being, eliminated. Differing national traditions and differing political perspectives still produce not insignificant differences in policy emphasis. That said, however, there have been few European governments, and no EU governments, which have not responded in recent years to the prevailing trend of placing increasing faith in the benefits of deregulation and free markets.

NATIONAL DECISION-MAKING PROCESSES

Three main generalisations can be made about business-related national decision-making processes in Western Europe, each of which will now be considered.

1.   Business itself invariably seeks, and in practice is usually accorded, involvement of some kind in relevant decision-making processes

Large and strategically important business firms are frequently accorded direct and privileged access to public decision-makers. National firms are usually accorded better access than foreign or multinational firms but this is by no means always the case. Certainly, there would be little difficulty in establishing direct and bilateral channels of communication at very senior levels if, say, Nestlé was to consider a major investment programme in Spain, of if Ford was to consider relocating car production from Belgium to Portugal.

More usually, however, communications between business and public decision-makers are not direct but are mediated via business, trade and employer associations. In all major and medium-sized West European countries there are hundreds of these associations, ranging in size and scope from peak associations covering all the main sectors of business, via sectoral associations, to associations representing small and highly specialised areas of business activity. The aims of the associations naturally vary considerably according to factors such as domain responsibilities and associational breadth and strength. Exchange and dissemination of information is one common aim. Another is the presentation of united positions to trade unions and other interested parties. Yet another aim, especially in concentrated sectors such as chemicals, is a strong input into the regulation of competition. Perhaps the most common aim of all, however, is the exercise of influence on public decision-making.

In seeking to influence public decision-making the main target of business lobbies at the national level is almost invariably national governments. Depending on domestic political circumstances, national parliaments can be a useful target too, particularly if, as in Italy, institutional arrangements give parliaments significant leverage over policy and party politics allow for manoeuvrings and effective pressurising on policy outcomes. Usually, though, parliaments are only a secondary target because it is normally governments which set the policy agenda, governments which determine the regulatory frameworks in which business is conducted, and governments which dispose of powers and resources that can be used to protect and to assist business activity.

For their part, governments are usually interested in establishing good relations with business. This is because the cooperation of business is necessary for a variety of policy purposes. For example, only business can provide much of the information that governments need in regard to such matters as investment, prices, output, sales and profits. Most crucially of all, business enterprises are the instruments via which so many governmental policies are given effect: if business does not find policies appropriate or sufficiently attractive it may be unable or unwilling to invest, to promote exports, to expand research, to take on more workers, to keep down prices, to buy on the domestic market, etc.

In consequence of this mutual dependence, a point which Grant (1987, p. 37) makes about the relationship between government and business in Britain may be said to apply, to at least some degree, to most West European countries: the relationship is not so much one of political struggle between the lobbied and the lobbyers, but is rather an exchange relationship from which both sides secure benefits. As will be shown below, the precise nature of that relationship can vary both between and within countries.

2. The influence of business on government tends to be in inverse relationship to the breadth and generality of the policies and decisions concerned

The influence of business is usually rather weak in regard to macroeconomic policy decision-making but can be quite strong in regard to middle range, specific, and technical policies and decisions.

At the macroeconomic level – where decisions are made about such matters as taxation rates, interest rates and exchange rates – governments have many considerations to bear in mind in addition to the needs of business. Moreover, much of the subject matter of macroeconomic policy is highly sensitive in nature, with the consequence that decision-making processes have to be restricted to a relatively few senior figures concentrated in the executive branch of government. A further factor limiting business influence on macroeconomic policies is that it is often the case that the room for manoeuvre available to governments, and the policy alternatives they are prepared to consider, are restricted by ideological priorities and political preferences. A very clear example of this was seen in the UK in the second half of the 1980s when Mrs Thatcher's government resisted strong business pressure for lower interest rates and greater exchange rate stability via entry into the ERM. To have 'conceded' would have meant abandoning the (then) central policy commitment of controlling inflation through domestic monetary policy and exchange rate flexibility.

At less exalted policy levels, where issues are less general in scope, less sensitive, and usually less politically partisan, governments tend to be more open and responsive to business lobbying. On matters as diverse as the licensing of dangerous substances, skilled labour shortages, and the employment conditions of part-time workers, there are many opportunities – from formally constituted advisory committees to informal telephone conversations – for representatives of business associations and individual firms to make contact with national and local politicians and officials. Occasionally, relations between business sectors and government departments and agencies become so close that the latter are almost 'captured' by the former and act virtually as their lobbies within the very framework and machinery of government.

As well as wanting good relationships with government so as to be able to influence policy content, business also often wishes for such relationships in order to be able to influence policy implementation. It can obviously be very advantageous for business sectors and firms to be well connected with, say, the officials who deal with applications for investment aid, or with the regulatory agency which monitors safety standards in the workplace. Good relationships and good connections of this kind can be established in many ways: from being a natural consequence of frequent communications over time to (a common practice in Italy) 'injecting' company employees into the public sector.

In certain circumstances business actually becomes part of the process of policy implementation. Most commonly this takes the form of business associations acting as communication channels for business policies and initiatives. Sometimes, however, as was shown earlier in the chapter, business undertakes – either by itself or in collaboration with government – regulatory functions. Where these functions involve not only applying standards and specifications but also playing a part in determining what the standards and specifications are, business is taken into that grey area where policy-making overlaps with and merges into policy implementation.

3. Decision-making approaches tend to be variants of one of three forms

It is to be emphasised that none of these three forms appears in a pure and unadulterated manner in any West European state. Furthermore, and as will be explained in greater detail below, decision-making forms do often vary within countries from sector to sector and from domain to domain. The forms are, therefore, perhaps best thought of as ideal types rather than as strict representations of reality. Their principal features, however, are present in different degrees in different states, and states do often tend towards the common use of one particular form. The three forms, or ideal types, are:

- *Étatisme*: Under this approach policy is made and implemented through strong and well-developed state structures. Ministers, in liaison with, and supported by, highly competent and relatively autonomous bureaucracies, may consult on policy with business and other interests but, for the most part, they push through their own policy preferences. This *étatiste* approach is naturally most associated with those countries – of which France is the best known example – which have traditionally taken a strongly *dirigiste* approach to economic management. In France, the *étatiste* tradition has been facilitated by circulation between, and high degrees of mutual identification and acquaintance amongst, senior bureaucratic, business and financial elites.
- *Corporatism*: Under corporatist approaches to decision-making government comes together with 'the social partners' – labour, business, and in a few

countries farmers – to make policy which is deemed to be in the collective and the national interest. The emphasis is on agreement, consensus and cooperation between the parties. In return for being given such an 'insider' role in decision-making, 'the social partners' are expected to play their part in ensuring decisions are applied. The European countries normally thought of as being the most corporatist are Sweden and Austria, but there are many others where elements of quasi corporatism are important. In Germany, for example, strong and centralised business and labour organisations, and large firms on a direct basis, have long worked closely with government – to such an extent that certain aspects of policy-making have been widely described as amounting to 'co-determination' and 'concerted action'.

• *Pluralism*: In most countries the basic pattern of decision-making is such that government takes the policy lead and makes the final decisions, but in so doing is influenced by pluralistic interests and pressures. Of course, there is considerable variation between countries, and within countries variations over time, regarding the nature of pluralistic activity and influence. In one variant – which was, for example, much used in Britain in the 1960s and 1970s – governments attempt to operate some sort of tripartite consultative relationship with business and labour elites on key economic and business policy questions. In a second variant – which has more or less been the prevailing system in Italy since World War II – business is a privileged partner of government in the sense that it enjoys much better access to, and influence over, decision-makers than does labour. And in a third variant – one which many West European countries have moved to over the last ten to fifteen years – there is only limited consultation between government and organised interests on general economic and financial questions, but there are many exchanges on middle-range and specific issues such as technological innovation, employment assistance, and regional development.

Where pluralist approaches are in place, their particular nature, and the influence that business is able to exert within them, is a consequence of a number of factors. Three factors are particularly important.

1. The coherence and solidarity of business. (A major reason why business in the UK has tended not to be politically strong is that it is internally divided – most notably between the interests of financial and industrial capital and also between the interests of large and small businesses.)
2. The coherence and solidarity of organised labour. (In France and Italy, for example, the trade union movement has been greatly weakened by both ideological and religious divisions.)
3. The ideological perspectives of governments. (The Netherlands is but one of many countries where conservative and right-wing governments have been more sympathetic to business interests and less sympathetic to labour interests than have been socialist and left-wing governments.)

The generalisations that have just been made about national decision-making processes were tentative and hedged even as they were being presented. They must now be further qualified by noting three factors which emphasise even more how so much of national decision-making varies according to time, place and subject matter.

1. National decision-making processes can vary over time

Although, as has been seen, it is just about possible to identify national decision-making patterns and styles, they are by no means permanently fixed. Changing socio-economic and cultural conditions, changing compositions of governments, and changing sectional representational strengths, are amongst the factors which can bring about significant changes over time.

The UK provides a good example of such a change. For much of the 1960s and 1970s business and trade unions were involved in extensive tripartite discussions with government on both broad policy issues – such as policies for growth, pay and labour relations – and specific policy issues – such as vocational education and job training. In 1979, however, the involvement in broad policy issues virtually ended when the Conservative Party came to power and took the view that there was no proper role for business or trade unions in national economic decision-making: it was the government's responsibility to govern and any involvement of sectional interests was to be confined to 'non-political' spheres of policy and decision-making.

2. National structures and mechanisms vary

There are considerable variations between countries in the institutional and structural aspects of their policy and decision-making arrangements. The following variations are especially worth noting:
• There are differences regarding the extent to which the many policy spheres which might be regarded as business related are, in organisational terms, brought together or are fragmented by government. For example, policy spheres such as trade, industry, employment, technology, research, and regional development are sometimes dealt with by separate ministries, sometimes by joined ones, and sometimes by 'super' or 'jumbo' ministries.

Governments frequently tinker with the organisational arrangements for such policy spheres. They may do so for one of a number of reasons: as part of a commendable search for improved organisational efficiency; because there has been an unhealthy build up of interdepartmental rivalries and tensions over who does what or what should be done; or even merely as a way of resolving domestic political difficulties. An example of this last sort of tinkering occurred in France in the spring of 1991: in May, President Mitterrand appointed Mme Cresson as Prime Minister; Mme Cresson had long believed that France should have a more active industrial policy and on assuming office she wished to give this belief organisational effect by strengthening the position of what had hitherto been the rather junior Industry Ministry; her organisational restructuring ambitions met with stiff political resistance, notably from the powerful and economically liberal Minister of Finance; the outcome of the political struggle was that Mme Cresson was obliged to retreat and industry was brought under the very same Minister of Finance's roof with the creation of a new 'superministry' embracing finance, telecommunications and foreign trade, as well as industry.

• Mechanisms for coordinating policies vary. A few countries – such as France via its Ministry of Finance – have strong ministries at the centre which can impose themselves on junior ministries and ensure there is a reasonable degree of consistency in the general direction of economic and financial policies. More usually, however, there is an absence of any such ministry with clear overall policy guiding and coordinating roles and powers. The result of this can be, unless there is firm political leadership from the top, tensions and struggles between ministries over policies and policy responsibilities. Such tensions and struggles have, for example, long been apparent in Germany between the liberal Economics Ministry and the more interventionist Research and Technology Ministry, and also between the Economics Ministry and the Environment Ministry.

• In some countries decision-making powers are very centralised, whilst in others there is a considerable measure of decentralisation to regions and localities. The UK and Ireland are prominent amongst the countries which are located towards the centralist end of the spectrum, whilst Belgium, Italy, Spain and, above all, Germany, are located towards the decentralist end. Where there is a significant amount of decentralisation there can be important differences between regions and areas of a country on such important matters for business as the availability of investment aid, the rigour of planning and development restrictions, and the strength of environmental protection laws.

A very distinct trend throughout Western Europe in recent years, in both centralised and decentralised countries, has been an increase in economic development activities at regional and local levels. Naturally, however, differences between countries regarding their regional and local governmental structures, and differences too between national governments regarding how tightly they have wished to control regional and local initiatives, have resulted in considerable variations in the nature and extent of such activities. In essentially centralised countries, such as the UK, the degree of real decentralisation has usually been limited, with key initiatives often being channelled via regionally and locally based, but ultimately centrally controlled and financed, enterprise and development agencies of various kinds.

• The national central banks – which are important for business primarily because of their roles in relation to the availability and price of credit – differ in terms of how closely they are 'plugged in' to governments. In regard to both the setting of targets for monetary growth and adjusting interest rates, there is a mixed pattern across EU countries, though with a gradual movement

– seen, for example, in recent changes in France and Spain – to greater central bank independence. Of the major banks, the Bank of England is subject to the greatest degree of governmental control, whilst the German Bundesbank – which is by far the most important of the European central banks because of the strength of the German economy and the power of the deutschmark – is the most independent in that it is generally able to discharge its responsibility for maintaining a stable currency and ensuring low inflation without having to bow to political pressure. (As its resistance to lowering interest rates in 1992–3 demonstrated.)

• The size and nature of national public sectors have implications for decision-making. In general, where governments run or control a business sector or activity they can normally take decisions affecting that business more quickly and, if necessary, more secretly than they can when dealing with the private sector. Their decisions, moreover, are more likely to be implemented. However, the extent of this decision-making 'gap' between the two sectors should not be overstated. Indeed, in certain respects it has narrowed in recent years. It has done so as a result of pressures from the EU for greater public sector transparency, the application of most EU regulatory and deregulatory legislation to both the public and private sectors, and moves by several governments to increase the business autonomy and market sensitivity of public sector firms.

3. National decision-making processes can vary between policy areas

As has been made clear, 'business policies' embrace a very broad range of policies: macroeconomic and financial policies, competition policy, trade policy, industrial policy, research and technological development policy, and employment policy are but the most obvious of a long list of policy spheres which have business-related matters at their heart, or at least as a very important element. With policies for, or affecting, business thus covering such a spectrum, it is not surprising to find that the associated policy and decision-making processes often vary considerably. They vary, for example, according to the importance of the policy matters under consideration, with decisions affecting strategic sectors being much more likely to attract ministerial attention than decisions which do not. In some cases, where sectors in different countries are subject to similar conditions and display similar structural features, sectoral similarities can be more important than national similarities – as is the case with chemicals which requires high levels of investment, which is highly internationalised, and where a few large companies are dominant.

Generalities about national decision-making patterns and styles can, therefore, often hide as much as they reveal, in so far as within countries significant differences often exist both between decision-making levels and between different policy areas and sectors. As Wilks and Wright (1987, p. 5) have observed in respect of industrial policy – which is just one of the policy spheres which make up 'business policies':

> In a policy area as large and as differentiated as 'industry', relations between government and industry are not conducted in one policy community or a single network of communications and influence, but several. Those communities or networks have different structures of relationships, characteristics, and personnel; their 'agendas' differ; and the policy processes by which they interact vary.

For those who wish to be acquainted with the specifics of business-related decision-making, it is thus necessary to probe beyond the generalities of ascribed national patterns and styles. Policy communities – which identify the actors who share a common identity or interest – and policy networks – the processes which link the actors together – must be explored at different decision-making levels and across policy sectors.

EUROPEAN UNION POLICIES

Protracted manoeuvrings and negotiations between the twelve member states of the European Community in the late 1980s and very early 1990s led, at the Maastricht summit in December 1991, to agreement on a Treaty on European Union (TEU). The Treaty was formally signed in February 1992 and, following a lengthy and difficult ratification procedure, came into operation in November 1993.

The European Union, which was created by the TEU, is a complex construction. It is based on three pillars:

1. The three constituent Communities of what came to be collectively and commonly referred to from the early 1970s as the European Community (EC). The three constituent Communities are: the European Coal and Steel Community (ECSC) which was established by the 1951 Treaty of Paris; the European Atomic Energy Community (Euratom) which was established by the 1957 Treaty of Rome (Euratom); and – most importantly – the European Economic Community (EEC) which was established by the 1957 Treaty of Rome (EEC). The founding Treaties of the three Communities have been amended over the years, most notably via the 1986 Single European Act (SEA) and via the TEU. The main purpose of the SEA and TEU amendments was to strengthen the policy and institutional bases of the EC/EU. Somewhat confusingly, one of the TEU amendments involved renaming the European Economic Community the European Community: with the consequence that the name European Community now refers to only one of the three European Communities, whereas up until the entry

into force of the TEU it was the commonly accepted term to describe all three.

2. Provisions on a common foreign and security policy.
3. Provisions on cooperation in the fields of justice and home affairs.

In this chapter, and indeed in the rest of the book, our main interest in the EU is with matters which fall under the first pillar of the TEU, and more particularly with matters which fall within the framework of the (renamed) European Community. So as to minimise confusion with use of names – a difficult task in the wake of the TEU – the acronym EU will be used to refer to the Union/ Community, except where circumstances make it clearly inappropriate to do so.

Some understanding of the 1957 EEC Treaty is necessary for an understanding of the nature of the EU's policy framework. Article 2 of the Treaty laid down the following broad objectives.

> The Community shall have as its task, by establishing a common market and progressively approximating the economic policies of Member States, to promote throughout the Community a harmonious development of economic activities, a continuous and balanced expansion, an increase in stability, an accelerated raising of the standard of living and closer relations between the states belonging to it.

Subsequent Treaty articles gave these general objectives a somewhat sharper focus by laying down guidelines for, on the one hand, the establishment of a common market and, on the other hand, the development of economic integration, between the member states of the EEC. They were only guidelines, however – not clear statements about what should be done – and as such were open to interpretation and disputation.

With the EEC Treaty being thus less than precise in its prescriptions, it is evident that the range of policy interests and responsibilities that the Community accumulated over the years, and which now constitute part of the EU's brief, are not to be explained purely in Treaty terms. Certainly the EEC Treaty acted, and the EU Treaty now acts, as an important stimulus to policy development, and certainly such 'core' EU policies as the Common Commercial Policy (CCP), the Competition Policy, and the Common Agricultural Policy (CAP), do find their roots, though by no means all of their principles, in the Treaty. But specific Treaty provision for policy development has not ensured that it has necessarily occurred: witness the only limited progress that has been made in developing transport policy, despite Article 74 of the Treaty (unamended by the TEU) which states that 'The objective of this Treaty shall, in matters governed by this Title (transport), be pursued by Member States within the framework of a common transport policy'. Nor has lack of Treaty provision necessarily prevented policy development: witness the emergence of policies for the environment and for research and development long before they were given a Treaty base via the SEA.

This development of some policies, and lack of development of others, is thus explained in part by 'non-Treaty' factors. Two such factors have been, and still are, especially important.

1. *The perceptions of the governments of member states as to what is desirable.* Policies are developed in the EU when the governments of the member states, or at least a sufficient number of them, judge that the advantages of operating at EU level, as opposed to national level, outweigh the disadvantages. The main advantages that are usually seen as accruing in regard to business-related policies are those that stem from having, in an increasingly interdependent and competitive world, a single and open internal market, a stable economic and financial environment, a common external trading stance, and some collective action and pooling of resources in particular functional and sectoral areas. The main disadvantages are the losses of national decision-making powers and of sovereignty, and hence also of national policy-making flexibility and manoeuvrability, that transfers of responsibility to the EU inevitably entail. When policies are initiated at EU level, states naturally often differ in their perceptions of the nature of the balance between the advantages and the disadvantages, but over time and in an increasing number of policy areas the advantages have increasingly been seen to prevail.

2. *The capacities of the member states to translate their perceptions into practice.* An incapacity to operationalise support for EU policy development may exist because of problems at either member state or EU levels. At member state level, a government may wish to support an EU policy initiative but be prevented from doing so, perhaps because of the known opposition of a powerful domestic interest group or because it might be electorally damaging. At EU level, opposition to a policy initiative from just one state can make policy development very difficult to achieve. This is partly because many decisions – though less since the SEA and TEU entered into force – require unanimous support, and partly because even where majority voting is permissible the preferred way of proceeding – especially on major issues – is by consensus.

The EU's present policy portfolio is thus largely to be explained in terms of the interaction of three factors: treaty provisions, political perceptions, and political capacities. This may be illustrated by briefly considering the development of the – crucially important for business – Single European Market (or internal market) programme.

A free and open Community market had been provided for in the EEC Treaty but by the early 1980s it had become quite clear that this would not be achieved unless a much more vigorous approach was taken to remove protectionist obstacles. A customs union had been established as early as 1968, when tariffs and quotas had been eliminated and a common external tariff imposed, but markets had remained divided and protected in important respects. This was mainly because states had maintained, and in the 1970s had even increased, non-tariff barriers to trade: notably in the form of national technical, safety and health regulations. During the 1970s the Commission had sought to remove these barriers by bringing forward legislation designed to harmonise standards, but progress had been extremely slow.

In the early 1980s a number of factors combined to convince the governments of the member states that a greater thrust was needed: economic growth had been disappointing for the best part of a decade; the Community was clearly falling behind its competitors, notably Japan and the United States, in the new technologies; there was an increasing appreciation that the continued fragmentation of the European market along national lines was having a damaging effect on the economic performances of the member states; and the accession to the Community of three new countries (Greece in 1981, and Spain and Portugal in 1986) made it clear to all that to continue on the same path and in the same way would mean that the common market would never be properly established.

To this background the Commission in April 1985 produced a White Paper entitled *Completing the Internal Market*. In the paper 300 measures were identified by the Commission as needing to be adopted if the internal market was to be completed. It was further suggested in the paper that 31 December 1992 should be set as the deadline for the adoption of the measures. The Heads of Government of the member states, meeting in the European Council in June 1985, accepted the White Paper, and in December 1985 they agreed that both the internal market objective and the 1992 deadline should be incorporated into the EEC Treaty via the SEA. As a result a new Article 8A was incorporated into the EEC Treaty. It included the following:

> The Community shall adopt measures with the aim of progressively establishing the internal market over a period expiring on 31 December 1992 . . . The internal market shall comprise an area without internal frontiers in which the free movement of goods, persons, services and capital is ensured in accordance with the provisions of this Treaty.

Notwithstanding, however, the White Paper and the new commitments in the Treaty to the completion of the internal market, the very slow pace of policy development in the 1970s and early 1980s suggests that progress on the completion of the SEM would have been very slow had a greater capacity not been made available to the Community to enable it to act upon its intentions. Such a greater capacity was made available and it has subsequently served to greatly speed up decision-making processes. Four aspects of this greater capacity have been especially important.

1.   Court of Justice judgements have saved the Community the need to make

law in respect of certain key SEM matters. A particularly influential judgement was issued in February 1979 in the now famous *Cassis de Dijon* case (Case 120/78) when the principle of mutual recognition was established. By this principle a product which is lawfully produced and marketed in one member state must be accepted in another member state unless it can be shown to be damaging to health, safety, the environment, or some other aspect of the public interest. As a result of the judgement, the need for legislation to harmonise standards so as to facilitate trade across internal Community borders was much reduced.

2. Where harmonisation is deemed to be still necessary, it is no longer done on the former basis of trying to harmonise standards in all respects. Under the 'new approach' the Community concentrates on setting the principles and parameters of standards and then leaves the detailed work to be undertaken by the appropriate European standards organisations (in which EFTA countries are also represented).

3. Since the early to mid–1980s the Council of Ministers – which is the EU's key decision-making body – has gradually dropped its former practice of taking decisions only by consensus and unanimity and has been willing to take decisions by qualified majority vote where there is an appropriate Treaty provision for so doing. Consensus is still preferred wherever that is possible, but in most circumstances it is now no longer regarded as permissible for one or two states to hold up an agreement when most states wish to press ahead and there is treaty provision for a vote. (Voting rules in the Council are considered in the next section of this chapter.)

4. Treaty amendments contained in the SEA and the TEU have greatly increased the circumstances in which qualified majority voting in the Council is legally permissible. Virtually all decisions which are directly related to, or which have implications for, the SEM are now subject to qualified majority voting rules, other than those which are concerned with fiscal matters or some of those which are concerned with free movement of persons.

So extensive have the EU's policy interests become that there are now few policy areas which have implications for business in which it does not have at least some involvement and responsibility. The nature of that involvement and responsibility takes many different forms. In its minimalist form – which is seen in areas such as education and health – there is only a very limited amount of EU policy activity and the member states are, in most respects, free to decide for themselves what policies are to be pursued and what decisions are to be made. In its intermediate form – which is found in areas such as industrial policy, policy for small and medium-sized enterprises, and energy policy – EU policy involvement is more extensive, but the involvement often stops short of formulating laws and is focused more on promoting consultation and cooperation. In its maximalist form, EU policy involvement is very extensive, and compulsion, through law, is an important part of the policy framework. Competition policy, commercial policy, agriculture policy and regional policy are examples of maximalist policy areas, with most of the important decisions which apply to them now being either taken at, or at least having to be approved at, EU level. In policy areas such as these the governments of the EU member states are greatly restricted in their ability to decide the policies and make the laws which apply in their countries.

The main policy interests and responsibilities of the EU can be grouped under five main headings: policies designed to establish the Single European Market, macroeconomic and financial policies, functional policies, sectoral policies, and external policies. Most of the policies that fall under each of these headings have at least some implications for business.[2]

Policies designed to establish the Single European Market

By far the most important of the many EU policies which are directed at, or which have implications for, business, are those which are associated with the creation of the Single European Market. Some of these policies predate the 1985 White Paper, some post-date it, whilst many were introduced, or were given a boost, by it. The policies are of three broad types.

First, there are policies designed to dismantle existing barriers to the free movement of goods, persons, services and capital between the member states. These barriers were identified in the White Paper as being physical barriers (primarily customs checks at borders), fiscal barriers (different national rates of Value Added Tax and excise duty), and technical barriers (different national standards and specifications for many marketable goods). Considerable legislative progress has been made in all three of these areas, though a few of the barriers identified in the White Paper, including border checks, have not yet (in early 1994) been completely removed. Moreover, there are barriers – most notably different rates of individual and corporate taxation – which the White Paper did not identify as priorities.

Second, and this overlaps in practice with the first type of policies, there are policies to approximate or harmonise such legal provisions in the member states as directly affect 'the establishment or functioning of the common market' (Article 100 EC). Harmonisation is resulting in the replacement of many national standards and specifications with European standards and specifications. As was explained earlier, the EU's approach to harmonisation has loosened in recent years following the establishment of the principle of mutual recognition and the 'new approach' to harmonisation legislation.

Harmonisation is not, it should be emphasised, solely concerned with opening up the market for the movement of goods, though that, indeed, is its main concern. Services and capital are also affected and legislation has been put in place in these spheres too. So, for example, in May 1993 the Council of Ministers adopted the Investment Services Directive which, in harmonising the conditions for authorisation and for carrying on business, provides for a single licence or 'European passport' for non-bank investment firms by enabling them to operate on a cross-border basis on the strength of the authorisation and prudential supervision of the competent authorities in the home state. The Directive, which is supported by a Capital Adequacy Directive, comes into force on 1 January 1996. It complements the 1989 Second Banking Directive which provides a single licence for credit institutions.[3]

Third, there are policies designed to promote competition. The principles of the EU's competition policy are set out in Articles 85–94 of the EC Treaty and are concerned primarily with: (a) the removal of restrictive practices (Article 85); (b) the prevention of abuses of dominant trading positions (Article 86); (c) the elimination of state aids which distort competition (Article 92–93); and (d) since 1990, when new legislation (Regulation 4064/89) based on Articles 85 and 86 entered into force, ensuring that large company mergers do not have anti-competitive implications. The EU's competition policy has become increasingly important as the creation of the SEM has been elevated to a central EU goal and this has been reflected in increasingly vigorous action in all four aspects of the policy: so, for example, the chemical industry, has been subject to penalties for creating and maintaining restrictive practices, notably in regard to price fixing and market sharing; national airlines have been obliged to liberalise and open up closed and protected routes because they were an abuse of dominant trading positions; the motor industry (most notably Renault, and British Aerospace in connection with its takeover of Rover) has had state aid cut and has been obliged to make repayments; and the merger control powers were first used to prevent a proposed merger in October 1991 when the Commission ruled against the proposed takeover of de Havilland, the Canadian aircraft makers, by Aérospatiale of France and Alenia of Italy on the grounds that the merged company would have a 50 per cent share of the world market and a 67 per cent share of the EC market for commuter aircraft of twenty to seventy seats. In the future, competition policy is likely to be much taken up with liberalising hitherto protected, and in many cases publicly owned or at least heavily publicly regulated, sectors. (Policies relating to the SEM are discussed further in Chapters 2 and 3.)

Macroeconomic and financial policies

As was noted earlier, membership of the ERM of the EMS limits the policy manoeuvrability to participating states – especially in relationship to exchange rate and interest rate policies. However, as the events of 1992–3 demonstrated – when sterling and the lira suspended their membership of the ERM (in September 1992), several other currencies were devalued (between September 1992 and May 1993), and the exchange rate bands for most participating currencies were widened (in August 1993) – the ERM is far from being a policy strait-jacket. Moreover, the limitations on national policy manoeuvrability which are a consequence of ERM membership, still fall a long way short of amounting to ERM participating states displaying coherent and consistent policies. Indeed, coherent and consistent policies have, in practice, proved to be very difficult to develop and the best the EU has been able to achieve in most macropolicy areas has been liaising mechanisms and informal understandings that are intended to try to ensure that national policies are in approximate harmony with one another.

This situation should change in the 1990s following the incorporation in the TEU of a scheme and a timetable for progression to Economic and Monetary Union. The main features of the scheme are a single currency and the establishment of a European Central Bank operating within the framework of a European System of Central Banks, and the main features of the timetable are a three-stage transitional process leading to the adoption of the single currency by 1999 at the latest. (See Chapter 2 for a fuller discussion of EMU.)

Functional policies

Functional policies are policies which have a clear functional purpose, but which are narrower in scope than macroeconomic policies. The functional policy which is most obviously applicable to business is industrial policy.

Until recently, EU industrial policy can hardly be said to have existed at all in the sense that there was no coherent or clearly defined set of goals and policy instruments for industry. What there was of industrial policy was basically made up of elements of market-related policies (with the SEM as its centrepiece), competition policy, and aspects of other functional policies – most notably regional policy (which is aimed mainly at improving regional infrastructures), social policy (which focuses mainly on job training and work conditions), and research and technological development policy (which is primarily concerned with encouraging and facilitating precompetitive research). In November 1990, however, an attempt was made to put industrial policy on a firmer footing when the Commission issued a Communication entitled, *Industrial Policy in an Open and Competitive Environment: Guidelines for a Community Approach* (Commission, 1990a). The guidelines contained in the Communication were focused on three goals, all of which had as a central aim the building of a favourable economic climate for private initiative and investment:

- *The improvement of the functioning of the internal market.* Measures which were seen as being necessary included the establishment of strict European standards to guarantee product quality, the opening up of public procurement, and the establishment of European company law.
- *The improvement of the functioning of the world market.* This was seen as including the continued opening and strict implementation of the multilateral trade system, the monitoring of dumping practices, and cooperation with international partners – especially countries in Central and Eastern Europe.

- *The pursuance of required structural adjustments.* Necessary steps to be taken were seen as including the improvement of trans-European networks (transport, telecommunications, energy), the strengthening of policies which take specific account of the needs of small- and medium-sized enterprises (SMEs), and increasing the involvement and contribution of firms in research and development.

The TEU also strengthened the EU's potential for promoting an active industrial policy. It did so in various ways, four of which are especially important. First, in the pre-Maastricht negotiations a source of some controversy was whether the EEC Treaty should be amended so as to make specific provision for an industrial policy. The 'free marketeers', led by the UK, were strongly opposed to the idea, whilst those who were more sympathetic to limited intervention, notably the Commission and France, were in favour. In the event, a compromise was reached whereby industry was added to the EC Treaty as a distinct policy area – in a new Article 130 – but the nature of the EU's commitment was only generally defined and any specific measures to be taken would have to receive unanimous support in the Council of Ministers. Secondly, provisions which had been first set out in the SEA for the Community to assume responsibilities for research and technological development were strengthened: under Article 130f of the EC Treaty 'The Community shall have the objective of strengthening the scientific and technological bases of Community industry and encouraging it to become more competitive at international level . . .'; under Article 130h 'The Community and the Member States shall coordinate their research and technological development activities so as to ensure that national policies and Community policy are mutually consistent'; and under Article 130i there was confirmation of the SEA requirement that the Council should adopt a 'multiannual framework programme setting out all the activities of the Community . . . The framework programme shall be implemented through specific programmes developed within each activity'. Thirdly, under Title VII of the EC Treaty (Social Policy, Education, Vocational Training and Youth), it was specified that 'The Community shall implement a vocational training policy which shall support and supplement the action of the Member States . . . (Article 127). And, fourthly, under Title XII of the EC Treaty (Trans-European Networks), the EC was required to 'contribute to the establishment and development of trans-European networks in the areas of transport, telecommunications and energy infrastructures' (Article 129b).

Most of the measures identified in the 1990 Communication and in the TEU called, in effect, for a strengthening of existing policies rather than the launching of new ones. Such a strengthening has since occurred, with several of the measures which were identified in the Communication and the TEU being taken up and incorporated into initiatives and programmes. Three examples may be cited by way of illustration. First, meetings of the European Council in 1992–3 reacted positively to Commission proposals for extra funds being made available for investment in infrastructure and trans-European networks.

Secondly, efforts to assist SMEs and to promote new business formation have been stepped up with, in June 1993, the Council of Ministers adopting a multiannual programme of measures to intensify 'the priority measures for enterprise policy' and to ensure 'the continuity and consolidation of enterprise policy in order to encourage the Europeanization and internationalization of enterprises, especially SMEs' (Council, 1993a).[4] The programme, which is to run from July 1993 to December 1996, includes amongst its specific objectives the improvement of the administrative, legal and financial environments for enterprises, the need to improve cooperation between enterprises via networks and databases, encouraging enterprises to adapt to structural changes and to changes brought about by the internal market, and ensuring EU initiatives and policies give full consideration to the interests of enterprises. Thirdly, Research and Development (R & D) has been given a slightly higher priority, with the allocation of 13 billion ECU (nearly £10 billion) to the Fourth Framework Programme which covers the years 1994–8. (Most member states would have preferred the Programme to have been allocated a much larger budget, but the UK in particular was strongly resistant and was able to reduce the figure since the Council decision was subject to a unanimity requirement.) The main themes of the Fourth Programme are the coordination of research activities in the member states, the concentration of funding on key technologies which could benefit many industrial sectors, and better dissemination of R&D findings via a European Technology Assessment Network.

The guidelines set out in the 1990 Communication and the provisions laid down in the TEU do not wholly resolve – and given the difficulties involved could not perhaps have been expected to resolve – the almost perennial question that arises in connection with industrial policy: where is the balance to be struck between market-based policies and interventionist-based policies? Differences on this have long existed within the Commission, between the member states, and between the member states and the Commission (or at least those parts of the Commission which have queried aspects of national policies – usually DGIV which is responsible for implementing the EU's competition policies and laws). The Communication and the TEU do, however, provide a framework for taking industrial policy forward. They do so in the context of a general acceptance by the governments of the member states of the merits of competition and of controlled deregulation, and of a widely shared presumption – which is not always fully applied in practice – that EU and national government intervention should be restricted in scope and should be designed primarily to promote innovation and to assist, rather than to resist, structural change.

Sectoral policies

Some EU policies are directed at particular economic sectors. By far the best known and most fully developed of these policies is the Common Agricultural Policy (CAP). Other sectors which have long received at least some attention are a number of 'sunrise' and 'rustbelt' industries which have been deemed to have special needs. The most important form of EU assistance to sunrise industries has been the promotion of precompetitive collaborative research across a range of high-tech areas. Assistance to rustbelt – or perhaps it is more accurate to describe them as declining industries since amongst their number are textiles and fishing as well as steel and shipbuilding – has usually taken the form of some sort of combination of protection from outside competition coupled with financial aid to promote restructuring and to soften the effects of contraction.

Within the general framework of the 1990 Communication on industrial policy, sectoral policy has been considerably developed in recent years through a series of Commission Communications and Council Resolutions on particular industries. Amongst industries which have been the subject of attention are the electronics and information technology industry, the aircraft industry, the motor vehicle industry, and the telecommunications industry (Commission, 1991, 1992a, 1992b, 1992c). The general thrust of the EU's approach in such sectoral areas has not been to impose tight sectoral plans or to provide massive injections of funds, but rather to concentrate on creating a favourable environment for the industries concerned by, for example, providing assistance in furthering cooperation between European undertakings and in promoting research programmes which will ensure the optimisation of research activity throughout the EU. The approach, in short, is characterised by a light interventionist touch: the central aim being to ensure that European business and industry takes full advantage of the increasingly integrated SEM.

External policies

There are many different aspects to the EU's external relations and policies. The aspect which is of most importance to business is external trade relations. The main pillars of these relations are the Common External Tariff (CET) and the Common Commercial Policy (CCP) which enable, indeed oblige, the member states to act as one on such vital matters as the fixing and adjusting of external customs tariffs, the negotiation of trade agreements with non-member countries, and the taking of action to impede import when unfair trading practices are suspected.

The CCP has led to some tensions in the EU. Agriculture has created the greatest difficulties in this regard because the special policy regime under which it operates, the Common Agricultural Policy, is based on pillars of protectionism and subsidisation – both of which are seen as being excessive in scope by non-EU agricultural exporting countries. Agriculture apart, however, the policy line pursued within the CCP has been fairly consistently based on the construction of an open, liberal and well-managed international trading regime. This policy line was clearly demonstrated in the Uruguay Round negotiations of the General Agreement on Tariffs and Trade (GATT), when the EU supported moves both to reduce restrictions on trade in spheres covered by existing GATT rules, and also supported the extension of GATT rules to such spheres as services and intellectual property.

EUROPEAN UNION DECISION-MAKING PROCESSES

There are five main EU decision-making bodies: the European Council, the Council of Ministers, the Commission, the European Parliament, and the Court of Justice. Their compositions, and their roles in relation to decision-making, are – in outline – as follows.

The European Council

The European Council brings together, on an at least twice yearly basis, the Heads of Government and the Foreign Ministers of the member states, plus the President and one Vice-President of the Commission.

When it was established in 1974 the intention was that the European Council would act as a relatively informal gathering for exchanging ideas, for giving direction to policy development, and perhaps also sometimes for breaking deadlocks and clearing logjams. In practice this intention has been only partially realised, for although the European Council does engage in the tasks originally envisaged, it has also become an extremely important decision-making body. It does not make laws and it is not involved in 'routine' decision-making, but it does make key political decisions on many of the most important, most sensitive, most controversial, and most difficult matters facing the EU.

The Council of Ministers

The Council of Ministers is the EU's principal legislative body and, in respect of matters not referred to the European Council, also its principal decision-making body.

The Council meets at three levels. At the lowest level, national officials examine the details of policy proposals in working parties. At the intermediate level, Permanent Representatives (ambassadors to the EU), meeting in the Committee of Permanent Representatives (COREPER), prepare ministerial meetings and attempt to reach agreements on issues which it has not been possible to resolve in working parties. At the topmost level, ministers – of trade, of industry, of finance, etc. – take all final decisions.

The ability of a state to defend its national interests in the Council of Ministers varies according to the policy matter under consideration. This is because in some policy areas decisions must be unanimous, whilst in others qualified majority voting rules apply. When qualified majority voting rules do apply – and, as was noted above, they do in respect of most SEM related matters – then 54 votes out of the total of 76 votes which are available constitute a qualified majority. (The 76 votes are distributed as follows: 10 to France, Germany, Italy and the UK; 8 to Spain; 5 to Belgium, Greece, The Netherlands, and Portugal; 3 to Ireland and Denmark; and 2 to Luxembourg).

The Commission

The Commission is the EU institution which deals most directly with business. It is also, in several key respects, the institution which is of most importance for business. It therefore merits a fuller consideration here than do the other institutions.

At the summit of the Commission are seventeen Commissioners, each of whom, rather in the manner of national ministers, has responsibility for a policy area or policy areas. Commissioners are nominated by national governments, with two from each of the five larger member states (France, Germany, Italy, Spain and the UK), and one from each of the seven smaller states.

Below the Commission is a relatively small supporting bureaucracy numbering around 16 000 staff. These are divided into Directorates General (DGs) which, like ministries in member states, deal with particular policies. There are twenty-three DGs, most of which deal with matters which are of interest and importance for business, for example, Internal Market and Industrial Affairs (DGIII), Competition (DGIV), Science, Research and Development (DGXII), Financial Institutions and Company Law (DGXV), and Enterprise Policy, Distributive Trades, Tourism and Cooperatives (DGXXIII).

All those who work in the Commission, from Commissioners downwards, are employees of the EU and are not expected to display national partiality in the exercise of their duties.

Of the many duties performed by the Commission five are of particular importance.

1. *Initiator of EU policies and laws*. Other institutions can request the Commission to bring forward policies and proposals for legislation, but it alone has formal initiation and drafting responsibilities.
2. *Executive functions*. The Commission has major responsibilities with regard to the management, supervision, and implementation of EU policies. These responsibilities include: exercising delegated law-making powers

in respect of 'administrative' and 'technical' legislation (the Commission issues between 6000 and 7000 legislative instruments each year – most of them in the form of regulations);[5] managing EU finances – this includes duties in helping to administer the funds which are available to assist business, notably in respect of regional development, training and retraining of labour, and research; and supervising, overseeing and coordinating the 'front line' implementation of EU policies and laws which is undertaken on behalf of the EU by appropriate national administrative agencies in the member states.

3. *Guardian of the legal framework.* The Commission shares with the Court of Justice responsibility for ensuring that EU law is respected. This can involve taking action against states (usually for not incorporating or not applying EU law in the proper manner), or against individuals, firms, or organisations. The most usual reason for taking action against business firms is for having engaged in restrictive practices of some kind. Where such action is taken, extensive informal processes always precede formal action, but firms can ultimately be fined and have often been so: in 1990, for example, Solvay of Belgium and ICI of the UK were fined 30m ECU and 17m ECU respectively for operating a market division cartel and offering price rebates to tie in large customers.

4. *External representative and negotiator.* The Commission represents the EU in many of its external relations. Of particular importance to business is that the Commission, on the basis of negotiating mandates given to it by the Council of Ministers and subject to a Council watching brief, conducts the EU's external trade relations. It does so both in formal negotiations, such as those that are conducted under the auspices of GATT, and in the more informal exchanges such as are common between, for example, the EU and the USA and the EU and Japan over access to each other's markets.

5. *Mediator and conciliator.* EU decision-making processes are often characterised by tensions and struggles between many different national, political and vested interests. The Commission, with its non-partisan stance and its pervasive presence (it is always represented at European Council, Council of Ministers, and European Parliament meetings), is well placed to oil the wheels of decision-making.

A problem with the Commission is that although it has very important tasks to perform it does not always have the necessary resources, policy and administrative instruments, or cooperation from member states, to be able to act with maximum effectiveness. Its position in relation to the implementation of the EU's competition policy illustrates this. DGIV is the Directorate General with the responsibility for applying competition law and it is, by comparison with most other DGs, well endowed with appropriate executive instruments. These are in the form of powers of investigation (into both business firms and governmental agencies as appropriate), powers of authorisation (over proposed large mergers, for example), powers to prohibit illegal arrangements and practices, and powers to issue fines. Such indeed are the powers of DGIV in relation to alleged breaches of EU competition rules that it is often accused, and not without reason, of being the prosecutor, the judge and the jury. However, although DGIV is reasonably well off as regards executive instruments, it is not well off as regards resources. Indeed, with only around 200 senior – or A grade – officials, it is understaffed. This means that it cannot properly monitor the application of competition policies and laws throughout the EU, and it is unable to investigate anything more than a small proportion of the many allegations of illegalities that are referred to it. DGIV's ability to ensure that competition policies and laws are enforced is further weakened by its not always receiving, especially in connection with state aid cases, adequate cooperation from member states. (A main reason for this is that although all member states support the broad thrust of most aspects of EU competition policies, in practice these policies can clash with national industrial policies designed to boost or to preserve what are seen by national governments as key sectors or firms. Italy, which dispenses far more state aid than any other EU country, has been a particular problem for the Commission in this regard.)

The European Parliament

The European Parliament (EP) is a directly elected parliament of 567 members. Germany has 99 members; France, Italy, and the UK each have 87 members; Spain has 64; the Netherlands has 31; Belgium, Greece and Portugal have 25; Denmark has 16; Ireland has 15; and Luxembourg has 6.

   Until the entry into force of the TEU the EP was essentially an advisory and pressurising body rather than a decision-making body. That is to say, the Council of Ministers had to consult it on most important matters, including significant legislative proposals, but was not usually obliged to accept its advice. Under the TEU, however, the role of the EP was considerably enhanced, with it assuming, for the first time, veto powers over certain types of EU legislation. Significantly, this included most SEM related legislation.

The Court of Justice

The Court of Justice has two main functions. First, it has a general responsibility for interpreting the provisions of EU law. In so doing it must attempt to ensure that the application of the law, which on a day-to-day basis is primarily the responsibility of national courts, is consistent and uniform in all member states. Second, it has specific responsibilities for directly applying the law in certain types of cases.

   In exercising these functions the Court has often contributed to the shaping and making of EU law. It has used the Treaties, and the somewhat unclear and incomplete nature of much of EU statute law, to, in effect, strengthen and extend EU competence in important areas, including competition law and law on free movement.

The role and nature of the Court are considered further in Chapter 3.

In addition to these five main EU institutions there are also several subsidiary institutions, two of which are of particular relevance to business.

The Economic and Social Committee is made up of 189 representatives of various types of economic and social interests. The representatives are drawn from the member states and are divided into three more or less equally sized groups: employers (just less than half of this group are drawn from industry); workers (the great majority of this group are officials of national trade unions); and various interests (about half of this group are associated either with agriculture, small- and medium-sized businesses, or the professions). The role of the Committee is primarily to make policy recommendations and to offer opinions on proposed legislation, especially in the social and economic spheres. The Committee's influence is much less than that of the EP, but it provides a useful forum for making views known to decision-makers and for establishing contacts.

The European Investment Bank has as its task to contribute, via the granting of loans and the giving of guarantees, to the 'balanced and steady development of the common market in the interests of the Community' (Article 198e, EC). What this means in practice is that the Bank acts as a source of investment finance for projects which advance specified EU goals. Loans are offered at highly competitive rates and on advantageous terms and are often available for projects which commercial banks would not wish to support. Large loans – of more than about 10 million ECU – are dealt with directly by the Bank, whilst smaller loans are dealt with by intermediary institutions acting as agencies of the Bank.

The EU's institutional structure is thus quite different in character from national institutional structures. This helps to produce, along with other factors, differences too in decision-making processes. Four of these differences are particularly worth noting.

- Decision-makers in the EU are not as accountable as are national decision-makers. The EU institution which has the responsibility for taking final decisions about most significant policies and laws – the Council of Ministers – is not a directly elected body and is not collectively accountable to an elected body. At best, the most senior figures in the Council – the ministers – are elected at two stages removed (by national electorates) and are individually accountable to their national parliaments.
- There is a much greater policy and decision-making role in the EU for non elected officials – in the Commission – than there customarily is in member states. The fifty or so officials in the Commission's Merger Task Force, for

example, have considerable room for exercising judgement in regard to determining whether proposed mergers should be permitted under the 1989 Merger Control Regulation, and in determining what conditions – in the form of sell-offs perhaps – should be attached to mergers which are authorised.

- EU decision-making processes are sometimes extremely protracted. This is especially so when unanimity is required in the Council of Ministers. Protraction can, of course, also occur at national levels, but not usually to the same extent. The difficulties of creating European company law illustrate the point: minor legislation, concerning such matters as one-man companies and the cross-border establishment of branches, have been adopted; legislation enabling European Economic Interest Groupings (EEIGs) to be established has also been approved – an EEIG is a loose form of cooperation allowing firms from at least two member states to come together for a specific purpose; but major company law directives for the creation of a European company statute or for a framework of worker participation have remained blocked for years (largely because of UK resistance).

- EU decision-making processes frequently attract the attention and participation of a great diversity of competing interests. The contrast here with what happens at national levels is, of course, one of degree, but EU processes have to cope not only with different ideological and sectional interests but also with different national interests. In consequence, successful decision-making at EU level is often very heavily reliant on compromises and complicated package deals.

These four factors go very much to the heart of what many observers have long believed are the major problems associated with EU decision-making: not enough democracy or efficiency. The SEA and the TEU made some attempt to rectify these deficiencies, notably by increasing the powers of the EP and extending qualified majority voting in the Council of Ministers to more policy spheres, but they certainly did not resolve all problems.

The business lobby

An important dimension of EU decision-making which merits comment is the input of business. The EU business lobby takes three main forms.

First, large and/or powerful business interests – both national and multi-national – frequently act in their own capacity. So, firms such as ICI, Renault and Siemens, generally have some sort of 'in house' lobbying unit, often as part of 'public relations' or 'external liaison' departments. The importance and lobbying strength of such interests mean they can usually get direct access to senior national and EU decision-makers when required.

Second, there are, as was seen earlier in the chapter, many national trade and business associations in the member states. Often it is necessary for them to be active not only at the national level but also at EU level, and they attempt this by keeping in touch with national governments (which provide the route to influence in the Council of Ministers) and, where possible, EU institutions – especially the Commission. A few of the larger national peak business associations maintain small offices in Brussels.

Third, there are numerous Euro-groups which seek to represent business interests at the EU level. The size, organisational structure, resources, representational strength, policy coherence, and influence of these groups varies enormously, but most share similar aims: to keep their members (which are usually affiliated national associations) informed of what is happening in the EU in their sphere of interest, and to feed the group's views into EU institutions and forums. The largest and best known business Euro-group is the Union of Industries of the European Community (UNICE) which is an umbrella group in the sense that it is made up of national peak business federations and attempts to represent the interests of business on a cross-sectoral basis. Of the numerous more sectorally focused business Euro-groups the following are amongst the more active and prominent: the European Centre of Public Enterprises (CEEP); the European Chemical Industry Federation (CEFIC); the European Insurance Committee (CEA); the European Federation of Pharmaceutical Industry Associations (EFPIA); and the European IT Round Table (which brings together, on a very loose and informal basis, the heads of Western Europe's main information technology companies).

The main EU target of the business lobby is normally the Commission, which may be approached for information, for advance notification of likely future developments, or in the hope that the views of business may be incorporated into proposed EU policies and laws. In reacting to the many approaches to which it is subject the Commission is normally receptive and responsive. Consultations and exchanges between the Commission and business occur at many levels and in many settings: from one-off meetings between Commissioners and leading businessmen – such as the meeting in June 1991 between the President of the Commission, Jacques Delors, and the heads of Europe's leading electronics companies (Bull, Thomson, Siemens, Olivetti and Philips) – to the regularised consultations which occur within the framework of the extensive consultative committee system that is clustered around the Commission.

A major reason why the Commission is so open is that its own limited resources means that it is often more dependent on business than are national governments to provide it with much needed information. Another reason is that EU policies and laws can be more easily developed and applied if affected interests are given some say in deciding what those policies and laws are, or at least can be satisfied as to the EU's good intentions.

Such is the potential assistance that business interests can give to the Commission that in a few policy areas – mainly specialised and technical areas where strong and widely encompassing groups exist – what might almost be described as neo-corporatist relations have been established between the Commission and Euro-groups. Pharmaceuticals is such an example: EFPIA has strongly influenced the Commission with regard to pricing, patents, medicine authorisation and marketing, and has been given agency powers in regard to the implementation of policy on drug information.[6]

By contrast with the receptivity of the Commission, the European Council and the Council of Ministers cannot normally be directly approached or lobbied by business. This is partly because they are not permanently constituted bodies but rather are, in effect, constant rounds of inter-state negotiations. (The Council of Ministers does have a permanent secretariat of just over 2000 officials, but this exists primarily to service Council negotiations and is not generally available for lobbying purposes.) It is partly also because neither body has wished to make itself available to outside interests. Business interests which wish to influence these bodies – and the Council of Ministers is a much more realistic target than the European Council – have, therefore, to make their approach through national governments. If governments do allow themselves to be persuaded by an interest's viewpoint, they may then present that viewpoint as the national viewpoint in the Council of Ministers.

In addition to being the way to the Council of Ministers, another reason for lobbying national governments is that they are the main agencies of EU policy implementation. It may well be advantageous for a business sector or firm if a government can be persuaded to, say, delay incorporation of an EU directive into national law, or to be not too vigorous in applying, for example, EU competition, environmental or consumer protection laws.

The European Parliament, rather like national parliaments, has traditionally been a secondary target for business lobbies. In recent years, however, it has received increasing attention as it has become a more influential, more powerful and more vigorous body. As this has happened, Members of the European Parliament (MEPs) have come to exercise important intermediary, liaising and channelling roles between business and the EU, EP committees have become an increasing focus of lobbying activities, and business lobbyists have become much thicker on the ground at the monthly plenary sessions of the EP in Strasbourg.

Business interests thus have several options available when they wish to press a case of some sort at EU level. Which is the most suitable and effective option varies according to circumstances.

CONCLUDING REMARKS

The political environment of business is in constant transition. An important aspect of the process of transition in recent years has been a reduction in policy differences between the states of Western Europe. There are, of course, still significant variations but they are not so great as formerly they were.

Three factors have been particularly important in accounting for this 'flattening out'. First, there has been the impact of international, and more particularly West European, interdependence. With trade barriers between countries being reduced, with finance being ever more global and footloose in nature, and with economic competition being ever more intense, it is now very difficult for any country to strike out against prevailing trends. Second, there has been some movement in the direction of political consensualisation in Western Europe. The extent to which this has occurred should not be exaggerated, but a mixture of political and practical factors have combined to bring about a narrowing in the range of economic, financial and social policies adopted by governments and advocated by major political parties. In this context, one of the most important political changes to have occurred has been the increasing acceptance of market principles by the major parties of the left in France, Spain, Italy and the UK. Third, there is the importance of the EU with, in many key policy areas, decisions and laws now being made at EU level and states being prevented from doing as they please.

The increasing importance of the EU has meant that business has increasingly had to be aware of developments at EU level, and has also increasingly had to direct its attention towards EU institutions if it wishes to influence the many aspects of the political environment in which it operates. This transference from the national to the EU level can be expected to continue, driven in no small part by ever greater consolidation of the SEM. However, it is likely that the transference will not be quite so rapid or so remorseless as was anticipated at the time of the signing of the Maastricht Treaty. The difficulties that were experienced in ratifying the TEU, coupled with the upheavals in the EMS, have put something of a brake on the integrationist momentum. Quite what force is in the brake, and for how long it will be felt, remains to be seen.

Notes

1. The terms 'policy community' and 'policy network' are examined at length in Wright (1988).
2. I have taken this framework for categorising EU policies from my book on the European Union (Nugent, 1994).
3. For the Investment Services Directive and the Capital Adequacy Directive see the *Official Journal of the European Communities* (OJ) L141, 11 June 1993. For the Second Banking Coordination Directive see OJ L386, 30 December 1989.
4. A fuller, if more dated, account of the Community's policy programme for SMEs can be found in the Commission's 1990 report on enterprise policy (Commission, 1990). See also the resolution of the Internal Market Council meeting of 11 November 1993, 'Strengthening the Competitiveness of Enterprises, in Particular of Small and Medium-Sized Enterprises and Craft Enterprises, and Developing Employment in the Community' (Council, 1993b).
5. The different types of EU legislation are explained in Chapter 3.
6. On the influence of the EFPIA see Greenwood (1991).

Guide to Further Reading

Studies which compare the institutional structure and policy approaches of several European countries with regard to business include: F. Duchene and G. Shepherd (1987); S. Wilks and M. Wright (1987); M. P. C. M. Van Schenden and R. J. Jackson (1987); and G. K. Wilson (1990).

Many general texts on the politics of individual countries contain chapters which deal with aspects of the business environment. For example, books in Macmillan's *Developments* series are useful and are periodically updated: see Dunleavy *et al.* (1993) on the UK, Hall *et al.* (1992) on France, Smith *et al.* (1992) on Germany. Grant (1987) provides a full length study of the business environment in the UK.

There are several studies of particular European industries which focus on the political environment. For example, Grant *et al.* (1988), Grant *et al.* (1989), and Martinelli (1991) all look at chemicals. Cawson *et al.* (1990) examine electronics.

Examinations of specific business related policies at European Union level include: on technology policy, Sandholtz (1992), Sharp and Pavitt (1993), and Petersen (1992); on shipping policy, Hart *et al.* (1993); on the common commercial policy, Hine (1989) and Maresceau (1993); on the special case of agriculture – which has spawned by far the greatest volume of sectoral studies – Fennell (1988) and Moyer and Josling (1990). See also the Commission Documents on industrial policy (1990a), on enterprise policy (1990b), on the electronics and information technology industry (1991), on the aircraft industry (1992a), on the motor vehicle industry (1992b), and on the telecommunications industry (1992c).

The general structure and policies of the EU are examined in many books and articles. See, for example, Nugent (1984), Nicoll and Salmon (1993), Tsoukalis (1993), and Harrop (1992).

Studies of business lobbying in the EU can be found in Mazey and Richardson (1993) and Greenwood *et al.* (1992).

The EU Treaties are published in several forms and editions. The EU's own publisher is the Office for Official Publications of the European Communities, which is based in Luxembourg.

Up to date accounts of EU activities, including policy and legislative developments, come in various forms. Major policy proposals are issued as Commission Documents (COM DOCS) and/or in the 'C' series of the *Official Journal of the European Communities* (OJ). New legislation is issued in the 'L' series of the OJ. *The Bulletin of the European Communities* provides a summary of EU activities, though it is published about six months after the activities in question. Excellent summaries and commentaries on what is happening in the EU are to be found in *Agence Europe* (daily), *European Report* (twice a week), and *European Access* (bi-monthly). The best newspaper reportage is in the *Financial Times*.

The economic environment

Rory O'Donnell

WHAT IS THE ECONOMIC ENVIRONMENT FOR BUSINESS?

In day-to-day economic commentary and discussion it is common to hear reference to a good or a bad 'economic environment' for business. This generally refers to the buoyancy of overall demand or, perhaps, the level of nominal interest rates. While these are, indeed, important elements of the economic environment, it is necessary to think more systematically about the economic environment for business activity in Europe. As was noted in the Introduction to this book, the conduct of business generally involves three elements or stages: the *acquisition* of resources; the *production* of a good or service; and *distribution* and sale. This suggests that many aspects of the economic environment beyond the buoyancy of aggregate demand and the level of interest rates affect the business environment. So, other macroeconomic factors, such as exchange rates, influence business decisions. The environment in which labour is hired is shaped by structural factors, such as skill levels and demography, and the *use* of labour is influenced by the social and legal norms which prevail. Technological capacity influences the availability and use of numerous assets which affect business activity. Patterns of consumer demand, which reflect cultural and demographic differences, can be seen as part of the economic environment. Finance is a key requirement of business and, consequently, the availability of financial services and the structure of the financial sector are also important aspects of the economic environment. Likewise, the existing structure of firms and industries shapes the opportunities for business. The geographical distribution of population and economic activity defines both opportunities for, and constraints on, business activity. Business is conducted in legal and social contexts which, taking a broad view, could also be seen as part of the economic environment.

Several of these dimensions of the economic environment are discussed in other chapters. This chapter provides a background to the more detailed analysis of these chapters by: (1) surveying the national economies of Western Europe, especially the economies of the member states of the European Union (EU); (2) examining the growing importance of market integration in Europe; (3) considering the nature and importance of key economic policy activities of the EU – notably the creation of the Single European Market (SEM), the attempt to control exchange rates by means of the European Monetary System (EMS), and the projected movement towards Economic and Monetary Union (EMU); and (4) placing the European economy in its global context.

In focusing particularly on policy at EU level, it is not being assumed that the EU by itself determines the economic and business environment. It is clear from Chapter 1 that the policy scope of the EU remains limited by national policy powers and involvement. Moreover, the process of formal European integration has coincided with a much wider internationalisation of economic and business life, with the consequence that the impact of the economic policies of the EU is also constrained by the globalisation of markets and firms. In short, economic and business life functions at a range of levels: the local, the regional, the national, the European, and the global. A central aim of this and other chapters is to identify the interaction of these different levels of the business environment, with particular emphasis being paid to the extent to which they relate to, and are affected by, integration at the EU level.

Two qualifications should be borne in mind when considering this account of the European economic environment. First, the economic environment for business in Europe is, like the economy itself, a subject on which there are alternative perspectives. Consequently, it is not possible to provide a purely factual and uncontested account of the economic environment for business in Europe. Any account is a combination of selected facts and interpretations, and different facts and interpretations could be chosen. Second, this account cannot do justice to the diversity of business activity. The relevant economic environment for the production and sale of motor cars for the European market is, for example, quite different from the economic environment which is relevant to running a restaurant in Dublin or a design consultancy in Copenhagen. A comprehensive account of the economic environment for business in Europe must disaggregate business by size, sector, stage of production, and nationality.

THE NATIONAL ECONOMIES OF WESTERN EUROPE

Size, economic significance, and prosperity

The overall significance of each of the national economies of Western Europe is indicated in Table 2.1. The four largest countries – Germany, Italy, France and the UK – contain 73 per cent of the population of the EU and over 66 per cent of the population of Western Europe. These four are each several times larger than all other countries, with the exception of Spain. This demographic significance is more than reflected in overall economic significance. The four large economies produce 78 per cent of EU Gross Domestic Product (GDP), with Germany alone producing over 25 per cent. The non-EU economies of Western Europe – of which Austria, Finland, Norway, Sweden and Switzerland are the most important – are of similar absolute size to several of the smaller economies within the EU.

TABLE 2.1   The economies of Western Europe: size, economic significance and prosperity

	Population 1991	GDP, 1992 billions US dollars[1]	GDP, 1991 per head[2] OECD = 100
Belgium	10.0	218	98
Denmark	5.2	142	99
Germany	79.8	1 763	110
Greece	10.3	79	44
Spain	39.0	580	72
France	57.1	1 336	103
Ireland	3.5	49	65
Italy	57.8	1 226	95
Luxembourg	0.4	11	120
Netherlands	15.1	323	93
Portugal	9.8	83	52
United Kingdom	57.4	1 039	88
EC	345.4	6 849	92
Austria	7.8	186	97
Finland	5.0	113	90
Norway	4.3	113	95
Sweden	8.6	246	94
Switzerland	6.9	244	122
US	252.7	5 881	125
Japan	123.9	3 699	108

NOTES
[1] Current prices and exchange rates.
[2] Indices using current PPPs (OECD = 100).

SOURCE   OECD (1993).

The third column of Table 2.1 shows an index of GDP per head, with the OECD average equal to 100. The richest countries in the OECD are clearly the US and Switzerland. Western Europe contains considerable disparity in income per head and this disparity is concentrated in the EU, with income levels ranging from 120 per cent of the OECD average in Luxembourg, to 44 per cent in Greece, 52 per cent in Portugal, and 65 per cent in Ireland. By contrast, the non-EU Western European countries are fairly uniformly prosperous. These data reveal a distinct geographical divide in Western Europe: less prosperous countries all lie on the southern or western periphery. This suggests that some systematic factors differentiate the Western European 'core' from its periphery.

Long-run economic growth

The rate of economic growth of the economies of the EU and of selected OECD countries is shown in Table 2.2. The most striking feature of these data is the marked slowing of growth after 1973, as the post-war 'golden age' came to an end. Since then, there have been periods of growth, but these have typically been short-lived and confined to a number of countries at any one time. In particular, the period since the second oil shock of 1979 and the deep recession of the early 1980s has seen an uneven pattern of growth in Europe. The overall growth of the EU was very slow between 1980 and 1985, at 1.4 per cent per annum, though a number of countries – the UK, Ireland and Denmark – managed to grow a little faster. From 1986 to 1991, overall growth in OECD-Europe was somewhat better, at an average of 2.8 per cent, but some countries experienced much stronger growth (notably Germany, Spain, Ireland and Portugal), while others (the UK, Denmark, Sweden and Greece) underperformed. Since 1991, there has been more uniformity of economic performance, except for the UK which has remained an outlier. (While most European countries experienced a fall in output in 1993 and continued recession in 1994, the UK was in the upward swing of the business cycle).

Numerous national and international factors have been cited to explain the slowdown of growth in the early 1970s and the fitful nature of economic performance since then. The increased national divergence in economic growth may reflect differences in fundamental national characteristics which shape economic life (see the discussion in Chapter 7 on 'national systems of innovation'); but it may also reflect the abandonment of national demand management in a context of very limited international policy coordination. In the 1980s, countries sought growth by means of competitive disinflation and diverse supply-side policies. More recently, most countries in Europe hope to emerge from the recession of the early 1990s by means of export-led growth, but, unless there is some source of additional demand, this cannot materialise for all countries. The continuing fitful and uneven growth performance – and, in particular, its implications for unemployment – is a central feature of the European economic environment. Only in 1993 did it find its way onto the agenda of the EU, and the formulation of an adequate response at EU level, and coordinated responses at national level, constitute perhaps the key economic issue in Europe in the 1990s.

TABLE 2.2   Economic growth, 1960–91

	Average annual percentage change of GDP at constant prices			
	1960–73	*1974–79*	*1980–85*	*1986–91*
Belgium	4.8	2.3	0.8	3.2
Denmark	4.6	2.0	2.6	1.1
Germany	4.7	2.4	1.1	3.5
Greece	7.3	3.8	1.3	1.7
Spain	7.0	2.3	1.4	4.3
France	5.6	2.8	1.5	2.7
Ireland	4.3	5.0	2.5	5.4
Italy	5.2	3.5	1.4	2.8
Luxembourg	3.6	1.3	2.5	4.3
Netherlands	5.3	2.6	1.0	2.8
Portugal	6.6	2.9	0.9	4.2
United Kingdom	3.3	1.6	2.0	1.9
EC	4.6	2.5	1.4	2.9
Austria	4.6	2.9	1.3	3.4
Sweden	4.4	2.0	1.8	1.3
Switzerland	4.5	–0.3	1.4	2.2
OECD Europe	4.7	2.6	1.6	2.8
US	4.1	2.4	2.4	1.8
Japan	10.1	3.7	3.7	4.9
OECD Total	5.0	2.7	2.4	2.6

SOURCE   OECD, *National Accounts*, 1960–1991.

Broad sectoral structure

The structure of the national economies of Europe is indicated in Table 2.3. Perhaps the most significant feature of this table is the degree of convergence in broad sectoral structure. In particular, services now make the major contribution to both GDP and employment in all West European countries, and this share has risen during the past two decades. The increase in the share of services in value added and employment reflects both an absolute increase in the amount and range of service activity and a relative decline in the share of both agriculture and industry. It also reflects, in part, the 'contracting out' of non-production activities from manufacturing. The most important inference to be drawn from the data in Table 2.3 is that national economic performances – in terms of incomes, productivity, trade and inflation – are not explained by differences in broad economic structure. It seems necessary to move to a finer level of detail to identify differences which might explain relative prosperity.

Despite the overall similarity in broad sectoral structure, Table 2.3 does reveal

TABLE 2.3   **Sectoral contribution to GDP and employment, 1991, percentages**

	Agriculture		Industry		Services	
	GDP	Employment	GDP	Employment	GDP	Employment
Belgium	1.8	2.6	30.1	28.1	68.1	69.3
Denmark	3.9	5.7	24.4	27.7	71.7	66.6
Germany	1.5	3.4	38.7	39.2	59.8	57.4
Greece	13.5	23.9	24.1	27.7	62.5	48.4
Spain	5.3	10.7	35.0	33.1	59.7	56.3
France	3.1	5.8	28.7	29.5	68.2	64.8
Ireland	9.0	13.8	33.4	28.9	57.6	57.2
Italy	3.3	8.5	32.1	32.3	64.6	59.2
Luxembourg	1.4	3.3	33.7	30.5	64.9	66.2
Netherlands	4.2	4.5	31.5	25.5	64.2	69.9
Portugal	5.8	17.3	37.8	33.9	56.4	48.7
United Kingdom	1.3	2.2	30.0	27.8	68.7	70.0
Austria	2.8	7.4	36.3	36.9	60.9	55.8
Finland	4.8	8.5	27.0	29.2	68.3	62.3
Norway	2.9	5.9	35.5	23.7	61.6	70.4
Sweden	2.6	3.2	29.5	28.2	67.9	68.5
Switzerland	—	5.5	—	34.4	—	60.1
US	2.0	2.9	29.2	25.3	68.8	71.8
Japan	2.5	6.7	41.8	34.4	55.7	58.9

SOURCE   *OECD in Figures*, Supplement to *OECD Observer*, June/July 1993.

important differences. For example, in two of the strongest world economies, Germany and Japan, industry continues to contribute about 40 per cent of GDP, and it is also significant in Spain and Portugal, which have not yet attained the large service sector typical of highly developed economies. In addition, the relative significance of different service activities differs between countries and this gives some indication of the nature of the national economies: finance, insurance, real estate and business services, contribute over 20 per cent of GDP in Italy, the UK and France, over 15 per cent in Denmark, The Netherlands, Sweden, Spain (and Japan), but only 12 per cent in Germany, 7 per cent in Greece and 6 per cent in Ireland.

Industrial and trade specialisation

The observation that differences in economic structure between the national economies of Western Europe do not explain differences in performance is confirmed even when the composition of industrial output and employment are considered. An analysis of the share of industrial output and employment accounted for by each sector in the standard international system of industrial classification shows a broadly similar pattern, especially among the four large European economies.[1] Certain differences are, however, apparent. The UK is relatively more specialised in extractive industries and chemicals, France in food products, Germany in engineering and chemicals, and Italy in clothing, textiles and footwear. Among other European economies, The Netherlands is more specialised in electrical machinery, Belgium in iron and steel, Spain in leather goods, Ireland in food, and Sweden in wood products, paper and furniture. Moving to a somewhat greater level of detail, it is still difficult to find differences in structures which reveal the nature of the national economies of Europe and are capable of explaining their past or future dynamic. Sharp (1992) reports the results of an analysis which divides the twenty-eight main (two-digit) branches of manufacturing into fast-, medium- and slow-growth sectors, ranked by their performance in the OECD as a whole.[2] This revealed, first, that the rank ordering of sector changed surprisingly little between 1963 and 1988 and, second, that most large European countries had a roughly comparable share of manufacturing capabilities in the fast-, medium- and slow-growth categories to the OECD in aggregate. To some extent this reflects the influence of the large economies *on* the OECD figures, and significant differences do emerge. Germany (along with Japan and the US) is more concentrated in high-growth sectors, particularly in capital goods, which have shown stronger growth than consumer goods. By contrast, Spain, Portugal and Greece are more concentrated in medium- and slow-growth sectors.

The need to delve in considerable detail in order to reveal the specialisation of the national economies of Europe, reflects the predominance of intra-industry specialisation and trade. The classical model of *inter*-industry specialisation and trade involves each country specialising in particular industries and forgoing others. By contrast, with *intra*-industry specialisation, each country retains a presence in most industrial sectors but specialises in narrow product categories *within* each industry. These highly differentiated products are then traded between countries. For example, both the UK and Germany sell each other cars and food products. Indeed, the trade figures for all West European countries show that each country has significant exports and imports in most product categories, and this intra-industry trade accounts for a high proportion of total trade.

The role of intra-industry specialisation further confirms the limited relevance of structural differences between the national economies of Europe. For example, despite its relative concentration in medium- and slow-growth sectors, Italy has performed extremely well in manufacturing industry. Its concentration on high value added segments of furniture (a medium-growth sector) and slow-growth sectors (such as pottery, clothing, leather goods and footwear) has yielded it outstandingly high world export market shares in these categories. What has happened is that many Italian firms have transformed these cost-sensitive, slow-growth industries by concentrating on categories where design, quality and delivery are key competitive advantages. Other patterns of particular specialisation, revealed by trade performance, include the UK in spirits, printing, publishing and tobacco; Germany in plastic products, metal products, industrial chemicals, transport equipment, furniture and textiles; France in wines and spirits, glass products, rubber products, food and steel; Italy in cement and clay products; and The Netherlands in petroleum refining, tobacco, food and industrial chemicals.

The limited ability of industrial and trade structures to explain the economic performance and prospects of the national economies of Europe has led to a focus on *factors which affect all industries,* such as technology and innovation, skill levels, labour market regulation, the relations between industry and finance, and corporate culture (Sharp, 1992). Indeed, an important idea in much recent economic analysis is that these phenomena may take distinct *national* forms (Porter, 1990). Some of these aspects of the national economies of Europe are described in subsequent chapters.

Openness and export orientation

The openness and export orientation of the national economies of the EU are shown in Table 2.4. There is considerable variation in exports as a percentage of GDP, from a low of 18.5 per cent in Spain, to almost 70 per cent in Belgium and 88.8 per cent in Luxembourg. Size is clearly a factor: all four large economies export between 21 and 27 per cent of national output, while the small economies, such as The Netherlands, Belgium, Ireland and Luxembourg, are more reliant on export markets. But size is not the only factor: the less developed economies (Greece, Spain and Portugal) have yet to develop large export markets, whilst the contrast between the export dependence of Ireland and Denmark (of roughly equal size) illustrates the difference between development based on indigenous competitive strengths and firms, and development led by the branch plants of multinational corporations.

There is also considerable variation in intra-EU and extra-EU exports. The four large industrial economies export almost as much outside the EU as they do within it – although this is somewhat less true of France. In the case of Germany and Italy, this reflects their remarkable shares in world exports of manufactured goods. In the case of the UK, it reflects historical links with non-EU markets. By contrast, Belgium, Spain, Ireland, The Netherlands and Portugal all export a far higher proportion of their national output to EU than to external markets.

Public finances

National public finance aggregates are an important indicator of economic performance and likely future economic policy. Consequently, public finance has considerable significance for business and is an important element in the business environment. Key indicators of the public finance position of the European economies are shown in Table 2.5. As will be seen in a later section on the macroeconomic and monetary environment, the ratio of debt to GDP and

TABLE 2.4   Openness and export orientation, 1993

	Export % of GDP	Intra-EC exports % of GDP	Extra-EC exports % of GDP
Belgium	69.4	41.0	13.1
Denmark	36.5	14.2	13.4
Germany	23.7	13.1	10.7
Greece	25.2	7.6	4.3
Spain	18.5	8.6	3.6
France	22.9	11.0	6.6
Ireland	63.1	42.2	14.6
Italy	21.0	9.0	6.8
Luxembourg	88.8	—	—
Netherlands	53.6	32.4	13.0
Portugal	27.9	15.8	5.3
United Kingdom	26.1	11.3	9.2
EC	26.6	13.5	8.5
USA	10.9		
Japan	10.1		

SOURCE   European Commission, *Annual Economic Report*, 1993.

the budget deficit are among the 'convergence criteria' for the EU's projected transition to Economic and Monetary Union. The path of the debt/GDP ratio is determined by four parameters:

- the rate of interest on national debt;
- the rate of growth of nominal GDP;
- the primary deficit (i.e. the difference between non-interest government expenditure and revenue);
- the initial debt/GDP ratio.

High interest rates tend to drive up the debt ratio by increasing servicing costs; high initial debt strengthens this effect; rapid growth tends to drive the debt ratio down; and, finally, a primary deficit adds to the debt, while a primary surplus pays back some debt.

During the late 1970s and early 1980s, conditions prevailed which tended to increase debt ratios: slow growth and historically high interest rates meant that even modest budget deficits set the debt/GDP ratio on an upward path. At the same time, deep recession and difficult problems of industrial restructuring tended to increase budget deficits. In the mid-1980s there was, with the exceptions of Greece, Italy and Portugal, a serious attempt at budgetary consolidation in Europe. However, it has proved difficult to generate big enough primary surpluses to reduce, or even stabilise, debt ratios. Since the mid-1980s this ratio has risen significantly in Belgium, Greece, Italy, Portugal and The Netherlands; has risen slightly in Germany and France; and has fallen in Denmark, Ireland and the UK.

TABLE 2.5   **Nominal convergence indicators: debt and deficits**

	Gross public debt % of GDP[3]	Budget deficit General government borrowing as % of GDP[1]	
	1994	*1993*	*1994*
Belgium	135.1	6.3	5.6
Denmark	64.0	3.2	2.6
Germany	47.2	5.5	5.0
Greece	86.1	13.1	11.1
Spain	51.5	7.2	6.4
France	53.4	5.4	5.5
Ireland	94.2	2.8	2.8
Italy	114.1	9.7	8.6
Luxembourg	8.6	2.0	1.7
Netherlands	80.2	4.0	4.5
Portugal	65.3	5.7	4.7
United Kingdom	51.5	8.3	6.4
EU[2]	—	6.3	5.8
Austria	49.0	2.0	2.7
Finland	40.0	9.5	6.5
Sweden	73.8	13.4	11.1
Switzerland	—	4.0	3.5

[1]SOURCE   *Economic Outlook for Europe*, Autumn 1993, Association d'Instituts Européens de Conjuncture Economique (AIECE). Figures for Greece, Luxembourg, Portugal and EU from *European Economy*, no. 54, 1993 and Supplement A, June/July 1993.
[2]European Union without Greece and Portugal.
[3]SOURCE   *Economic Outlook*, December 1992; figures for Luxembourg and Portugal from *European Economy*, no. 54, 1993.

Estimated budget deficits for 1993 and 1994 are shown in Table 2.5. These figures reflect deep recession, with all countries, including Germany, France and Denmark, experiencing sizeable budget deficits. While the economic cycle will probably return these countries to near budget balance, others have deficits which are clearly structural rather than cyclical. Belgium, Greece, Italy – and, to a lesser extent, Portugal, The Netherlands and Spain – have run large budget deficits in every year since 1985, or earlier. Where this is combined with large annual costs of servicing outstanding debt, it indicates a severe public finance problem which will last for many years to come.

MARKET INTEGRATION IN WESTERN EUROPE

Background

The European Economic Community (EEC) Treaty of 1957 expressed the determination to 'lay the foundations of an ever closer union among the peoples of Europe'. The principal means chosen to achieve this was the establishment of a European Economic Community, the central element of which was to be the creation of a common market – an integrated market without obstacles to the movement of goods, persons, services and capital.

The relatively integrated economy of what is now the European Union developed largely out of the provisions of the EEC Treaty. It is an economy which should be seen as part, albeit by far the most important part, of a large, prosperous West European zone of advanced economic activity. The relatively homogeneous and highly integrated nature of this zone has been obscured by the division of Western Europe into two trade groupings, the European Communities (EC) and the European Free Trade Association (EFTA), but the two groupings have, in practice, long been closely associated with one another via trading agreements. In January 1994, a new trading agreement – the European Economic Area (EEA) – officially started functioning, which means that there is now virtually unrestrained circulation of manufactured goods, services, capital and labour between EFTA (minus Switzerland) and the EU.

The formation of the EEC in 1957 and of EFTA in 1960 had significant effects on trade. During the 1960s and early 1970s, trade inside each group increased relative to trade between the EC and EFTA. For example, the share of exports from each EC–6 member that went to other members roughly doubled between 1958 and 1987. After 1973, when free trade agreements on industrial goods were concluded between the EC and EFTA countries, trade *between* the two blocks grew significantly. One interpretation of these and other developments is that the core of Western Europe, with Germany as its pivot, grew in the 1970s and 1980s to include the UK, and this enlarged and more cohesive core exerted a strong gravitational pull on the periphery of Western Europe. The countries of the southern periphery – Greece, Spain and Portugal – joined the EC in the 1980s and several EFTA countries, notwithstanding the EEA, seem set to join in the 1990s. These enlargements may further increase the gravitational pull of the EU, presenting all countries in Europe with the choice of becoming either full members or satellites (Wijkman, 1990).

The emergence of a single trading area combining the EU and EFTA is not the only significant element of market integration to have occurred in Europe. A third regional trade arrangement, formed in 1949, was the Council of Mutual Economic Assistance (CMEA). This eventually contained Albania, Bulgaria, Czechoslovakia, the GDR, Hungary, Poland, Rumania and the Soviet Union, but it collapsed after the political institutional transformations in Central and Eastern Europe in 1989 and was formally dissolved in 1991. The following year, Czechoslovakia (now the Czech and Slovak Republics), Hungary and Poland – the so-called Visegrad states – signed Association Agreements with the EC, and these, as well as providing various forms of economic and technical assistance to the Visegrad states, provide for a gradual dismantling of trade barriers (with the EU dismantling its barriers at a more rapid pace). Association Agreements have subsequently been negotiated with other Eastern Europe states.

The crisis of the Community and the costs of 'non-Europe'

In response to the economic difficulties which were experienced in Western Europe in the 1970s and early 1980s, the European Parliament, in 1982, commissioned a group of economists to draw up a report on the economic crisis affecting the European Community and on ways of bringing about a resumption of growth. The report, by Albert and Ball, confirmed that the economic performance of the EC was significantly worse than that of its major trading rivals, Japan and the US. Their analysis led them to argue that 'the main obstacle to the economic growth of European countries is what we must call "non-Europe" '. By 'non-Europe' they meant the low level of cooperation between Community members and the weakness of common policies. States had resorted to measures which, though they did not contravene the Community's rules, amounted to protection via non-tariff barriers (NTBs). Important examples were the use made of state aids, state procurement, and national technical and professional standards. In addition, member states had been less than *communautaire*, with the result that 'Europe has for ten years been virtually paralysed by hair splitting and protracted disputes and interminable budgetary debates, all of ridiculously small importance compared with the major challenges facing it' (Albert and Ball, 1983).

One of those major challenges was the wave of technological change and innovation. As a result of non-cooperation between the different firms and states, Europe, though spending as much on research as Japan, was effectively being left behind – especially in the field of information technology. Through most of the 1980s, EC imports of high-technology products grew at an annual average rate of 11.4 per cent, almost double the rate of growth of EC exports. In particular, imports significantly outpaced exports in trade with Japan, EFTA, and the most competitive developing countries. The implication of these adverse rates of growth of exports on trade levels or trade balances is shown in Table 2.6. An export/import ratio greater than one reflects a trade surplus, a ratio less than one shows a trade deficit. The overall decline of the EC trade ratio from 1.1 in 1982 to 0.8 in 1991, reflects a shift from surplus to deficit in high-tech products. Only with the US did the Community's position improve during the 1980s. The most dramatic deterioration in the trade balance of the EC occurred with the group of fifteen competitive developing countries (denoted MC15 in Table 2.6). As noted in the early 1990s by the European

TABLE 2.6   EC trade in high-tech products: export/import ratio

	1982	*1991*
Extra-EC	1.1	0.8
USA	0.4	0.5
Japan	0.2	0.1
EFTA	1.2	0.9
MC15	2.0	0.7

SOURCE   'The European Community as a World Trade Partner', *European Economy*, no. 52.

Commission, 'all indicators point to a weakening of the EC competitive position and an increasing dependence on foreign suppliers' (Commission, 1993, and see below).

In devising a strategy for recovery Albert and Ball laid stress on two sets of measures: the creation of a unified internal market, and new Community-level cooperation in a number of important fields – specifically high-technology sectors such as information technology, energy, biotechnology, aircraft and space research. These two elements became the central thrust of the initiatives which culminated in the Commission's 1985 White Paper *Completing the Internal Market* and the 1986 Single European Act (SEA).

The 1992 project: completing the internal market

In 1985 the incoming Commission, led by Jacques Delors, presented a White Paper to the European Council entitled *Completing the Internal Market*. It emphasised that the EC must, in the interests of efficiency and competitiveness, remove internal barriers by 'completing' the internal market. There were three aspects to this 'completion':

– welding together the twelve individual markets of the member states into one single market of 320 million people;
– ensuring that this single market was also an expanding market;
– ensuring that the market was flexible so that resources, both of people and materials, and of capital and investment, flowed into areas of greatest economic advantage.

The White Paper set out in great detail the measures necessary to achieve the first of these objectives and a timetable for their legal enactment. It grouped the 300 measures necessary to complete the internal market under three headings:

• the removal of physical barriers to trade and competition, including the removal of border posts;

- the removal of technical barriers to trade and competition – the most obvious of these barriers being different national standards adopted for health or safety reasons or for environmental or consumer protection;
- the removal of fiscal barriers to trade and competition – in particular, the approximation of indirect taxes across the EC.

An important innovation in the White Paper was the adoption by the Commission of a 'new approach' to the removal of technical barriers. Up to that point the attempt to remove technical barriers had taken the form of harmonisation of countries' technical standards. This proved to be an extremely lengthy and difficult process. The 'new approach' moved away from the concept of harmonisation to that of mutual recognition. The principle of mutual recognition means that member states must give access to their market to any product which satisfies the requirements of any member state (see also Chapter 3).

Another important innovation in the White Paper was action on public procurement. In principle, public bodies were already forbidden to discriminate between suppliers from EC countries and were required to advertise major contracts, but in practice public procurement in all countries usually favoured national companies. In addition, important areas such as telecommunications, water, energy and transport were exempt from the Community's requirements for open tendering. The White Paper proposed that existing regulations for open competition would have to be enforced and that these exemptions would be eliminated.

While the White Paper was concerned mainly with the SEM, it did link this to three other policy approaches. It stressed that the suspension of internal borders must be accompanied by actions which strengthened the research and technological base of industry in the EC. It argued that the integration of national markets must be accompanied by a strengthening of the coordination of economic policies and the European Monetary System (EMS). Finally, the Commission noted the risk that, by facilitating the movement of resources to areas of greatest economic advantage, the completion of the internal market could widen the existing discrepancies between regions of the Community. In the Commission's view, this enhanced the importance of the Community's Structural Funds.

Most of the measures in the White Paper were adopted by the December 1992 deadline and attention has since moved to the member states, which have to transpose the EU directives into national law and ensure implementation. The Commission has identified delays in five areas: suppression of border checks, indirect taxation, the creation of a EU patent and trademark, abolition of double taxation on firms, and company law.

Over the years a number of measures have been added to the SEM as originally outlined by the Commission. For example, a greater realisation of the link between external trade policy and internal market fragmentation has led to action on car quotas and air transport (see below). Proposals for a single market for energy have also been added and, recently, the role of infrastructure, and in particular of trans-European networks, in making the single market a reality has been emphasised by the Commission.

Firm size in the internal market

In 1988 the European Commission undertook a major study of the SEM entitled the *Economics of 1992*.[3] This included an inventory of the main non-tariff barriers, estimation of the losses in welfare resulting from the fragmentation of European markets – the so-called 'costs of non-Europe' – and analysis of the likely effects of the SEM programme. The analysis identified two main channels through which the SEM programme would impact on business and the economy – 'size' and 'competition'. 'Size' referred to the possibility that reduced costs, increased demand, and better market access would allow firms to exploit economies of scale. The competition to acquire scale and the subsequent competition to lower costs could initiate a major restructuring. 'Competition' referred to the possibility that increased competition would force previously sheltered firms to differentiate their product by means of innovation. The operation of this mechanism led some to expect that the SEM programme would have a major dynamic impact on those sectors in which NTBs were high, technological development was significant and the outlook for market growth was good (Emerson *et al.*, 1988).

While exploitation of economies of scale and increased competition are not necessarily inconsistent – so long as the market can sustain enough firms – there are, in fact, considerable differences in thinking between those who stress the benefits of *economies of scale* and those who emphasise *competition* and *innovation*. This was reflected in the *Economics of 1992*, which was assembled from the research of many different economists. In the report there was a clear tension between the view that further concentration of industry would be likely in the SEM (because significant economies of scale remained to be exploited) and the view that the larger market would increase the *variety* of products available, and hence that small- and medium-sized enterprises would benefit most (because they suffered most from non-tariff barriers and they have a particular ability to innovate). This is one of the most important questions concerning the European economic environment and the impact on it of the integrated market. If a significant part of the increased competition created by completion of the market takes the form of cost reduction based on scale expansion, then the fear naturally arises that small firms will find it very difficult to compete. Furthermore, if completion implies increased firm size, then *barriers to entry* of various sorts may increase – even though market completion also means increased competition *between those dominant firms* in a given industry (Venables, 1985). If, on the other hand, those who stress competition and innovation are correct, then the increased competition resulting from market completion will be based only to a small extent on exploitation of scale economies and will take a number of other forms, such as technological activity aimed at product and process development, product differentiation, market segmentation, and redefinition of firms' specialisation (Ergas, 1984; Geroski and Jacquemin, 1985). The argument between these two views turns on a number of theoretical and empirical points concerning the effects of the SEM on the size of firms, the relationship between competition and innovation, the historical significance of economies of scale, the effects of technical and organisational change on scale economies, and the role of small firms in economic development. While these are complex phenomena, some impression of the role of firm size in the European economy can be gained by reviewing recent patterns of mergers, acquisitions and alliances in Europe.

Cross-border mergers, acquisitions and alliances in Europe

An important feature of the European economic environment is the wave of mergers, acquisitions and strategic alliances (MAAs) which has occurred since the late 1980s. In contrast with earlier periods of MAA activity, the recent boom has witnessed a high proportion of cross-border deals. In considering the implications of this for the European business environment a number of features of the phenomenon should be noted.

- While much of this activity has certainly been prompted by the completion of the SEM, there is, almost always, a significant global dimension to the restructuring which occurs within Europe (Young, 1992).
- In pursuit of European and global strength, both EU and non-EU firms have been involved in European MAAs.
- The recent wave of mergers and acquisitions has very distinct national, sectoral and structural characteristics.

This section will illustrate these features and assess what MAAs tell us about the emerging European economy. It will conclude with a discussion of the policy issues which MAA's create for the European Union.

The national and sectoral characteristics of recent MAAs can be summarised as follows. The acquiring firms come principally from the UK, France, the US, Switzerland, Sweden and Germany. A very large proportion of the acquired companies are British, with German, French, Spanish and Italian firms also proving attractive acquisitions. This confirms Britain's role as both a major international investor and a major location for inward investment. However, a large proportion of British acquisitions have been in the US rather than Europe. Mergers and acquisitions are concentrated in a few industries, reflecting particular circumstances and motivations. Among these are the chemical sector (where economies of scale exist), food products (in which there have traditionally been high NTBs) and the defence industry (in which the opening of government procurement and the end of the Cold War have created fear of international competition). In general, mergers and acquisitions have risen significantly less quickly in fast growth sectors than in the rest of industry (Jacquemin and Wright, 1993).

There has also been a rapid increase in the number of strategic alliances in Europe. Among the most notable of these are the partnerships of GEC and Siemens, and Volvo and Renault. Many economists see joint ventures and other types of cooperative arrangement as important ways of anticipating the SEM. Jacquemin and Wright argue that these operations can, in certain circumstances, promote synergies through complementarity, making it possible to disseminate technological information more widely, and to reduce the time required to bring a new product or process to market. Alliances and joint ventures can also ensure that risks are more widely distributed among partners and can facilitate entry, especially for small- and medium-sized firms, in high-tech activities, such as information technology, new materials and biotechnology. Jacquemin and Wright (1993) also note, however, that management problems and regulatory and political differences constitute obstacles to cooperation agreements. Kay goes further, arguing that the direct effect of the SEM will be to *diminish* the frequency of industrial collaborative activity in general, and joint venture arrangements in particular: 'Where 1992 is successful, its direct effect should be to switch the emphasis in corporate strategies from cooperation to competition' (Kay, 1993, p. 177).

Given the diversity of markets and firms, it is not surprising that the motivations for MAAs vary considerably. Two possible motivations are strategic and economic. Strategic motivations include growth of market share, diversification, competitive considerations and defensive moves. Economic motivations include the desire to exploit economies of scale and to acquire resources (such as technology, products, brands and skills) held by the target firm. Examining European MAAs in the light of these motivations, Hamill concludes that there is, indeed, an important SEM dimension to the recent wave of cross-border deals:

> Competitiveness in a 'Europe without frontiers' will be dependent on the strength of a company's product (market share) and its geographical market coverage within Europe. Companies positioned to gain most from the Single market are those with strong product portfolios across most of the major markets in Europe. In many of the cases presented below, cross-border MAAs have taken place to increase market share, strengthen products and extend geographical market coverage prior to the removal of internal trade barriers. (Hamill, 1992, p. 143)

This has been important both for cross-border MAAs within Europe and also for non-European companies, especially Japanese and US firms, which have acquired or formed alliances with European partners because of the fear of 'Fortress Europe'. But research in this area stresses that, despite the role of the SEM, there remains an important outward-looking, global, dimension to most recent MAAs.

Hamill's survey includes MAAs in the European defence industry, airlines, pharmaceuticals and packaging. It is worth looking briefly at each of these. In *defence equipment* European companies, such as GEC, Plessey, Daimler-Benz, Thomson and Siemens, have responded to the SEM, particularly the liberalisation of government procurement, by merging or forming partnerships to achieve the critical mass necessary for global competition. In the *airline* industry, a wave of American acquisitions and mergers, following deregulation, has been echoed in Europe by a wave of cross-border strategic alliances. This has, in part, been prompted by the deregulatory effect of the SEM on a previously highly regulated industry. But Hamill notes that there has been an important international dimension as well. The larger European airlines, such as BA and SAS, have aimed to globalise their operations by strengthening their market position in the US, but especially in the rapidly growing Far Eastern market. In other industries the European dimension seems less significant than global, technological and strategic developments. In *pharmaceuticals*, for example, the increasing cost of R&D has been among the factors which have motivated recent MAAs. This has prompted the large multinationals to acquire developing biotechnology companies, and to form alliances with each other. *Packaging* is an example of an activity in which a process of Europeanisation has spread from one industry to another: this industry has traditionally been highly fragmented but, as a consequence of recent MAAs, the European industry is becoming increasingly consolidated into fewer, larger companies providing pan-European coverage. Hamill notes that the 'major motivational factor in this respect has been the shift towards pan-European strategies by major packaging customers, especially European food and drink companies, which itself has been the result of mergers and acquisitions' (Hamill, 1992, p. 153).

The *food industry* presents a particularly interesting example of the emerging European economic environment and its implications for business (see also the discussion of this sector in Chapter 6). The industry is one which has traditionally been fragmented along national lines, because of differences in tastes, standards, regulations and policies concerning food production and sale. At the same time, within the larger European economies, the industry has undergone significant evolution and consolidation.[4] Future development will be determined by the response of companies to three types of change: strategic and technical possibilities, competition from the major food multinationals, and the SEM programme. With regard to the latter, the Commission's research shows that the indirect effects of the SEM – such as the broadening of consumer choice, an increase in trade, efficiency gains and improvement in the competitiveness of EU food companies *vis-à-vis* the rest of the world – are likely to be significant. This, and the convergence of consumer tastes in Europe, suggests that large economies of scale might be exploited by replacing national brands with pan-European brands. However, companies taking this route may, in turn, be squeezed – on the one side by pan-European own-label suppliers and, on the other, by restructured multinationals supporting global brands (McGee and Segal-Horn, 1992). Recent MAAs provide evidence for each of these possibilities. While the absolute number of domestic MAAs has increased sharply, the proportion of MAAs which are cross-border has risen also. These have been interpreted as attempts to build pan-European positions from which to dominate particular food categories. But there is also evidence of major firms seeking to build international rather than purely European positions, suggesting an agenda which is global rather than regional. The result of these MAAs has been to further consolidate the European and US consumer packaged good's markets into fewer hands – Philip Morris (USA), BSN (France), Nestlé (Switzerland), Unilever (Anglo-Dutch) and Pepsico (USA). For example, half of Unilever's acquisitions in the past five years have been in Europe, but the biggest have been in the US, suggesting 'that multinational and transnational portfolios are becoming very much more important... There appears to be little hard evidence yet for the rise of the genuine pan-European brander' (ibid., p. 44). These developments in the food industry confirm the general observation that the emerging environment for any particular line of business in Europe will be the outcome of a complex interaction between the undoubted Europeanisation prompted by the SEM programme, autonomous technical and other changes in each industry, and the tendency to globalisation which is strong in many lines of business.

Mergers, acquisitions and alliances raise important issues for EU competition policy. They also bring to light significant disagreements about the actual and desirable nature of the economic environment for business in Europe. The policy issues concern the balance between competition in the *internal* market, on the one hand, and the competitiveness of Europe *vis-à-vis* the US and Japan, on the other. A central instrument in the creation of the common market was competition policy: Article 85 of the EU Treaty prohibits any agreements and concerted practices which restrict and distort competition in the EU and which may affect trade between member states, whilst Article 86 prohibits abuse of dominant position which may affect trade between member states. When the SEM programme was removing non-tariff barriers to intra-EU competition, it was considered important to prevent new impediments to competition arising from collusion or monopoly power. Consequently, the traditional pillars of EC competition policy were buttressed in 1989 by the introduction of new legislation on mergers and acquisitions. This so-called 'Merger Regulation' dictates that all mergers and acquisitions with a 'Community dimension' must be notified to the Commission, which then decides whether the deal constitutes a threat to effective competition in the EU.[5] However, if improved European competitiveness is to be achieved by overcoming the fragmentation of the internal market, thereby throwing European firms into competition with one another, this is believed to involve an inevitable trend towards industrial concentration. This has led the Commission to favour MAAs which create pan-European firms and corporate structures suited to the SEM and large enough to compete with major non-European players. In its study of horizontal mergers, the Commission says, 'It is probable then in many cases mergers simultaneously produce some efficiency gains, notably in the form of cost reductions, and some increase in monopoly power which may manifest itself in higher prices. There is thus the question of a trade-off between the two kinds of effects' (Commission, 1989, p. 45). The Commission's approach has been to develop indicators of the relative likelihood of increased monopoly power and efficiency gains. It considers that efficiency gains are likely where there are large economies of scale and learning effects, substantial excess capacity, and high capital intensity and technological content. It assigns most of the high-tech industries (including chemicals, pharmaceuticals, computers, telecommunications, electronics, the motor and aerospace industries, and precision instruments) to the category of industries 'in which there is less danger of a reduction in competition and mergers offer real prospects of efficiency gains' (ibid., p. 29).

In conducting competition and merger policy the Commission can take advantage of the fact that Article 85(3) stipulates that the prohibition on restrictive practices may not apply if an agreement between firms 'contributes to improving the production or distribution of goods or to promoting technical progress'. In the very first case to be considered under the 1990 Merger Regulation, the Commission approved the cross-shareholding agreement between Renault and Volvo on the grounds that its positive effect on international competitiveness would outweigh any negative effect on competition. Overall, the Commission reviewed fifty-four proposed deals in the first year of operation of the Merger Regulation: of these, the vast majority were approved without change and three were approved after modification. Up to the end of 1993, only one had been blocked.

Some economists dispute the empirical and analytical basis of the Commission's approach to MAAs. Kay argues that 'the Commission has adopted too permissive an attitude towards European merger and acquisition activity and that there is a real danger that the emerging Europe-wide merger wave may sacrifice some of the gains in productive efficiency and consumer welfare that 1992 is intended to generate' (Kay, 1993). In support of this view, he cites evidence that mergers frequently have little positive effect on profitability and rarely lead to an increase in efficiency. If this is the record of single-country mergers, there may be even greater problems with cross-border mergers because of the added complications of different cultures, languages, legal systems and political conventions. Economists like Kay also reject the argument that the threat of takeover disciplines European management and encourages it to pursue profit-oriented behaviour. The relatively well-developed markets for corporate control in the UK and the US are not typical of the European situation, and development of an active market for corporate control at European level could seriously detract from the very objectives of competition and efficiency embodied in the SEM programme, by promoting short-termism and a concern with financial transactions (ibid.). This scepticism about the Commission's favourable attitude to MAAs is based, in part, on doubts about the Commission's estimate of the extent of economies of scale and rejection of the Commission's argument that mergers can be beneficial in high-technology industries.

Kay traces the positive attitude to MAAs to the intertwining of two separate EU agendas: competition in the *internal* market and competing in the *external* market. For those who believe that European strength depends on 'mergers and takeovers ... [which] create truly European companies which have no special links to a particular country' (Emerson *et al.*, 1988), there is indeed a trade-off between competition and competitiveness. Kay sees the Commission being willing 'to subvert' the internal market objective to the external market objective. 'Ironically, however, if the Commission's enthusiasm for stimulating cross-frontier mergers post-*1992* is allowed full rein, all the evidence cited above suggests it could have profoundly deleterious consequences, not only for competition within the internal market, but also for Community competitiveness *vis-à-vis* the rest of the world' (Kay, 1993, p. 176).

The internal market programme in perspective

There can be little doubt that the legislative programme to complete the internal market was a very significant step in European economic integration. Whether it will fulfil the hopes of its authors, by reviving the competitiveness and dynamism of Europe, remains to be seen and certainly cannot be taken for granted. In this, and a number of other respects, it is important to keep the SEM programme in perspective when considering the European economic environment for business.

First, research suggests that while the terms 'completion of *the* internal market' and '*single* European market' are unavoidable, they may create the misleading impression that since January 1993 there has been a single or unified European market of 340 million people for almost all manufactured goods and services. But the fragmentation of the European market is only partly a result of the trade barriers which have been removed in the SEM programme. Much of the fragmentation arises from the diversity of cultures, traditions and consumption patterns in Europe and, consequently remains after 1993. Conversely, there was already a unified European market for some commodities, such as aircraft and oil. The extent to which the SEM programme is creating a unified European market in each product is a question for expert industry-specific analysis. Kay shows that the 'strategic market' may have very different geographic and population dimensions in different industries and, indeed, segments of industries (Kay, 1990; see also Chapters 5 and 6).

Second, it is important to appreciate that economic analysis cannot predict the precise effects of the SEM on each industry and country in Europe. Even if we were content to apply the traditional factor proportions theory of trade, or a modified version of it taking account of human capital, etc., we are faced with the problem identified by Pelkmans: 'variants of this theory always explain comparative advantage at a high level of aggregation; not at the level relevant for deciding industrial production and marketing' (Pelkmans, 1984). If the *new* approach to understanding trade, with its emphasis on intra-industry trade, is considered relevant, then this problem is even more acute. As Ergas says 'it has to be conceded that intra-industry trade is a more complex phenomenon which does not lend itself as readily as the inter-industry trade model to predictions of shifts in competitiveness and comparative advantage' (Ergas, 1984).

Third, the completion of the SEM must be seen in the context of other changes in the general economic environment affecting businesses, such as technical change, organisational change, macroeconomic conditions, and the emergence of important new producers from Asia. One of the most significant features of current technological change, and the associated organisational restructuring, is that it seems to be *inherently international* or, perhaps more accurately, supranational (Perez, 1983). This arises, in part, from the provision of unprecedented data-management capabilities and telecommunications infrastructure, which allows the efficient management of transnational firms (see Chapter 6). In addition, the productivity increases, made possible by computer-aided design and manufacturing, mean that for businesses to reach viable size the volume of output and the range of products of a given plant must serve an international market. The same applies in the production of services, such as information and telecommunications. In short, national markets, particularly small national markets, are a hindrance to the full deployment of the new technologies.

Recognition of these facts allows us to see the SEM as Europe's response to a set of changes which are occurring in any event and which will inevitably increase the international aspect of economic life. In this context, the movement to completion of the internal market would seem to do two things. First, it is helping to ensure that these new developments in business occur fully in Europe, rather than influencing Europe but partly passing it by. Second, while no single national government in Europe can greatly influence the economic environment, or fashion the social developments which a rapidly changing economy produces, it seems likely that the European Union could. Whether the Union has sufficient authority, effectiveness and legitimacy to do this is, however, open to doubt.

THE MONETARY AND MACROECONOMIC ENVIRONMENT

Introduction

The monetary and financial system forms an important part of the economic environment for business in Europe. It is possible to identify four ways in which this is so. First, almost all business activity involves both equity and debt and, consequently, the availability and cost of finance is a significant factor in business decisions. Second, business involves transactions and the ability of the financial system to handle multiple and complex payments shapes the environment for business. Third, aggregate monetary magnitudes have a bearing on the macroeconomic environment through their influence on output, employment, interest rates and inflation. Fourth, the geographical space in which the European economy operates contains many jurisdictions, each of which has its own currency. The existence of different currencies, each underpinned by a different state is, in and of itself, an important feature of the European business environment. Furthermore, where national governments control monetary policy then the macroeconomic environment is likely to be different in each country.

The 1992 Treaty on European Union (TEU) contains a blueprint for transition to full Economic and Monetary Union (EMU) by 1997 or, at the latest, by 1999. However, in 1992 and 1993 the European Monetary System (EMS), a key vehicle to EMU in the Treaty, experienced severe turbulence: two currencies (sterling and the lira) left the system, several realignments occurred and, in August 1993, the margins within which currencies are permitted to fluctuate were dramatically widened. Grave doubts now exist about the economic and political possibility of moving to EMU in accordance with the Maastricht timetable. Despite these doubts and uncertainties, however, there is likely to be continued interest in exchange rate stability in Europe. In this context, the EMS and the TEU plan for EMU will remain relevant. This section therefore concentrates on these aspects of the European monetary and macroeconomic environment.

The European Monetary System

After revaluations of the mark and a devaluation of the French franc in the 1960s, the 1969 Hague summit of Community leaders decided that the Community should seek to move towards EMU. To this end, restrictions on exchange rate movements were introduced, but the project proved to be unsuccessful and was shelved at the Paris summit of 1974. A much more modest attempt to limit exchange rate volatility – the 'Snake', – was tried between 1972 and 1979 but it too had only limited success. Notwithstanding those two episodes, general dissatisfaction with the floating exchange system which had replaced the fixed rates of the Bretton Woods era in the 1970s produced pressures for change: exchange rate movements disrupted production and trade and seemed to reflect speculative whims more than underlying economic conditions. This was the context in which the EMS was devised in 1978 and introduced in early 1979.

The purpose of the EMS is to minimise fluctuations between currencies, thereby creating a 'zone of monetary stability'. A central feature of the system is the European Currency Unit (ECU). This is a composite currency made up of specified amounts of all member state currencies. At any point in time, each currency participating in the EMS has a given value – called a 'central rate' – in relation to the ECU. These values, once fixed collectively, have to persist until a decision is made by the participating states to alter them. The central rates, expressed in terms of the ECU, are then used to establish a grid of exchange rates between each pair of currencies in the system. The general means used for a country to meet its exchange rate obligations is for national fiscal and monetary policy to be conducted in such a way as to ensure that the currency's market value does not rise or fall beyond its specified limits. However, should this occur, the country concerned is obliged to intervene in the foreign exchange markets or to undertake other measures, such as changes in interest rates or fiscal policy. In order to facilitate these interventions, the EMS has some shared foreign exchange reserves and has facilities to provide credit to countries having to undertake balance of payments financing.

Although all member states' currencies are represented in the ECU, only eight countries – West Germany, France, Belgium, Luxembourg, The Netherlands, Denmark, Ireland and Italy – initially participated in the ERM of the EMS. Spain joined in June 1989, the UK in October 1990 and Portugal in April 1992, all three opting for the wider 6 per cent band, not the narrower 2.5 per cent band. In September 1992, sterling was 'suspended' and the Italian lira was withdrawn from the mechanism. In August 1993, the fluctuation band for the whole system was widened to +/–15 per cent.

The EMS has been the subject of a vast literature, examining its creation, its working and its ability to achieve its goals. This voluminous literature is now cast in a new light by the crises which hit the system from September 1992 and led to its dramatic alteration in August 1993. The crises, and their implications for EMS and EMU, have now themselves become the subject of analysis. It is not possible here, in an overview of the European economic environment, to provide a thorough account of the EMS and the way it has been understood by economists. However, students of the European business environment should be aware of some of the key features of the system and the issues which they have thrown up.

One of the most important features of the EMS is that it has functioned in different ways at different times during the period from 1979 to the present. Consequently, there are few general propositions which are true of EMS *per se*. The following chronology has been suggested for the development of the EMS:

- From 1979 to 1983 inflation differentials were broadly accommodated by frequent realignments.
- From 1983 to 1987 the system experienced more stability and less frequent realignments. Anxieties about asymmetry (see below) led to reform of the system in 1987.
- From 1987 to 1992 there was significant convergence of inflation rates, interest rates and budget deficits, and *no* realignments.
- In 1992 and 1993 the system came under severe strain as a result of remain-

ing differences in inflation, high interest rates associated with German unification and political doubts about the ratification of the TEU.

• Despite increased intra-EMS exchange rate stability, over the years from 1979 to 1993 there was a significant cumulative appreciation of the mark (and the Dutch guilder), and a trend depreciation of the lira, the French franc and the Irish punt.

As regards the impact of the EMS on the economic and monetary environment, five effects which are fairly widely accepted by observers, and which are relevant to any future attempt to establish European-level management of the macroeconomic and monetary environment, are worth listing:

1. Although the EMS has probably assisted disinflation in some countries, and the maintenance of low inflation in many, there is little evidence that it has reduced the *cost* of disinflation, in terms of increased unemployment.
2. The EMS has displayed significant asymmetry in that Germany has retained the ability to set monetary policy independently, and other countries have pegged their currencies to the deutschmark.[6]
3. This asymmetry has not been constant. Between about 1987 and 1990, monetary leadership was more widely shared, but leadership shifted back to Germany after re-unification because of Germany's need to conduct the tightest monetary policy in the EC.
4. Asymmetry has both advantages and disadvantages. It is the asymmetry of an exchange rate system which produces its disciplinary, anti-inflationary, role. But it can also increase volatility in peripheral economies.
5. There is some evidence that the EMS has lent a deflationary bias to the European economy, because each country has believed that the benefits of fiscal expansion would accrue to its neighbours.

EMU in the Treaty on European Union

The Treaty on European Union contains a blueprint for EMU. Although the events of 1992–3 have cast doubt on the feasibility of fully implementing this plan – both in terms of its context and timetable – the EU is, at present, pressing ahead. Consequently, despite a degree of uncertainty, the Maastricht blueprint for EMU is likely to remain an important element of the economic environment for business.

Three reasons can be identified for the willingness to proceed to EMU. First, after a period of naïve and dogmatic belief in the general floating of exchange rates in the 1970s, there developed widespread disillusionment with this idea in Europe and, by and large, this remains. Second, the liberalisation of capital markets as part of the SEM project is widely believed to alter the conditions for the conduct of domestic monetary policy, in such a way that it requires either the abandonment of fixed exchange rates or greater coordination of monetary policy.[7] Third, the more the SEM programme has proceeded, the more have many influential people come to believe that many of its possible benefits will be lost if separate currencies continue to exist.

The Treaty articles which deal with EMU may be classified into five categories: objectives; principles; instruments; rules; and transitional provisions. The *objectives* are to contribute to the achievement of the goals of the EC, which are set out in Article 2 of the EC Treaty as follows:

– balanced economic development;
– sustainable and non-inflationary growth respecting the environment;
– a high degree of convergence of economic performance;
– a high level of employment and of social protection;
– the raising of the standard of living;
– economic and social cohesion and solidarity.

In designing the Treaty basis of EMU, several economic and monetary *principles* were agreed and these are now incorporated in the Treaty:

– the parallel development of economic and monetary integration;
– price stability as the main objective of monetary policy;
– central bank independence;
– sound public finances and monetary conditions;
– a sustainable balance of payments;
– an open market economy with free competition.

In order to pursue the objectives outlined above in accordance with these principles, the EU requires certain policies and instruments. Although the full range of Union policies are relevant to pursuit of the stated objectives, the incorporation of EMU into the Treaty has resulted in the definition of new or enhanced *policy instruments* in two particular areas:

Monetary policy

• Establishment of a single currency, the ECU.
• The establishment of a European Central Bank to manage this currency, and definition of its rules.

Macroeconomic policy

• Surveillance of national macroeconomic policy and performance, formulation of broad guidelines for the economic policy of the member states and the Community and control of 'excessive' budget deficits.

The Treaty defines certain *rules* governing both membership of monetary union and behaviour within it. In order to participate in the adoption of the single currency, a country must meet the following 'convergence criteria':

- inflation close to the three best performing member states;
- public finances without excessive deficits or debt;
- a currency within the normal EMS fluctuation margins for at least two years, without devaluation;
- interest rates which suggest that the convergence is durable.

Within EMU and, indeed before the final stage is reached, member states must conduct their economic policies:

- as a matter of common concern and coordinate them within the Council;
- with a view to contributing to the achievement of the objectives of the Community;
- in accordance with the broad guidelines set by the European Council and the Council of Finance Ministers;
- without monetary financing or budgetary deficits;
- without being bailed out by the Community;
- avoiding 'excessive deficits'.

The Treaty, and an attached protocol, define an excessive deficit as either a government deficit significantly above 3 per cent of GDP, and not declining substantially and continuously towards that level, or public debt greater than 60 per cent of GDP and not approaching that value at a satisfactory pace.

The final element of the Treaty concerns the *transition* to EMU. There are two dimensions to the transition to a single currency. The first is definition of the *method* of transition; the second concerns the *speed* of transition and *the procedures* for moving forward. In defining the method of transition, the TEU follows closely the three stages suggested in the 1988 Delors Report on EMU. Stage one, which began in 1990, involved adherence to the ERM and the gradual removal of controls on the movement of a capital between member countries. Stage two, which began in January 1994, has seen the establishment of a European Monetary Institute, as a forerunner of the eventual European Central Bank, and is also intended to include closer coordination of the macroeconomic policies of the EU member states. In the third and final stage, exchange rates will be locked irrevocably, EU rules on macroeconomic and budgetary policy will become binding, and the new European Central Bank (ECB) will prepare the transition to a single currency. The TEU stipulates that the European Council must decide, before the end of 1996, whether a majority of member states fulfil the necessary conditions for the adoption of a single currency and, if so, set a date for the beginning of stage three. But the Treaty makes clear that 'if by the end of 1997 the date for the beginning of the third stage has not been set, the third stage will start on 1 January 1999' (Article 109 J.4). At that point, any number of states can proceed to EMU. The Treaty ensures that non-participating states cannot prevent others moving to the third stage.

The British Conservative Government has consistently opposed the idea of a single currency. In recognition of this, the TEU included a special procedure for the UK in the form of a 'Protocol'. The procedure stipulates that the UK 'shall notify the Council whether it intends to move to the third stage of economic and monetary union before the Council makes its assessment', towards the end of 1996. If the UK indicates that it does not intend to move to the third stage, then it will be excluded from the majority and weighted majority voting procedures on matters concerning EMU. The Treaty also contains a Protocol on Denmark – in recognition of the fact that the Danish constitution may require a plebiscite prior to Danish participation in the third stage of EMU. Following the June 1992 referendum in Denmark, in which ratification of the TEU was narrowly defeated, the Danish Government was, in December 1992, granted a clearer 'opt-out' from EMU.

The macroeconomic and monetary environment after the crises of 1992–3

There can be no doubt that the exchange rate crises of 1992–3 significantly changed the European macroeconomic and monetary environment. In describing the emerging macroeconomic and monetary environment it may be useful to distinguish between the macroeconomic environment as it directly affects business and the longer term question of the prospects for EMU as designed in the Treaty on European Union.

The implications of exchange rate regimes for business

Exchange rate regimes are an important element of the business environment. However, their impact on the economy is potentially complex; indeed, in *One Market, One Money* (1990) the Commission identified sixteen mechanisms through which a move to EMU would impact on the European economy.

While it has been argued that exchange rate uncertainty reduces international trade, the evidence in favour of this is weak. Greater emphasis is now placed on the harmful effects of exchange rate uncertainty on investment. This uncertainty increases the risks attached to both domestic investment (especially where it is hoped to export) and of international investment. Consequently, the effects on business of a move to stable exchange rates, or EMU, arise because of reduced uncertainty concerning relative prices and, in the case of full EMU, the elimination of the costs of buying and selling different currencies. This suggests that the exchange rate regime in Europe is an important element of the economic environment and that, in general, business would benefit from less exchange rate uncertainty.

However, the direct implications of exchange rates for business cannot be separated from other economic variables, such as inflation, interest rates and the level of demand. When the interactions of these four are taken into account, it is less easy to say what exchange rate regime is most advantageous to business activity. For example, the reduced uncertainty yielded by fixed exchange rates would be of limited value to business if it involved a significantly *overvalued* exchange rate, or if maintenance of a fixed rate involved very high interest rates. Likewise, the absence of both transactions costs and uncertainty in EMU may be of limited value to businesses in a country or region which suffers a specific negative shock if no alternative policy instruments have been devised to replace exchange rate changes. Consequently, in thinking about the implications of the exchange rate regime for business in Europe, one is drawn into complex macroeconomic arguments.

Looking at inflation, exchange rates, the level of demand and interest rates in the EU since the 1992–3 crises, the most significant change is in the UK and Italy, which have not only had a large devaluation and a reduction in interest rates, but have moved from a pegged to a floating exchange rate regime. In other counties, a devaluation *vis-à-vis* the deutschmark and a move to a fluctuation margin of +/– 15 per cent were, of course, important changes, but their significance may lie more in the relief they afford from speculative attacks and associated high interest rates, than in increased exchange rate volatility. After the initial devaluations, interest rates fell, but there was limited exchange rate volatility. More significantly, there has been little evidence that governments wish to use the wider margins of fluctuation actively to pursue a devaluation strategy. Consequently, one possible change in the macroeconomic environment – a switch from an anti-inflation policy involving real appreciation, to a growth-oriented policy of competitive devaluations – seems not to have transpired. Although Britain might be said to have pursued such a policy in 1992

> most other EU countries have more anti-inflationary credibility to lose than the U.K. had, and most realise that their mutual trade is sufficiently great that the effect of widespread devaluation will be much smaller than that of any individual devaluation. Competitive devaluation is therefore unlikely, so long as countries are not seen to be competing unfairly. (Winters, 1993, p. 3)

The realignments of 1992–3 have more than accommodated differences in underlying economic performance and the new parities should, therefore, be considerably easier to defend than those which prevailed between 1987 and 1992.

However, it seems unlikely that the EU states will in future be able, or indeed be willing, to defend exchange rate parities by means of an asymmetric system. The problems of monetary control that arise in an asymmetric system, when asymmetric shocks occur, are likely, as De Grauwe (1992, p. 121) has argued, to lead to conflicts about the kind of monetary policy to be followed for the whole system:

> Pressure on the centre country will certainly be exerted. These conflicts of interest

have to be dealt with in one way or another. [This] suggests that an asymmetric system may not survive in the long run. Too much conflict will exist about the appropriate monetary policies for the system as a whole. Peripheral countries especially if they are similar in size to the centre country (as in the case in the present EMS), may not be willing to subject their national interest to the survival of the system. In the end, more explicit co-operative arrangements may be necessary.

The events of 1992 and 1993 suggest that a central issue in the European economic environment is whether more explicit cooperative arrangements will be designed.

In this respect, some economists can envisage a reformed EMS working well and, possibly, leading to EMU. Thygesen (1993) makes the point that there are two types of mistake an exchange rate system must attempt to avoid. The first is to defend rates that are perceived to be misaligned. The second is to give in to speculative pressures when rates are in good correspondence with fundamentals. It is important to recognise that these dangers tend to alternate. Although the crises of 1992–3 confronted the EU with the first of these dangers, it is next likely to face the second. Among the reforms which are proposed to enhance the system's ability to handle turbulence is a maximalist use of the powers conferred on the EMI in the Treaty on European Union. Thygesen outlines an optimistic scenario in which central banks become more independent of their governments, but more dependent on each other, and currencies one by one return to the earlier margins. In that context, the incentives and capacity for collective action would be enhanced. Although monetary leadership shifted strongly back to Germany after unification, Thygesen argues that 'this phase now appears to be over':

> As German interest rates decline in recession and the German stability performance is no longer superior to that of several other Member States, the anchor function will widen to comprise all the countries conducting stable exchange rate policies – whether this development is planned or not. Germany will obviously continue to exercise the influence that its financial weight accords, but that is inevitably smaller than corresponding to the role in the past. (ibid., p. 470)

Thygesen goes on to argue that not only can the EMS be made to work again, but reform of the system in the direction of more symmetry can overcome a major problem in the transition to EMU. Recognition of 'the new reality that there is no longer an obvious tendency for Germany to retain the leadership role in the EMS' could lead Germany to be less hostile to monetary cooperation prior to full monetary union. It was largely the German doctrine that monetary policy is indivisible (i.e. conducted entirely by either a national authority or a full European Central Bank) that caused the second, transition stage to EMU to be so empty in the TEU.

Although the experience of cooperation in the EMS has built up a measure of consensus among European governments on macroeconomic management, and although competitive devaluations seem unlikely, it would be unwise to rule out exchange rate changes. Real economic developments may well occur which push currencies to the limits of the +/–15 per cent band, or perhaps even beyond. If economic pressures were to build up, it will now be harder (after the crises of 1992–3) for governments to guarantee that macroeconomic policy will not change, and this alone will prompt financial markets into trading currencies, thereby changing exchange rates. As has recently been said, 'If we have learned one thing about freely floating exchange rates, it is that they are volatile' (Eichengreen and Wypolsz, 1993, p. 9). But, in the absence of a definite existing misalignment or a clearly distinctive policy approach (such as might be attributed to the UK), it is not possible to predict the timing, size or, perhaps, even the direction of future exchange rate changes.

One thing that has changed since the late 1980s and, indeed, since the design of the TEU, is the level of European governments' concern about unemployment and economic growth. While control of inflation was the primary policy goal in the 1980s, this was largely achieved by the early 1990s. Table 2.7 shows a very considerable degree of inflation convergence in the EU in 1993 and 1994. While unemployment remained high by historical standards in most EU countries in the 1980s, the recession of the early 1990s produced a new surge in unemployment in Europe. In consequence, there was something of a change in policy priorities, which was marked at the EU level by the presentation of the Commission's White Paper, *Growth, Competitiveness and Employment*, to the Brussels European Council in December 1993. However, neither the White Paper nor the reactions of governments to it produced any consensus on how the problem should be tackled. Proposals for a major coordinated expansion were, once again, rejected because of existing deficits and doctrinal rejection of Keynesian ideas. It seems more likely that the EU will follow individual European governments in reacting to problems of slow growth and unemployment with supply-side measures, rather than with macroeconomic policy. Indeed, the EU initiative on growth, unemployment and competitiveness has brought forward arguments for deregulation of European labour markets, increased training and the enhancement of European infrastructure. If common policies are not implemented, or do not work, the danger is that member states will resort to supply-side measures which undermine the SEM.

Prospects for monetary union

Turning to the second dimension of the post–1993 macroeconomic environment, the prospects for transition to a single currency, there is considerable uncertainty, with the plan for EMU embodied in the TEU coming under critical scrutiny. The possibility of a gradual transition to EMU by means of a progressive convergence of macroeconomic performance, and tightening of the ERM, has been questioned. Related to this, it has been argued that the minimal institutional developments envisaged in stage two of the EMU transition cannot produce a sufficient pooling of instruments and responsibilities to advance much beyond the achievements of stage one. Furthermore, some economists

TABLE 2.7   Inflation (deflator of private consumption)

| | Annual percentage change | | | |
	1981–90	1991	1992	1993	1994[2]
Belgium	4.6	2.9	2.4	2.8	2.7
Denmark	5.8	2.4	2.1	1.6	2.0
Germany	2.7[1]	3.9[1]	4.7	4.1	3.5
Greece	18.4	18.4	16.0	13.5	9.0
Spain	9.3	6.3	6.0	5.5	5.0
France	6.4	3.2	2.6	2.7	2.5
Ireland	7.0	3.2	2.9	2.2	2.2
Italy	9.9	6.8	5.3	5.8	4.7
Luxembourg	5.1	2.9	3.4	4.7	3.2
Netherlands	2.2	3.3	3.1	2.7	2.5
Portugal	17.1	11.9	9.1	6.8	5.7
United Kingdom	6.0	7.2	5.1	5.1	3.0
EU	6.5[1]	5.3[1]	4.6	4.5	3.5

NOTES   [1] Excluding Eastern Germany.
        [2] Commission forecast, January 1993.
SOURCE Commission Services.

have argued that the convergence criteria and the Treaty rules governing national fiscal policy are arbitrary, unnecessary, and likely to lend a deflationary bias to the European economy throughout the 1990s. Indeed, as shown in Table 2.5, in 1993 and 1994 only Luxembourg simultaneously met the convergence criteria on public debt and deficits. The experience of 1992–3 has already reawakened fears that the Treaty has designed a somewhat unbalanced system, in the sense that there may be more coherent institutions and policy on the *monetary* than on the *economic* side. Will the Union's economic policies be sufficient to pursue goals other than price stability – especially employment, growth, competitiveness and cohesion? Concern has been expressed too about the fiscal requirements for a successful EMU: can the European Union hope to create an economic and monetary union without the system of fiscal federalism which is found in almost all successful monetary unions? Finally, several of these questions are closely related to issues of political union. Many would doubt that the, largely intergovernmental, decision-making procedures which apply to the EMU provisions of the TEU have the authority, legitimacy or effectiveness to progress to and, more importantly, *govern* an economic and monetary union.

Faced with these doubts, few economists believe that the EU, or even a majority of its member states, will proceed to EMU in accordance with the Maastricht plan. While some see recent problems as evidence that a European economic, monetary and political union was never meant to be, it seems likely that this reflects a prior opposition to the idea. Indeed, many still believe that the *eventual* monetary integration of Western Europe is virtually inevitable. But no one seems clear on how and when this might be achieved. If the crises of 1992–3 simply implied a slower transition to EMU there may be no great difficulty. However, questions have been raised which cast doubt on the *strategy* and *method* of transition chosen in the Treaty of European Union. Consequently, the prospects for EMU may depend on the design of an alternative strategy and the achievement of political agreement on it. This confirms the extent to which EMU is a political project, dependent on political will as much as economic convergence.

THE WESTERN EUROPEAN ECONOMY IN A GLOBAL CONTEXT

Western Europe's place in the international trading system

Western Europe is one of the most significant areas of economic activity in the world. This can be demonstrated in various ways. First, as was seen in Table 2.1, the European Union, plus Austria, Finland, Norway, Sweden and Switzerland, contains a population of over 370 million. Second, although numerous external factors influence the European economic environment, discussion of this subject tends to focus on economic relations between Europe, the US and Japan. These industrial giants account for the bulk of Europe's external economic transactions – both trade and investment flows – and it is with these countries that Europe has its most significant economic policy and exchange rate relationships. The population of Western Europe is 40 per cent larger than that of the US and three times that of Japan. The Gross Domestic Product of the EU is over twice that of Japan and slightly ahead of that of the US. The income or product of the whole of Western Europe is larger than that of the United States and Canada together. Third, the EU economy accounts for almost one quarter of world GDP and this is reflected in its role in international trade. In 1993, exports accounted for 8.9 per cent of European Union GDP, while imports to the EU accounted for 9.8 per cent. In the same year, EU merchandise trade accounted for 20.7 per cent of world trade, compared to 16.8 per cent for the US and 9.7 per cent for Japan. The EU accounts for over 27 per cent of world trade in commercial services, ahead of the United States (16 per cent) and Japan (10 per cent).

The geographical structure of EU external trade is outlined in Table 2.8. In 1990, EFTA countries represented the largest supplier of imports (23.5 per cent), while the US remained the single most important trading partner (supplying 18.4 per cent of EC imports and taking 18.2 per cent of EC exports). The geographical structure of EU exports is similar to that of imports. In 1990, almost 60 per cent of EC exports went to industrialised countries, an increase of over 10 percentage points since 1980. EU exports have expanded most rapidly to fast growing markets, many of them in the Far East, including, in decreasing order, South Korea, Taiwan, Japan, Turkey, Singapore, Hong Kong,

Israel and China. Overall, the top six trade partners of the EU are the US, Switzerland, Austria, Sweden, Japan, the former Soviet Union, and Norway.

TABLE 2.8   Geographical structure of EC trade, 1990, per cent of total extra-EC trade

	Industrialised Countries				Developing countries	Eastern Europe
	USA	Japan	EFTA	Total		
Imports	18.4	10.0	23.5	59.7	31.1	6.8
Exports	18.2	5.4	26.5	59.8	32.0	6.7

SOURCE   'The European Community as a World Trade Partner', *European Economy*, no. 52.

The product composition of EC imports in 1990 was 78 per cent manufactures, 16 per cent energy, and 5.9 per cent agricultural products. This represents a significant increase in the share of manufactured goods: an increase which is paralleled by similar developments in other industrialised economies. Unlike imports, the product composition of EU exports has remained relatively stable over time, with manufactures accounting for 94 per cent of total merchandise exports in 1990. Industrial machinery (15.3 per cent) and chemicals (12.3 per cent) are the two largest exporting sectors in the EU.

Trade patterns give an idea of Europe's place in the international division of labour and this, in turn, highlights significant external factors in the European economic environment. It is clear, for example, from Table 2.8, that European trade has a strong regional character: a large proportion of European external trade is within the EU, within EFTA, or between the EU and EFTA. Most of this trade is in industrial goods and, not surprisingly, it is *intra*-industry rather than *inter*-industry trade. When considering European trade with the outside world two features are notable: first, the EU (which may be taken here as a proxy for Western Europe) runs a large and rising trade deficit with Japan and, second, its trade balance with the US has, since the early 1980s, been strongly influenced by the volatile exchange rate between the dollar and European currencies.

There is clear evidence of a considerable competitive trading pressure on the EU. It has lost market share in strong demand, high technology sectors, particularly to Japan and the newly industrialised countries. It has a weakened position in the motor industry. At the same time, it is under growing competitive pressure from less developed countries in labour intensive, low R+D products. Its strength, as Tsoukalis (1993, p. 256) says, seems to lie in the upmarket end of relatively weak demand sectors such as textiles and clothing, leather, footwear, furniture and chemicals. These are the adverse trade developments which prompted the Community to embark on the ambitious SEM programme.

There are some important asymmetries in economic relations between the

EU, the US and Japan which, in the view of Holmes and Smith (1992), play a major role in shaping policy relations between them. While both the EU and the US have had persistent trade deficits with Japan, in the case of the US, but not the EU, this is part of an overall trade deficit. Thus, to some degree, the US deficit with Japan is a reflection of the *macroeconomic* contrast between a high-saving Japan and low-saving US. In the case of the EU, the deficit with Japan is more than matched by a surplus with the rest of the world. The real problem which both the US and the EU face is, as Holmes and Smith say, that imports from Japan are concentrated in particular sectors, especially cars and electronics. 'In contrast to the general pattern of trade between advanced economies, Japanese-EC/US trade is to a great extent based on inter-industry rather than intra-industry trade.' In other words, Japan has a competitive advantage in whole sectors and where this advantage increases it tends 'to threaten the extinction of whole industries and therefore, whole lines of technological development' (ibid., p. 189). Finally, the counterpart of these asymmetries in trade is a strong pattern of capital flows. Given its large trade surplus, Japan is by definition a major source of outward investment.

European Union trade policy

The customs union

An important element of a common market is a single set of arrangements for trade with non-member countries. In consequence, Article 113 of the EC Treaty requires the Union to have a Common Commercial Policy (CCP). The Commission conducts this policy on the basis of mandates agreed by the Council of Ministers. In managing what is thus a customs union, the EU can make use of common external tariffs, import levies, export subsidies (in the case of agriculture), anti-dumping measures and counteracting measures against subsidies in other countries. Article 115 provides for the continuation of national trade policies in certain circumstances, including cases where the execution of the common commercial policy leads to economic difficulties in one or more member state. In addition, Article 115 allows member countries to pursue other policy measures which directly affect trade, such as technical standards, administrative restrictions, 'voluntary export restraints' (VER's), and many others.

In the case of most goods entering the EU from third countries, tariffs are now of limited significance. There are two reasons for this. First, as a result of successive rounds of negotiations in the General Agreement on Tariffs and Trade (GATT), tariffs in the EU and elsewhere are now fairly low (though see the references to agriculture, textiles, clothing, and consumer electronics below). Almost a third of EU imports bear a tariff of 5 per cent or less, and 90 per cent of imports face a tariff of 15 per cent or less. Second, greater restrictions to trade now arise from non-tariff barriers. Many of these arise as a result of a range of government interventions in the economy. Consequently, the attention of GATT has shifted towards NTBs. Although the Tokyo Round (1975–9) focused on NTBs and, indeed, yielded various agreements on technical regulations and standards, customs valuation, import licensing procedures, anti-dumping charges, subsidies and public procurement, these seem to have had limited impact. As a result, similar issues arose, and were in large part resolved, in the Uruguay Round negotiations, which were completed in December 1993.

It should be emphasised that, important though GATT is in the context of international trade, its impact has been limited by two related factors. First despite the principle of multilaterism, there has been a proliferation of bilateral and multilateral trade agreements of various sorts over the years. Second, a number of sensitive sectors have remained outside, or have not been resolved within the context of, the standard GATT process of tariff reduction. The EU has participated in these developments but has been no more responsible than others for any weakening of the GATT regime.

As regards bilateral and multilateral agreements to which the EU is a party, the most significant are: (1) The European Economic Area which, as noted above, brings all EFTA states (except Switzerland) into a virtual free trade area with the EU and also extends to them most aspects of the SEM programme. (2) Cooperation and Association Agreements which the EU has contracted with the countries of Central and Eastern Europe. These agreements provide, amongst other things, for trade preferences and, in the case of the Association Agreements, for a gradual movement to free trade (with EU barriers being dismantled the faster). (3) Trade agreements with Mediterranean countries, which are based on an attempt to develop an overall approach to trade with these countries. The trade agreements signed under this heading generally permit industrial products, subject to some exceptions, to be imported into the EU duty free, but restrict the access of agricultural products which are covered by the Common Agricultural Policy (CAP). (4) Trade arrangements with less developed countries. There are two main components to the EU's trade policy with the developing world: the generalised system of preferences and the Lomé Convention. Very briefly, the generalised system of preferences allows duty free entry, subject to ceilings, to a wide range of manufactured exports from a list of developing countries. The Lomé Convention provides non-reciprocal duty free access to the EU for almost all products originating in the sixty-nine, so called, African, Caribbean and Pacific countries (ACP) – many of which are former British or French colonies.

European Union policy in sensitive sectors

As regards sensitive sectors, agriculture is the best known, but it is less well known that its exclusion from GATT, prior to the Uruguay Round, was largely at the behest of the United States. Nevertheless, the CAP – a continuation of a long history of agricultural support in Europe – has by now served to give the EU a protectionist image, primarily because an important element of the CAP is the exercise of 'Community preference', which is achieved mainly through import levies and export subsidies. Although other countries, such as the US, Canada and Japan, offer considerable support to their agricultural producers, the EU has come under particular pressure because growing European self-sufficiency has meant that the CAP not only protects European farmers from *import* competition, but subsidises EU *exports* on to world markets. Since the CAP offers greatest support to temperate products, such as beef, dairy produce, lamb, sugar and cereals, it was countries such as the US, Canada, Australia and New Zealand which insisted that agriculture figure prominently in the Uruguay Round. The agreement reached in December 1993 will gradually reduce the export subsidies, import barriers and domestic farm supports of both the EU and the US.

Other sectors which were not included in the progressive reduction of trade policy interventions until the Uruguay Round are textiles, clothing, steel, cars and electronics. Trade in textiles and clothing was governed by a special, more restrictive, regime known as the multifibre arrangements (MFA). These were bilateral agreements between importing and exporting countries imposing quantitative restrictions on low-cost products originating in developing countries. Their existence reflected the resistance of developed countries to import penetration and job loss in labour intensive sectors, where competition is based on cost. The Uruguay Round agreement involves the progressive phasing out of the MFA quotas and reduction of tariffs over a ten year period from 1995. In the case of steel, the EU has something approaching an industrial policy which is protected by bilateral VERs with the main world suppliers of steel. Indeed, VERs have become one of the most important instruments of trade policy, given that countries are 'bound' under GATT rules from any increase in tariffs.

A major concern of trade policy has been to protect the motor industry in Europe from intense Japanese competition. The European car market has traditionally been heavily fragmented by differing technical standards, state aids, taxes and the restrictive dealership system used by the major European motor manufacturers. Until recently, the market was further fragmented by the negotiation of national VERs, which imposed limits on Japanese import penetration into Italy, France, the UK, Spain and Portugal. By contrast, in small European countries, with no motor industry and consequently no interest in trade policy discrimination against Japan, Japanese imports have up to 30 per cent of the local market. The case of cars provides a good example of the nature of the European economy and the way in which it shapes the European business environment. Not only do different member states pursue radically different trade policies with respect to international competition in cars, but within those countries which have a significant motor industry, diverse responses can also be found. While some have sought to strengthen their 'national champions' through policies to aid rationalisation and restructuring, others have devoted considerable effort to attracting Japanese investment. The British have seen UK-based Japanese car production as a means of retaining a domestic motor industry, while the Japanese see it as a way of circumventing the import barriers raised by several EU countries. This has given rise to protracted disputes in the EU, with the French and Italian producers arguing that exports of 'Japanese' cars from the UK should be counted in the overall Japanese quota. As Tsoukalis says, 'Long intra-EC disputes about rules of origin and minimum local content have created a picture of complete disarray with respect to one of the most important industrial sectors where the customs union has remained largely a myth' (Tsoukalis, 1992, p. 263).

A related element of the European trade environment is the use of anti-dumping instruments by the EU. A particularly important development of recent years has been the extension of anti-dumping duties from final products to imported components, in an effort to deal with the problem of 'screwdriver plants'. These are foreign-owned plants which assemble components imported from the parent company. Both the EU and the US have imposed anti-dumping duties in order to protect themselves from what they see as 'unfair trade practices' in Japan and the newly industrialised countries. In deciding on trade policy in sectors such as textiles, clothing, steel, cars and electronics the EU, and indeed member states, must be aware of the fact that although anti-dumping actions and VERs tend to create cartels and other anti-competitive effects, they do tend to attract inward investment. Some economists believe that a significant proportion of Japanese investment in the EU is motivated by the desire to circumvent actual, or expected, EU protectionism. Others argue that such investments mainly reflect a process of globalisation which would proceed regardless of EU commercial policy.

Relations between external and internal policies

It is important to appreciate that, because of the complex and multiple inter-action of states and markets, trade policy, technology policy, industrial policy, competition policy, and even migration policy, are all interrelated. This confronts national governments and the EU with the difficult task of finding a coherent and non-contradictory combination of policies in each of these areas. An illustration of the link between internal and external policy is seen in the way the completion of the SEM has had implications for the EU's external trade regime. In thinking about these implications attention is turned to a controversial issue which has confronted European governments: whether regional integration and international liberalisation are complementary or competitive objectives.

The SEM programme has implications for the EU external trade regime because some of the fragmentation of the EU market was caused by the limited nature of the Community's Common Commercial Policy and the exercise of national policies under Article 115. For example, where a member state had a national barrier to external imports recognised under EU law, it could apply to the Commission to have controls on an *intra*-EU border, in order to avoid import penetration via another EU country. Consequently, the failure to have a sufficiently broad CCP undermined the achievement of a common internal market. The SEM programme, and more particularly the dismantlement of border controls, should end this practice of individual member states negotiating with the Japanese (and others) on measures such as VERs to 'moderate' their exports to the EU. Another example of the implications of the SEM for EU trade policy is seen when a liberal intra-EU regime is established in an area such as services, for the EU has to decide whether this regime should be extended to third countries. This was an important issue in the liberalisation of financial services under the Second Banking Directive (see Chapter 5), in the opening of public procurement to international competition, in the harmonisation and mutual recognition of technical standards, and in the treatment of foreign subsidiaries as European economic agents under Article 58 of the EEC Treaty.

In general, EU decisions in the areas discussed above confirm the validity of the EU's stated policy that the SEM programme will not lead to greater protectionism. Indeed, many of the measures removing barriers to intra-EU trade will automatically facilitate access to the European markets from outside. The economic and political possibility of not extending internal market measures to third parties has turned out to be less than was feared by the US and Japan (Mayes, 1990). Indeed, two important aspects of the internal market can offer distinct benefits to third countries. First, EU companies are constrained by European competition policy and by restrictions on state aids. Their non-EU rivals will, in some circumstances, be able to benefit from a monopoly position in other parts of the world and government supports of various kinds. Second, the EU does not have a sufficiently well-defined set of industrial policy goals to use external trade and other instruments in pursuit of a policy of 'European champions'. Consequently, the accusation that the SEM implies a 'Fortress Europe' does not seem well founded. There are, of course, sectors, such as cars, in which future European trade policy remains unclear and others, such as agriculture, textiles and clothing, in which it depends more on the outcome of international negotiations than on the SEM programme. In such sectors the EU will remain under pressure to change its existing stance, but it must do so in ways which reconcile its diverse internal interests.

In considering the implications of closer European integration for economic relations between the EU and the rest of the world, Mayes has argued that the most important question is the degree to which integration promotes growth in the European market (ibid.). If it does so, there is likely to be a net gain to most third countries and the application of trade policy measures need not be unduly contentious. If, however, the European economy does not grow, either because of integrative measures or for some other reason, then external economic relations become more of a zero sum game. The impact of integration on growth is less a mechanical necessity than a function of the *response* of firms and, particularly, of *governments* to the cost reductions, price reductions, and improvements in trade balance which market integration causes. As is well known, the rapid growth of the European economies in the late 1980s – widely seen as, in part, a *1992* effect – has since given way to recession and severe macroeconomic difficulties.

Summary on the global context

Overall, the external trade regime of the European economy is one of a low CET, supplemented by fairly extensive use of instruments of external protection. This protection is most significant in three kinds of sectors: first, agriculture; second, labour-intensive products (such as clothing, textiles, footwear and shipbuilding) in which Europe is threatened by import penetration from developing countries; and, third, high-technology products such as consumer electronics, office equipment and telecommunications, in which Europe has lost market share to Japan and the US. Considering this situation, Tsoukalis says 'European countries seem to be squeezed from both sides' (Tsoukalis, 1992, p. 266). He also notes some significant differences between Europe's economic relations with Japan and the US. European trade policy towards Japan has been marked by strong discrimination against Japanese imports, but also deep internal disunity within the EU. This reflects the particular sectors in which Japan is strong, the dominance of Japanese exports to Europe rather than Japanese foreign direct investment in Europe, and, of course, the weakness of EU decision-making procedures and the fragmented nature of policy in Europe. By contrast, European relations with the US have been more harmonious. While agriculture has been the most contentious issue, it has been kept in perspective by close political ties, the lack of substantial and persistent trade imbalances, and the existence of very large trans-Atlantic investments.

A final point to note is that the economic environment for business in Europe will be significantly altered by the re-establishment of capitalism in Central and Eastern Europe. It is, however, extremely difficult to predict how these economies will evolve and how they will affect Western Europe. Research on these questions is in its infancy and faces the difficult, if not impossible, task of predicting future comparative advantage. The research which has been done points to, amongst other things, the high average levels of education in Poland, Hungary and the Czech Republic and suggests that these countries are unlikely to base their comparative advantage on cheap, unskilled, labour (Hamilton and Winters, 1992).

CONCLUSIONS

This chapter has characterised the European economic environment by considering particularly the three key economic policy areas of the European Union: the SEM, exchange rate management, and external trade policy. Within each of these broad policy areas – which involve market regulation, macroeconomic management, and external economic relations – national governments retain considerable policy competence. Furthermore, these three policy areas by no means exhaust the scope of economic policy, and, as other chapters of this book demonstrate, in other areas – such as labour market policy, social policy and technology policy – national governments are much more significant than the European Union. From this there emerges a picture of a partial *European* economic environment.

The existence of a distinctively *European* economic environment is also qualified by the prevalence of international or global business and markets. The environment for business is significantly shaped by trade patterns, investment flows, technological changes, corporate structures and strategies, which are essentially global, and certainly not confined to Europe or any of its national economies. There is, of course, some uncertainty and debate about whether markets and firms really are truly *global*, but this in no way undermines the observation that the European economic environment for business is shaped by *external* factors.

Overall, the economic environment contains local, national, European and global elements and is shaped by an interaction of forces which operate at these different levels. However, it should not be thought that there is necessarily symmetry or uniformity in the nature of the forces at each of these levels. Each tends to provide different kinds of inputs to the economic and business environment. The local environment provides natural resources such as land, human inputs and skills; the social *milieu* of the firm; and certain policy inputs, such as local taxes, incentives and infrastructure. The cultural and institutional factors in the economic environment for business are largely shaped at the national level, as are laws and a vast range of policies which affect the economic environment. The European level also determines some legal and policy factors, as well as creating a context of trade and international investment opportunities. But it has been noted that only a limited range of policies are determined at EU level, and some of these, such as exchange rate policy, lack authority, effectiveness and, perhaps, legitimacy. Finally, the forces operating at an international or global level are very largely commercial, economic and technological, and have little policy content. Although all four levels – the local, the national, the European and the global – are at work, the balance between them, and between their associated social, institutional, technological, market, and public policy elements, is quite different in particular economic and business contexts.

Notes

1. NACE is the official general industrial classification of economic activities within the European Union, first established by Eurostat in 1970. It divides economic activity sectors in ten very broad divisions (one-digit level), subdivided into more detailed industrial classes (two-digit level) and further divided into groups and

subgroups (three- and four-digit level). This system of classification of industrial employment and output differs somewhat from the system used to classify international trade. Trade is generally classified according to the United Nations Standard International Trade Classification (SITC).

2. In the 1980s this rank ordering was as follows: *Fast growth*: (1) electrical machinery, (2) plastic products,(3) non-electrical machinery, (4) printing and publishing, (5) other chemicals, (6) scientific instruments. *Medium growth*: (7) paper products, (8) transport equipment, (9) industrial chemicals, (10) rubber products, (11) wood products, and furniture, (12) food, (13) non-ferrous metals, (14) beverages, (15) furniture, (16) fabricated metal products, (17) glass products. *Slow growth*: (18) non-metallic mineral products, (19) pottery and china, (20) other manufacturing, (21) textiles, (22) iron and steel, (23) tobacco, (24) coal and petroleum, (25) clothing, (26) leather products, (27) petroleum refining, (28) footwear.

3. This study appeared in *European Economy*, no. 35, March 1988. It is sometimes referred to as the 'Cecchini Report', after the Chairman of the overall 'Costs of Non Europe' project. The *Economics of 1992* was subsequently published by Oxford University Press (see Emerson *et al.*, 1988).

4. A period of wholesaler domination was followed by manufacturer domination in the 1960s, which was in turn succeeded by the rise of the retailer (McGee and Segal-Horn, 1992).

5. A merger is deemed to fall within the competence of the Union authorities if the combined worldwide turnover of the companies is ECU 5 billion or more, and EU turnover of each of at least two of the companies is ECU 250 million or more. However, a merger is exempt from EU jurisdiction if each company has more than two-thirds of its EU turnover in one country.

6. In any exchange rate system involving N currencies, there are only N–1 exchange rates. The system must determine these N–1 exchange rates and the overall money supply. The asymmetric solution is that one country sets the monetary policy for the whole system and all the others simply adjust their monetary policy so as to maintain a fixed exchange rate against that central currency. In a symmetric system, all N countries might agree collectively on the thrust of overall policy and all are equally responsible for defending exchange rates.

7. The Padoa-Schioppa report of 1988 argued that free trade, free capital movements, fixed exchange rates and national monetary policy autonomy constitute an 'inconsistent quartet'. Once the first three are established, it is necessary to strengthen the macroeconomic policy function of the Union. Otherwise, the conduct of separate national monetary policies would, sooner or later, force a move from fixed exchange rates. The removal of capital controls, as part of the SEM programme, does seem to have prompted governments and central banks to coordinate monetary policy somewhat more closely. This meant that the inconsistency of the quartet was concealed, until the crises of 1992–3.

Guide to Further Reading

There are a number of excellent general texts on the economics of European integration. The most satisfactory general account, combining economics with political and institutional analysis, is by Tsoukalis (1993). Swann (1992) offers a comprehensive account of EC policies and issues, while both Robson (1987) and Molle (1990) provide somewhat more technical treatment. Dyker (1992) is a collection of papers on aspects of the European economy. Critical accounts of the European Community can be found in Cutler *et al.* (1989) and Grahl and Teague (1990).

There are a number of general sources of information and analysis on the European economy. *The Journal of Common Market Studies* (hereafter *JCMS*) is the most important of these, combining political, economic, legal and historical work. The journal, *Economic Policy*, has a strong European focus and presents analytical economics in a readable form. Another journal which should be monitored is the *Oxford Review of Economic Policy*. The Centre for European Policy Studies (CEPS), based in Brussels, publishes studies on all aspects of European integration, while the Centre for Economic Policy Research (CEPR) is a network of European economists, coordinated from London, which publishes books and papers on the European economy. The European Commission publishes a quarterly journal, *European Economy*, which is a key source of economic data and analysis.

The common market and the project to complete the SEM are discussed in all the sources listed above. The analytical basis of trade liberalisation is explained in intermediate textbooks, such as Markusen and Melvin (1981), and in surveys by Grossman (1992) and Kierzkowski (1987). The implications of the 'new trade theory' for policy are discussed in the volume edited by Krugman (1987a), in Krugman (1987b) and in Bliss (1987). Jacquemin and Sapir (1989) is a collection of readings which trace the development of the theory of market integration. The paper by Krugman, also available in Padoa Schioppa (1987), is a valuable introduction to the conceptual issues in the microeconomics and macroeconomics of integration. While many feel that the key Commission study, *The Economics of 1992*, exaggerates the benefits and diminishes the costs of the SEM (see Flamm 1992; Kay, 1989), Baldwin (1989) uses recent developments in endogenous growth theory to argue that the long-run, dynamic effects of trade liberalisation will be even larger. Helm (1993) provides a neat analytical overview of the internal market and considers its extension to public utilities.

Policy issues arising from the SEM – concerning the balance between deregulation and reregulation and between member states and the Union – are discussed by Helm and Smith (1989) and Kay and Posner (1989). Geroski (1989b) asks to what extent the EC requires an industrial policy. The CEPR have recently published an assessment of the EU merger regulation (Neven, Nuttall and Seabright, 1993).

On the role of firms and firm strategies, the journal *Transnational Corporations* is a valuable and very readable source. In addition to the sources cited in the chapter, Caves (1991) analyses corporate mergers in international economic integration, while Streeton (1992) discusses the relative roles of states and firms in economic interdependence and integration. Two useful collections of papers on the role of multinational investment in the European economy, and the impact of European integration on multinational strategies, are those edited by Cantwell (1992) and Young and Hamill (1992). Amin and Dietrich (1991) present a set of critical papers on structural change in the European economy. Kay (1990) is excellent on the geographic and produce scope of the 'strategic market'.

There are many dimensions to the external economic relations of the European economy. Most of these are addressed in a special issue of the *JCMS* (Hine, 1992). Other special issues of the *JCMS* are devoted to relations between the EC and EFTA (vol. 28, no. 4, June 1990) and the implications of the 1992 programme for developing countries (vol. 29, no. 2, December 1990). Mayes (1993) contains papers which examine most of the key aspects of the external impact of closer European integration. The role of multinational corporations is covered in Dunning and Robson (1988), Yannopoulos (1990) and Robson and Wooton (1993). The international dimension of EU competition policy is analysed by Jacquemin (1993). The European Commission has devoted an issue of *European Economy* (no. 52, 1993) to the EU as a world trade partner.

There is an enormous and growing literature on the EMS and economic and monetary union. The analytical issues are well explained by De Grauwe (1992), while the most comprehensive account of both the history and literature is Gros and Thygesen (1992). Cobham (1991) offers a shorter recent survey of the literature. Blanchard and Muet (1993) provide a trenchant criticism of the policy of 'competitiveness through disinflation' pursued by France and other countries in the EMS. The concept of EMU and the issues which shaped the TEU are explained in O'Donnell (1991), Britton and Mayes (1992) and Eichergreen (1993). The Commission's evaluation of the potential benefits and costs of EMU are presented in *One Market, One Money* (Commission, 1990) and reviewed by Bean (1992). The TEU convergence criteria, especially the rules on 'excessive deficits', are criticised by Buiter, Corsetti and Roubini (1993), and the political and economic conjuncture which led to agreement on EMU is analysed by Sandholtz (1993).

The legal environment

Walter Cairns

THE DIFFERENT LEGAL TRADITIONS WITHIN THE EUROPEAN UNION

Since the original six member states of the European Community (EC) had very similar legal systems based on the codified law model, it is this system which dominates European Union (EU) law. However, the enlargements of the EC in the 1970s and 1980s made it necessary to assimilate new legal concepts, particularly those on which the Anglo-Saxon systems are based.

The present-day EU, therefore, consists of countries belonging both to the codified law model (France, Belgium, Luxembourg, The Netherlands, Spain, Italy, Portugal, Germany, Greece and Denmark) and to the common law model (the United Kingdom and Ireland). It should also be noted that certain differences arise within the codified law group, mainly between those whose law is based on the Napoleonic codes (France, The Netherlands, Belgium, Luxembourg, Spain, Italy, Portugal) and those which developed their own codification movement (Germany, Denmark and Greece). The differences between them appear at various levels of the legal process, as will be explained in greater detail below.

These differences are obviously reflected in the business law which applies under each of these systems, and, ultimately, they have repercussions for the attempts made at the EU level to harmonise the legal system of the member states in this area. They appear at the level of the substantive law, the legislative techniques employed, the structure of the courts, and the linguistic difficulties involved.

Substantive law

Substantive law comprises those legal rules which lay down the rights and obligations of persons. By 'persons', we mean both natural persons and legal persons, i.e. associations formed by natural persons which, from a legal point of view, lead a separate existence: for example, companies, partnerships and even non-profit making associations. The substantive law does not include procedural law, which enables persons to enforce these rights and obligations.

The main difference between the common law and the civil law systems resides in the hierarchy between the two main sources of law, i.e. legislation (rules laid down by the parliamentary authority) and case law (rules developed by the courts).

In the civil law system, legislation enjoys absolute supremacy. This implies that: (1) no court decision may override legislation; (2) every court decision must be based on a law; and (3) courts are prohibited from issuing statements by way of general provisions.

By contrast, under the common law there is no clear hierarchy between the courts and the legislature. In those areas of the law covered by legislation, the relevant Acts take precedence over the case law. However, in spite of an increase in all West European countries since World War II in legislation commensurate with a greater degree of state interference in social and economic activity, considerable areas of the law are governed only by the rules and principles developed by the courts, i.e. the law of precedents.

The difference between the common law and civil law systems is also reflected in the hierarchy which exists within the case law itself. In the civil law countries, no court decisions can take precedence over others; in principle, the judgments of the French *Cour de Cassation*, or the Dutch *Hoge Raad*, have no greater authority than those of the *Tribunal d'instance* (which is the lowest type of French court) or the *Arrondissementsrechtbank* (which is the lowest type of court in The Netherlands). In the common law system, however, there is a distinct hierarchy between court decisions: in England, for example, the judgments of the High Court take precedence over those of the County Courts.

Legislative techniques

The manner in which legislation is drafted also differs from one system to another. In the civil law countries, the practice is for the legislature to content itself with the bare outlines of a law (*loi-cadre* – *Rahmengesetz* – *Legge delega* – *Ley de bases*), leaving the executive to work out the details by means of regulations. The common law tradition, on the other hand, is for the legislature to draft Acts in a detailed manner, leaving as little as possible to be regulated by the executive.

The structure of the courts

At the level of court structure, the main difference between the two systems lies in the degree of specialisation. In the common law countries, there is just one set of judicial bodies which adjudicates in any type of litigation. The civil law countries, on the other hand, have a different system of judicial organisation according to the subject matter of the dispute to be settled. Thus in many Continental states there are separate courts for disputes between the individuals and the authorities (administrative courts) or for those between traders amongst themselves or between traders and ordinary citizens (commercial courts).

Linguistic differences

That linguistic differences will present certain difficulties in any attempt to compare and harmonise legal systems within an EU numbering nine official languages may appear to be the elucidation of the obvious. However, the accession of Britain and Ireland presented linguistic differences of another kind (which were not encountered on the subsequent accessions of Greece, Spain and Portugal). Although the legal systems of the original six (and the three countries which joined the EC after the United Kingdom and Ireland) contained a number of important differences, the language barrier posed no particular legal problem since nearly all legal concepts used in one language had a one-to-one equivalent in the other official languages of the original EC.

The arrival of English, however, presented a fresh linguistic challenge, because in many cases the legal concepts of the 'Six' did not correspond to any equivalent term, or were matched by terms which only partially covered the specific meaning of the term in question. An example of the former is the term *acte* in French (*Akte* in German, *atto* in Italian, *acto* in Spanish), which is a fundamental legal concept in France, Germany, Italy and Spain, meaning any document which has legal implications. There is no equivalent for this term in English, and the frequently used substitute 'act' is an unsatisfactory, nay incorrect, translation. Of terms which have only a partial match in English, the French concept of '*hypothèque*' is a good example. This term, which means a security for a debt taken on a real property, is often translated as 'mortgage'; however, the English term can mean not only a security against property but also a loan for the purchase of the property.

The importance of the differences which have just been identified for the legal environment of business in Europe should not be overstated. Three observations are appropriate in this regard.

* As regards the differences in legislative techniques, there has been an increasing trend for the common law systems to resort to the framing of

legislation in general terms, leaving the details for governments to implement by means of delegated legislation.

- In practice, the difference in the role of the courts and the use of legislative techniques between the common law and the civil law states is less pronounced than the relevant theory might suggest. For example, although in France there is officially no hierarchy between the courts, it is inconceivable that an interpretation adopted by the *Tribunal d'instance* could be on equal terms with – let alone override – an *arrêt* of the *Cour de Cassation*. (In fact, the latter was specifically created in order to impart as much unity as possible to the case law of the lower courts.) Although the French courts are prohibited from substituting themselves for the legislature, they have often in practice been compelled to do so by the extremely general nature of some legislative provisions. Obvious examples of such rules are Articles 1382 (tort liability) and 544 (rights of ownership) of the *Code Civil*.

- Business law is a legal area which has traditionally lent itself to comparative law – and consequently also to harmonisation – better than such legal fields as administrative law or criminal law. Since international trade is a phenomenon which has existed for centuries, necessity has dictated that contracts be drawn up and corporate structures devised which give rise to as little unavoidable litigation as possible. It is also a fact that Anglo-Saxon law has exercised a considerable influence over continental legal systems in matters commercial, particularly in the field of company law. In addition, German law has been a prominent influence in attempts at EU harmonisation in the field of company law.

GENERAL PRINCIPLES OF BUSINESS LAW IN THE MEMBER STATES OF THE EUROPEAN UNION

In this section, such general principles of business law as can be distilled from the legal systems of the EU member states will be summarised. It is these principles which form the fundamental legal environment of the European business world, as well as constituting the basis for the legal philosophy of the main Founding Treaty of the EU – the 1957 Treaty of Rome (EEC). This section will not, however, concern itself with the rules developed under the EEC Treaty which form the subject matter of the final section. Nevertheless, it is important to point out at this stage that some of the principles common to the member states are the subject of attempts at harmonisation under the EEC Treaty, the Single European Act (SEA) and the Treaty on European Union (TEU). Thus, for example, whereas the law of corporate structures and competition law are subject to an intense effort at EU harmonisation, the law of contracts has thus far – and is likely to remain for some considerable time – largely immune from the EU integration process.

In general, the business law of the EU states reflects a Western desire to allow business activity to flourish in as unregulated a manner as possible, whilst providing adequate safeguards aimed at protecting the public interest, the consumer, and the employee. Viewed in this light, the general principles of European business law can be grouped under the headings which now follow.

Freedom to enter into contractual obligations

In all member states, the freedom to contract – that is, to conclude agreements – is regarded as one of the basic economic freedoms which is fully protected by the legal system of the state in question.

This freedom has many implications. In the first place, it means that no prior authorisation needs to be obtained before agreements are concluded. Second, it implies that contracts as such require no special form; indeed, they do not even need the formality of a written document. Third, the parties to contracts are free to choose the subject matter of the contract and to stipulate such terms and conditions as are mutually advantageous to them. Fourth, the parties may, by express provision, depart from the ordinary law of contracts, since the latter is intended to supplement rather than regulate the parties' contractual behaviour. Finally, contracts are restricted in scope to the parties involved; in other words, they cannot bind third parties.

The general rules stated above apply in principle, that is, they are the norm which remains subject to exceptions. Thus there are cases in which contracts require official authorisation, such as building contracts which are subject to planning permission. Certain contracts require not only to be written, but also to contain certain particulars, for example contracts regarding the disposition of land. Some areas are prohibited as subject matter for contracts, such as indecent publications and other matters which affect the public interest, whilst some terms and conditions of contracts may impair the lawfulness of the agreement, for example the sale of land which manifestly disadvantages one of the parties. There are also certain provisions of contract law which cannot be circumvented by private agreement, such as the 'cooling-off' period in consumer credit agreements. Finally, although contracts cannot bind third parties, the latter must respect the existence of agreements and may not seek to subvert them.

Protection of private property

Every EU member state assumes that private property is a precondition for business growth and prosperity, and must therefore be protected by law. So, the basic property law provision in the French Civil Code, Article 544, states that 'the right of ownership is the right to use, enjoy and dispose of property to the maximum possible degree, provided that this right is not used in any way which is prohibited by laws and regulations'. This is a principle which *mutatis mutandis* applies in every Western European state.

The manner in which persons endeavour to maximise the use of their property for business purposes assumes various forms, in respect of which the law, in most cases, restricts itself to supplying guidelines and complementing the property owner's wishes. The most common forms which the legally protected use of property rights takes are: (1) the lease of property, under which the object in question is hired to another person, who in turn may use the property for commercial or non-commercial purposes; (2) sale of goods; (3) the granting of easements, i.e. restricted use by third parties of the property in question; (4) succession, by which the goods in question are assigned to the owner's heirs and legatees after his death.

However, this right to the protection of private property is also subject to restrictions based on public interest. Here, an important distinction is made in all legal systems between moveable property and real (unmoveable) property, with the latter generally being subject to greater restrictions than the former. This is not only true in relation to transactions involving land, but is also seen in building planning restrictions and in registration formalities.[1] Three important caveats, however, must be entered in relation to this distinction between moveable and real property. First, all EU member states are gradually realising the outdated nature of the distinction and have given legal recognition to the fact that certain items of moveable property – securities, for example – deserve as equal a degree of protection as real property in view of their economic importance in present day society. Second, the distinction between real and moveable property is not as rigid as it might appear, since the law considers certain categories of moveable goods to be so closely identified with the real property in which they are located that real property status is also conferred on them. Third, not all property rights concern material or tangible goods. Ideas, designs and inventions, which are the product of the human brain, form the substance of intellectual property rights, which are also subject to a special system of protective rules.

The recognition of corporate personality

In order to facilitate the flow of business activity, the law bestows recognition not only on natural persons, but also on combinations of natural persons for a specific purpose – which in the vast majority of cases is for a business purpose. This has led to the concept of corporate personality, that is, a personality which for legal purposes is distinct from the natural persons which constitute it and whose actions are legally restricted to the specific objective for which they were created.

Had the law not done this, business activity would seldom have risen above the artisanal level. Large companies would have been extremely difficult to establish, since shareholders would have been personally committed not only to a company's profits but also to its debts. Thanks to the development of corporate personality, it has been possible to create large corporations based on the financial contributions of persons who cannot be held liable for more than their input, that is, their shares. The result has been the widespread formation of medium-sized and large business enterprises. The former mostly are confined to 'limited companies' or 'cooperatives', whereas the majority of the latter take the form of 'public limited companies'.

However, the very fact that the law allows such an appreciable degree of liability limitation lays it open to abuse. This is why those business operations to which the law has granted corporate status are subject to a strict regime of legal control, regulation and publicity with a view to protecting the public interest.

The principle of individual liberty

Because persons are, in principle, free in the manner in which they conduct their affairs, they must also bear the responsibility for their individual actions. The manner in which the law regulates this responsibility can be either criminal or civil in kind. Criminal liability concerns the action which will be taken by the public authorities against persons who infringe the rules of criminal law. Civil liability entails that all persons who commit damage to others – that is, either to their person or to their property – must compensate the latter for their loss. In the majority of cases this compensation is expressed in financial terms. With the expansion in business activity, the scope of liability was also extended to the consequences of the damage caused by the goods manufactured by a person. This has given rise to the concept of product liability in all EU member states. (This area will be discussed more extensively in a subsequent section as one of the areas which is increasingly the subject of EU harmonisation.) All EU member states have also developed the concept of 'strict liability', which means that, in certain cases, the law vests liability in a certain person regardless of whether he or she was at fault or not. Strict liability most frequently applies in relation to the possessors or operators of dangerous items, and has been the determining element in the development of employers' liability. Interestingly, the concept of strict liability has been the product of the case law in both the common law and the civil law countries.

Free and fair competition

It is implicit in the legislation of EU member states that anyone may engage in trading activity anywhere within the national territory. Even in a federal system such as Germany, restrictions on trade between federated members have disappeared. In recent years, however, it has been realised that it is not enough to safeguard free competition; it must also be fair. Precisely because free and unfettered capitalism tends towards the elimination of smaller business units or their assimilation into large ones, legislative intervention has been deemed to be necessary in order to prevent the abuses which are inherent in a monopolistic or oligopolistic economy. As a result, legislation has been widely enacted aimed at preventing either the occurrence of large monopolies and/ or at curtailing the misuse of monopolies, as well as other restrictive practices such as price fixing and territorial exclusivity agreements.

State intervention on social grounds

In the modern business world, the law no longer accepts that firms' obligations begin and end with trading in a free and fair environment. The obligation of business enterprises towards the community is entrenched by taxation and by legislation in such areas as social welfare and social security, industrial relations, and the protection of the environment and of the consumer. These are all obligations which require a large measure of state intervention, although it should be noted that the extent of the intervention varies considerably between EU member states. Germany and Denmark, for example, have much more interventionist systems than Spain and Portugal – a fact which has led countries such as Germany and Denmark to press for more EU legislation in these policy areas, on the grounds that countries such as Spain and Portugal which have 'lower standards' thereby obtain certain trading advantages in the Single European Market (SEM).

VARIATIONS IN THE BUSINESS LAW OF THE MEMBER STATES

It was noted earlier in the chapter that business law is international almost by definition and requires a good deal of *de facto* harmonisation for the good conduct of commercial relations. Substantial differences do, nevertheless, exist between the legal systems of member states of the EU in the area of business law, though it is interesting to note that many of these differences cut across the common law/civil law divide.

Even a brief description of the differences between the various aspects of business law within the EU would far exceed the space available in this chapter. Attention will, therefore, be directed towards those aspects which are the most relevant from a practical viewpoint, and to those aspects which are not covered in other chapters of this book (see, in particular, Chapter 4 for an examination of labour law, and Chapter 5 for an examination of financial and taxation law).

Law of contracts

The area of contract law which has the greatest possible relevance to European business is that which establishes what remedies may be used if the other party to a contract breaches the terms of the agreement.

It is generally accepted in all the legal systems of the member states that the unexcused failure to perform one's contractual obligations constitutes breach of contract, and that the innocent party must be protected against such a contingency. As to the remedies available, there are essentially three courses of action open to the aggrieved party. First, he may claim specific relief, that is, actual performance of the defaulting party's undertaking. Second, he may be awarded compensation, which in the majority of cases will be financial. Third, the innocent party may require a combination of the two first-named, that is, a refusal to accept further performance from the other party, combined with a claim to recover any performance which may actually have taken place.

The main difference between the various legal systems on this question reside in the precise conditions in which each remedy is available, and the exact effect of the remedy when granted by the courts. Four differences are particularly worth noting:

1. *Monetary compensation for breach of contract*. If a French, Italian or Spanish court awards financial compensation for breach of contract, it draws a distinction between the *damnum emergens* (actual loss) and the *lucrum cessans* (lost earnings). This distinction is unknown in the common law countries, whose courts base any compensation on the general concept of 'expectation interest' to cover the amount which the aggrieved party may expect. The German system, however, applies a combination of all these notions: any compensation takes into account the *Erfullungsinsteresse* (actual loss), *Vertrauensinteresse* (expectation interest), and the *entgangener Gewinn* (loss of earnings).

2. *Reflecting defaulting party's liability in award*. Differences also emerge in the proportion between the defaulting party's liability and the contractual reward which must be expressed in the amount of any damages awarded to the aggrieved party. In general, German law is less concerned with the problem of proportionality than 'Napoleonic law' countries such as France, Spain or Italy, or the common law countries. In Germany, recovery must be available for losses which an experienced observer would consider to be a likely consequence of the defendant's error. In the 'Napoleonic law' and the common law countries, on the other hand, recovery is more strictly limited to damages which were, or could reasonably have been, foreseen as likely by the obligor at the time of contracting.

3. *Termination of contract*. In certain cases, the various legal systems allow the aggrieved party to terminate the contract where the other party defaults on its terms. However, the 'Napoleonic law' countries require

much greater formalities for the termination of a contract as a remedy for breach of contract than either the common law or German law.

4. *Procedural differences.* Here, the main differences between the systems in the matter of contract enforcement reside in the special nature of certain courts. Business contracts involving traders are, in some cases, heard by specialist commercial courts – such as *tribunaux de commerce* in France and *Handelsgerichte* in Germany – whereas in other countries – such as the UK, Ireland, Spain and Italy – the ordinary courts deal with 'business' and 'civil' contracts alike.

There is as yet no attempt at harmonising the law of contracts at the level of the EU. In view of the relatively low number of difficulties encountered in accommodating national differences in this area, this would appear not to be a priority area for the approximation of laws.

Corporate structures

As was explained earlier, there are, for the most part, few differences in principle between the member states in respect of corporate structures, mainly because of the dominant influence exercised by English company law in the course of the nineteenth century which affected nearly every West European country. There are, however, two sets of differences which are important as they have significant practical implications.

Acquisition of shares

There are differences between countries on the question of whether companies are authorised to acquire shares in other companies. Differences are particularly sharp between Germany and the other EU member states.

In Germany, the Board of Management of a company usually possesses broad and substantial powers to represent the company in whatever manner it deems to be appropriate. If, to this end, the board considers it appropriate to acquire shares in another company, it may do so entirely of its own initiative.

In the other EU countries it is a company's Articles of Incorporation which, in principle, determine whether it is so authorised. If no such authority can be derived from the Articles, the legal power of a company to acquire shares is open to debate. In the UK, the ability to acquire marketable shares is listed among the company's express powers, which means that a company may not acquire marketable shares unless specifically authorised to do so in the Articles of Incorporation. In France, it is generally felt that the acquisition of marketable shares represents an indirect pursuit of the company's objective and therefore it is not necessary for the company to have specific provision in its Articles in order to allow it to acquire shares in another company with similar business purposes. Italian law prevents companies from acquiring shares if the scope and nature of the acquisition would cause a major change in the objective of the organisation as laid down in the Articles (*International Encyclopedia of Comparative Law,* vol. XIII, chapter 7, p. 9).

Management structures

Here, the major differences appear between Germany and Italy on the one hand, and the other EU countries on the other. In most member states, company management is entrusted to a Board of Directors, such as the *Conseil d'Adminis-tration* in France and the *Consejo de Directores* in Spain. The Chairman of the Board is also the Chief Executive, who determines the general direction of the company and is responsible for the day-to-day management, as well as representing the corporation with regard to third parties. In Germany and Italy, however, management is formed by two mandatory bodies – the *Vorstand* (executive board) or the *Consiglio d'Amministrazione* (board of directors) on the one hand, and the *Aufsichtsrat* and the *Collegio Sindicale* (supervisory committee) on the other hand. The *Vorstand* and the *Consiglio d'Amministrazione* form the most important administrative organ, in that they make the major policy decisions and run the company. The main function of the *Aufsichtsrat* and the *Collegio Sindicale* is to supervise the executive board/board of directors and to monitor constantly the company's corporate affairs. However, whereas in Germany the members of the *Vorstand* are appointed and dismissed by the *Aufsichtsrat*, in Italy the *Consiglio d'Amministrazione* is appointed by the general meeting of shareholders. For the purpose of keeping the executive board/ board of directors strictly separate from its supervisory organ, it is normally forbidden for one person to be concurrently a member of both bodies. The relations between them are complex and governed by detailed provisions (*International Encyclopedia of Comparative Law,* vol. XIII, chapter 4, p. 4).

Tort liability

The rules of tort liability seek to regulate the compensation which is due by the author of an unlawful act to his victim. They concern merely the *private law* aspects of such unlawful acts, that is, they do not govern their implications in terms of the criminal law.

In principle, there are considerable differences between the various legal systems in this area – hence the attempts currently being made at harmonisation at the EU level. However, these differences are greater in theory than in practice. This is especially the case in that aspect of the law of torts which is of particular interest to business lawyers, namely the liability for damage caused by things, since both product liability and the liability for dangerous things fall within the area of the law of torts.

As a general rule, it can be said that German law is less strict than the other legal systems in the EU in relation to the liability for damage caused by things.

In the 'Napoleonic law' countries, the courts have, since the 1930s, sought constantly to extend the scope of the relevant provisions in their Civil Code to cover virtually all dangerous things. Thus in France, the *Cour de Cassation* established in 1930 the rule that Article 1384(1) of the Civil Code had to be extended beyond its original terms of reference, that is, liability for damage caused by animals or ruinous buildings, to include liability for things under a person's guard. Moreover, the *Cour* has also established that in such cases the principle of strict liability should apply. This means that it is no defence for the person who has custody of the thing in question to prove that he/she took all precautions which a reasonable person would have taken.

English law also applies the principle of 'strict' (i.e. no-fault) liability. In the landmark decision on this subject, the House of Lords ruled that any person who for his own purposes brings on his land and collects and keeps there anything likely to do mischief if it escapes, must restrain it at his/her peril and, where he/she fails to do so, may be held liable for the damage which results whenever something harmful emanates from the dangerous object in question (*Rylands* v. *Fletcher* (1868) LR 3 HL 330).

German law, on the other hand, has never retreated from the principle that liability for damage caused by things is subject to the general principle of normal fault liability, as expressed in Article 823 of the Civil Code. However, the German Parliament has provided for a large number of exceptions which impose strict liability in case of damage caused by electricity, gas, pipelines, aircraft, water pollution, etc. The German courts have also shown a tendency for entertaining an increasingly strict interpretation of the owner's liability where the risk inherent in the thing in question so warrants. However, strict liability has never been established as a general principle in the same way as has been the case in virtually every other West European state.

It should be stressed that the importance of the differences which have just been noted should not be exaggerated. The business person in every West European state is now well aware that the liability for things produced or used by him/her will no longer be dependent on the damaged party having to prove that the business in question was subjectively at fault.

THE SOURCES OF EUROPEAN UNION LAW

What could be termed EU business law is still, relatively speaking, in its infancy. In spite of the considerable volume of legislation which followed upon the Commission's 1985 White Paper *Completing the Internal Market*, the laws which regulate business activity remain predominantly national. A key reason for this is that, in spite of the long-term goal which many advocate of the creation of a European federation, the scope of the three Founding Treaties was, and as amended by the SEA and the TEU still is, restricted. Essentially, the EEC Treaty (now renamed EC Treaty by the TEU) sets itself the priority of ensuring that trade between the member states is not distorted by restrictions on goods, capital, persons or services, be they a result of unfair competition or discrimination on grounds of nationality. However, as can be seen from the previous section, this only covers part of the essence of business law.

There are three main sources of EU law.

First, there is what is customarily referred to as *primary law*. This consists of the Founding Treaties plus supplements and amendments to them. As was explained in Chapter 1, the Founding Treaties consist of the 1957 European Economic Community (EEC) Treaty and the Treaties setting up the European Coal and Steel Community (1951) and the European Atomic Energy Community (1957). The main supplements and amendments to the Founding Treaties are the Merger Treaty (1965), the Budgetary Treaties (1970 and 1975), the various Acts of Accession (1972, 1979 and 1985), the Single European Act (1986), and the Treaty on European Union (1992). Together, the Founding Treaties and their subsequent supplements and amendments constitute, as it were, the 'constitution' of the European Union. They take precedence over any other form of EU law.

Second, there is what is known as *derived legislation*, which is legislation which the Council and the Commission enact on the basis of the Treaties. This legislation is made up of regulations, directives, decisions, recommendations and opinions.

Regulations are laws which apply throughout the EU. Being binding and directly applicable, they take effect without requiring enactment at national level. Most regulations – and there are up to about 5000 in an average year – are concerned with the detailed application of law and are highly technical and specific in character, but some are of a broader nature and set out principles of EU law. Many of these broader regulations have been of considerable importance to the development of EU business law. They include regulations on competition law (e.g. the regulations granting block exemptions for certain categories of agreements such as Regulation 4078/88), on the free movement of goods (e.g. the various regulations on customs valuation, such as Regulation 1979/81), on the free movement of workers (e.g. Regulation 1390/81 on social security for self-employed families and their families), and on company law (e.g. Regulation 2137/85 on the European Economic Interest Grouping).

Directives are binding on the member states only as to the result to be achieved, and allow the national authorities a discretion as to the means of implementation, that is, by legislation or by administrative action. Directives are the means which are usually used for establishing legislative frameworks and principles and they have played a key role in building up EU business law, especially in relation to the SEM which was virtually achieved at the end of 1992 by a rolling programme of 300 Directives (e.g. Directive 89/336 on electromagnetic compatibility, Directive 89/392 on the safety of machinery, and Directive No. 88/357 on non-life insurance).

Decisions are addressed to either member states or individuals. They have binding force and are not subject to any further implementation at the national level. Usually they are concerned with detailed matters of policy application.

Two general observations should be made on the subject of derived legislation:

(i) *Only regulations, directives and decisions are legally binding*. Under Article 190 of the EC Treaty, those enacting such legislation must state the reasons for which they have been adopted and mention any proposals or opinions which are required under the Treaty. Recommendations and opinions are not legally binding, although they are persuasive and not entirely devoid of legal significance. Thus, for example, the coal and steel products which are covered by EU anti-dumping legislation are dealt with in Recommendation 3018/79.

(ii) *The legislation which is relevant from the point of view of EU business law often takes the form of framework legislation*, that is, instruments enacted by the Council of Ministers or by the Council of Ministers and the European Parliament which set out the main principles and which leave the details to be filled in by legislation delegated to the Commission. Framework legislation usually takes the form of directives (such as Directive 88/361 on capital movements) but not always (e.g. Regulation No. 4064/89 on merger control).

Third, there is *case law*. This does not only mean the decisions of the European Court of Justice (ECJ) but also case law developed by the national courts, since they also are expected to apply EU law.[2]

The ECJ is the chief judicial body of the EU. Its main task is to ensure that EU law is applied uniformly throughout the member states and to arbitrate in disputes between the member states and EU institutions, and also between the institutions themselves. It consists of thirteen judges – who sit mainly in Chambers made up of between three and five judges – and six Advocates-General, who submit reasoned opinions to the Court on the cases on which it must give a ruling. Only the most important of cases are dealt with by the Court sitting in plenary session.

The individual EU citizen has direct and indirect access to the ECJ. He or she may bring direct actions against certain instruments of derived legislation under Article 173 of the EC Treaty; he/she is also an indirect party to ECJ proceedings where he/she is involved in a dispute which a national court decides to refer to the ECJ for a preliminary ruling. For example, if an EU citizen sought to import a consignment of computers from Germany into France, and was faced with a demand for a duty which could be regarded as a charge with equivalent effect to a customs duty, he/she could take the French customs authorities to the French courts on the basis that this duty infringed Article 13(2) of the EC Treaty. The French court in question would probably seek the assistance of the ECJ in deciding whether or not such a payment was contrary to EU law, and would therefore refer the case to the ECJ for an authoritative interpretation in the shape of a preliminary ruling. This is precisely what happened in Case 1/83, *IFG* v. *Freistaat Bayern*, in which the Court decided that German customs law infringed Article 13(2) of the EC Treaty.

Similar decisions have been reached by the Court in disputes between EC nationals and the authorities of the member states as regards the prohibition of import restrictions (Case 145/88), the free movement of persons (Cases 389 and 390/87) and the free movement of capital (Joined Cases 286/82 and 26/83).

THE RELATIONSHIP BETWEEN EUROPEAN UNION LAW AND NATIONAL LAW

The EEC Treaty was not the first international agreement to lay down provisions affecting business life in signatory states. However, it was the first international treaty to give judicial protection to the individual citizen, who is able to invoke its provisions before his or her domestic courts and does so in the knowledge that EU law overrides any national legislation which conflicts with it. This is thanks to two key concepts, both developed by the ECJ in relation to EC law, direct effect and primacy.[3]

Direct effect was the first specific concept of EU law to emerge from the case law of the ECJ. In a suit brought by a Dutch transport firm against its national fiscal authorities, the Court, for the first time, 'emancipated' EU law from traditional international law by making the following statement:

> the Community constitutes a new legal order of international law for the benefit of which the States have limited their sovereign rights, albeit within limited fields, and the subjects of which comprise not only Member States, but also their nationals. (Case 26/62)

The ECJ also recognised that by creating this legal order, the member states had acknowledged that Community law could be relied upon by the member states' citizens before their own domestic courts.

Not every EU law provision, however, is capable of producing direct effects. In the same decision, the Court stipulated four conditions which must be satisfied before the provision in question qualifies for direct effect. The rule must: (1) be sufficiently clear and precise for judicial application; (2) establish an unconditional obligation; (3) be such that the obligation it contains is complete and legally perfect; and (4) its implementation must not depend on the subsequent adoption of measures by either the Community institutions or the member states having discretionary powers in the matter (Case 26/62).

Thanks to a liberal interpretation by the ECJ of these criteria, many provisions of the EEC (now EC) Treaty which are particularly important to EU business law have been given direct effect – even where their meaning is not entirely clear or after the implementation date of the provision in question has expired. Thus it was possible to establish the direct effect of Treaty provisions on the free movement of goods (in particular Articles 30 to 34), the free movement of persons (Articles 48 and 52), and competition law (Articles 85 and 86). As a result, the EU citizen can enforce his or her business law rights before domestic courts.

The attribution of direct effect was not, however, by itself sufficient to establish the true scope of Community law. Let us suppose that on a certain legal point an EU law provision having direct effect and national law are in conflict with each other. Since both rules could be invoked before the domestic courts of the member state in question, to which rule should that court give precedence? The answer was provided by the ECJ in the famous *Costa* v. *ENEL* decision (Case 6/64). In this landmark decision, the Court repeated its view that the member states had limited their sovereignty for the benefit of a new legal order, but drew the additional conclusion that

> the integration into the laws of each Member State of provisions which derive from the Community, and more generally the terms and the spirit of the Treaty, make it impossible for the States, as a corollary, to accord precedence to a unilateral and subsequent measure over a legal system accepted by them on a basis of reciprocity.

The case thus established the principle of the primacy, or supremacy, of Community law.

Two observations must be added here. First, although these principles of direct effect and supremacy have been decreed as constituting a rule of thumb by the ECJ, not all the member states have accepted the principles to the same extent. Second, in order to avoid EU law being applied in disparate ways in the various member states – a real danger in view of the general differences between the various legal orders – the ECJ plays a unifying role in the interpretation of EU law. This it does especially through the mechanism of Article 177 (EC), under which the courts of the member states may – and in some cases must – refer any question of EU law which occurs in a dispute brought before them to the European Court for an authoritative interpretation.[4]

SUBSTANTIVE CONTENT OF EUROPEAN UNION BUSINESS LAW

As was noted earlier, the main purpose of EU business law is to promote free trade and fair competition throughout the European Union. The substantive rules seeking to achieve this end can be grouped under five headings: (1) the 'four freedoms'; (2) the customs union; (3) competition law; (4) corporate structures, and (5) fiscal measures.

The 'four freedoms': movement of goods, persons, services and capital

The EC Treaty provides for the creation of a common market. This involves free movement of goods, persons, services and capital across EU borders. The legal provisions governing each of these will now be considered.

Free movement of goods

The EC Treaty lays down a wide range of rules to ensure the free movement of goods. They fall into two broad categories.

First, customs duties and charges with equivalent effect to customs duties are prohibited between member states (Article 13(2) EC Treaty). The concept of 'charges with equivalent effect' is fraught with difficulties of interpretation, and the ECJ has repeatedly been called upon to rule whether or not a particular charge falls within this category. In so doing, the Court has filled the gap left by the extremely vague nature of the relevant Treaty provisions. At a very early stage it defined the prohibited charges as duties, whatever their description or technique, imposed unilaterally, which (1) apply specifically to a product imported by a member state, but not to a similar national product, and (2) by altering the price have the same effect upon the free movement of goods as a customs duty (Cases 2 and 3/62). In a subsequent decision, known as the 'Diamond Workers case', the ECJ shed further light on this concept by holding that the prohibition in question related to any pecuniary charge, other than a customs duty in the strict sense, imposed on goods circulating within the Community by reason of the fact that they cross a frontier, in so far as such a charge is not permitted by a specific provision of the Treaty (Cases 2 and 3/69). These clarifications by the Court, however helpful, appear to have had little effect since the number of ECJ cases on this subject continues to grow year by year.

Second, as regards import and export quotas (quantitative restrictions on imports and exports), the Treaty applies the same approach as it does to the removal of customs duties. Quantitative restrictions within the strict sense of the term were eliminated within a relatively short period among the original Six (and well within the transitional period in the case of more recent members). However, the Treaty also addresses itself to the 'measures equivalent to quantitative restrictions', and here too it has been the ECJ which has been called upon to clarify this concept.

On this subject, the Court has also attempted to add a few general criteria for future guidance in order to complement a rather vaguely worded Treaty commitment. The most important of these was formulated in the 1974 Dassonville case, where the Court held that 'all trading rules enacted by member states which are capable of hindering, directly or indirectly, actually or potentially, intra-Community trade are to be considered as measures having an effect equivalent to quantitative restrictions' (Case 8/74). In the opinion of the present writer, this general statement has almost acquired the status of an additional Treaty article, so conclusive has it been for the subsequent development of the case law on this subject.

One factor, however, places a potential restriction on the scope of the ban on import or export quotas which does not apply in the case of customs duties. Article 36 of the EC Treaty states that its provisions on trade quotas do not preclude prohibitions or restrictions on imports, exports or goods in transit justified on grounds of public morality, public policy or public security. In the event, this has not provided member states with an easy mechanism for circumventing the prohibition on quotas, since here again Article 36 is applied under the watchful eye of the ECJ. In addition, the Court has always applied the principle that exceptions to the rule must be strictly interpreted, which also serves to restrict the member states' scope for evasion.

In addition to the case-by-case work of the ECJ, the EU institutions have taken legislative and regulatory action aimed at the harmonisation of member states' legislation so as to enhance the free movement of goods. Three initiatives have been particularly important in marking progress made in this field.

The first took the shape of two general programmes which were launched in 1969 for the removal of technical barriers to trade: one on industrial products, the other on foodstuffs. Under the original timetable, these programmes were to have been completed in the early 1970s, but it soon became apparent that this was an unrealistic aspiration, and the programmes are still in the process of being implemented.

The second initiative came in the form of a Commission letter (*EC Bulletin*, 1980) which followed the 1979 ECJ *Cassis de Dijon* decision (Case 120/78). In this ruling, the Court had stated that technical and commercial rules, even those which are equally applicable to national and imported products, may be used to create barriers to trade only where the rules are necessary to satisfy mandatory requirements and to serve a purpose which is in the general interest and for which they are an essential guarantee. From this ruling, the Commission concluded that a member state may not in principle prohibit the sale in its territory of a product lawfully produced and marketed in another member state, even if it is produced according to technical or quality requirements which differ from those imposed on its domestic products. The Commission's 1985 White Paper, *Completing the Internal Market* (which will be returned to shortly), gave official recognition to this new approach and proposed a distinction between areas in which *harmonisation* is essential and those in which it is sufficient to accept the principle of *mutual recognition* of the various fundamental requirements laid down by national law. Most SEM legislation, covering areas as diverse as health controls and financial services, is now based on this approach. As a result, the EU does not now seek to harmonise everything, but rather seeks to establish 'essential requirements', leaving the detailed standardisation measures to the various European standardisation bodies.

The third initiative came with the adoption of the Commission's 1985 White Paper and the enactment of the 1986 Single European Act. The background to these measures was as follows. The Treaty rules relating to the 'four freedoms', the customs union, fiscal measures and company law were aimed at creating in the Community an internal market which would resemble as closely as possible market conditions which prevail within a nation state. However, as was shown in Chapters 1 and 2, it came increasingly to be appreciated that progress was too slow, and that what was needed was a definite target date for the creation of this internal market. A significant step in this direction was taken with the White Paper, *Completing the Internal Market*, which was issued by the Commission in April 1985 and which was adopted by the European Council two months later. It laid down an ambitious programme of 300 directives which were to be enacted before 30 December 1992. The White Paper included the following measures (see also Chapter 2 on this):

• the removal of physical and technical barriers to trade – for example, phytosanitary regulations, rules on the use of dangerous substances such as asbestos, and safety measures for such utensils as pressure vessels and tower cranes;
• free movement of capital;
• harmonisation of company law and related measures such as trademarks, the structure of public limited companies, etc.;
• conditions for the cross-border provision of services such as banking and insurance;
• fiscal harmonisation, such as the collection and rates of VAT;
• removal of internal frontier controls on persons.

The White Paper was soon followed by the SEA, which brought about changes in the procedures of the EC institutions which would facilitate the completion of the internal market. As was explained in Chapter 1, the SEA provided that certain decisions which previously had required unanimity be made subject to the qualified majority rule. It also laid down a cooperation procedure between the Council and the European Parliament which gave the latter more input into decisions affecting the internal market.

Progress made in implementing this ambitious programme was so satisfactory that virtually all 300 directives proposed in the White Paper were adopted by the official target date of 31 December 1992, and approximately 90 per cent of these directives had been incorporated into the national law of the member states by the end of 1993. The following examples give an idea of the range of measures adopted:

• *Physical barriers:* Directive on the Holding, Movement and Control of Excise Goods in the Single Market, which simplifies the fiscal procedures relating to the movement of excise goods across intra-EU boundaries.
• *Veterinary and phytosanitary controls:* Directive on Animal Health Requirements, which lays down veterinary health requirements for trade in live animals not covered by other measures.
• *Food law:* Directive on Extraction Solvents, which establishes the approximation of the laws of the member states relating to extraction solvents used in the production of foodstuffs and food ingredients.
• *Technical barriers:* Directive on the Approximation of Laws of the Member States Relating to the Safety of Machinery, which lays down certain technical standards which must be incorporated into the relevant health and safety legislation of the member states.

• *Sectoral measures:* Directive on Medical Devices, which provides for the harmonisation of existing national systems to minimise technical barriers for medical devices.
• *Public procurement:* various measures which, in conjunction with existing directives on the subject, seek to open up the EU market in public purchasing. The main objective is to achieve fair competition in this field through improving transparency, the application of EU purchasing rules to such utilities as water, energy and transport, and by providing adequate remedies enabling suppliers and contractors to pursue complaints regarding alleged discrimination.
• *Financial services:* the Non-Life Insurance Services Directive, which lays down rules under which the freedom to provide services within the EU is applied to non-life insurance business. Thus, for the first time, EU insurers have a legal basis enabling them to cover the risks of potential policy holders residing in any member state.
• *Consumer affairs:* Directive on Unfair Contract terms, which provides for the approximation of laws of member states concerning unfair terms in contracts between a consumer and a seller or supplier.
• *Copyright:* Directive on Rental and Lending Rights, which gives copyright owners and performing artists the right to control the renting or lending of their works, and to claim remuneration for these activities.
• *Transport:* Directive on Motor Exhausts, which approximates the laws relating to the permissible sound level and the exhaust system of motor vehicles.
• *Environment:* Directive on the Consumption of Energy by Household Appliances, which provides for the indication by labelling and standard product information of the consumption of energy and other resources by household appliances.

Free movement of persons and services

A distinction must be drawn here between salaried workers and self-employed persons. As to the former, Article 48 of the EC Treaty provides that workers of the member states shall be free to accept employment offers anywhere in the EU, and that they may move freely within the territory of member states for that purpose as well as residing there in order to pursue their employment. It also prohibits any discrimination based on nationality between workers of the member states as regards any aspect of employment. It even gives workers the right to remain in a member state after their employment there has finished. This freedom is subject to two reservations: it does not apply to the public services, and it contains a similar 'public policy' exception to the one found in Article 36.[5] The Court of Justice has developed an extensive case law on this subject, some of it quite controversial (see for example the famous van Duyn decision (Case 41/74)).

In order to make the free movement of workers a practical reality, the EC Treaty requires the Council of Ministers to enact harmonising legislation in the field of social security. This legislation has two objectives: (1) to aggregate all the periods covered by social security contributions paid in more than one member state; and (2) to secure the payment of social security benefits anywhere within the EU.

In relation to self-employed persons, Articles 52–8 seek to ensure their freedom of establishment anywhere within the EU. Subject to the same 'public policy' provision which applies to workers, the Treaty gives EU citizens the right in principle to take up and pursue self-employed activity, and to set up and manage firms and companies. Articles 59–66 confer on them the right to provide their services across EU frontiers, regardless of their nationality and where they are established. Here again, the EU institutions have adopted positive harmonising steps which complement the work of the Court in calling to order those member states which maintain discriminatory practices in this field. Two types of measures need to be distinguished in this context.

First, in 1960 the Council enacted two general programmes: No. 32/62 on the Abolition of Restrictions on Freedom to Provide Services, and No. 36/62 abolishing restrictions on freedom of establishment (Lasok, 1986, p. 323). The latter programme, in particular, seeks to give priority to activities which are especially valuable to the development of production and trade, and to enable the setting up of agencies and branches, as well as facilitating the entry of management or supervisory personnel in such agencies or branches.

Second, legislation has been enacted establishing the mutual recognition of diplomas, certificates and other evidence of formal qualifications. Normally, each sector envisaged is covered by a double directive: one seeking to secure the mutual recognition of qualifications, the other aimed at the coordination of the legislative and administrative provisions concerning the actual contents of these qualifications. In this way, sets of directives have, for example, been adopted in the medical professions and in relation to architects, pharmacists and insurance agents. Here too SEM legislation adopted pursuant to the SEA has had a major impact, with the adoption of a general Council directive which applies to a wide range of professions and which is making it easier for professionals to work in member states other than their own.

Free movement of capital

The free movement of capital is widely seen as a necessary corollary to the free movement of goods, persons and services, and the rules seeking to achieve it are contained in Articles 67–73 of the EC Treaty. It is important to point out that these rules are much less strict than those relating to the other freedoms, no doubt because the drafters of the Treaty considered that this was a particularly sensitive area in view of the importance of capital movements to the political economy of the member states. Thus Article 67(1) contains no unconditional requirement that all capital movements must be liberalised, since this must only be done 'to the extent necessary for the proper functioning of the common market'. The Treaty provides no further clarification on the scope of this qualification in the absence of a clear dividing line between 'necessary' and 'other' liberalisation measures.

However, very early on the Council did adopt two directives providing for the gradual abolition of restrictions on detailed lists of capital movements. Subsequently, a more general directive removing controls from all capital movements was adopted in June 1988.

Closely related to this issue is the question of the movement towards Economic and Monetary Union (EMU) and the TEU provisions for so doing. Chapters 1, 2 and 5 give consideration to this.

The customs union

The EU is a customs union, that is, an area in which not only do goods, persons and capital move freely between member states, but also an area which applies common customs rules and rates in relation to products emanating from outside this area. These common rules and rates take the form primarily of harmonised legislation in three main areas: customs tariffs, definition of origin and customs valuation. Each of these will now be briefly considered.

The common customs tariff

Common customs rates applied by the Community take the form of the Common Customs Tariff (CCT). The CCT came fully into operation on 1 January 1968, when it replaced all the member states' individual rates towards non-EC products. Its nomenclature is based on that of the Customs Cooperation Council, which is a non-EU body established in 1951 (but of which all the EU members states are signatories). It is subdivided into ninety-nine chapters, the first twenty-four of which cover agricultural products and products of the food industry. The remaining chapters cover all industrial products, for example, minerals, chemical products, wood, paper, textiles and metals. The initial CCT nomenclature, established by Regulation 950/68/EEC, has undergone considerable change as a result of its annual review which is published in the *Official Journal of the European Communities*. These changes have been caused not only by the bilateral and multilateral trade agreements of the EU, but also by the generalised preferential systems under which the EU grants tariff reductions – in most cases to Third World countries. In spite of the extensive rules of interpretation which are stated in Part I of each CCT Regulation, frequent disputes occur between businesses and the national customs administrations on the classification of their produce under this nomenclature. The Court of Justice, under Article 177 of the EC Treaty, gives the decisive ruling.

Definition of origin

One of the difficulties involved in interpreting the CCT is determining the origin of a particular product as it enters the territory of a member state, as two or more countries could be involved in the manufacture or processing of the product. Another area of difficulty is to ensure that any procedure seeking to establish this origin must be identical throughout the EU. This was the subject matter of Regulation 802/68/EEC which was adopted a few days before the CCT came into operation. Generally speaking, the Regulation provides that the relevant country for determining the origin of goods shall be that in which the last substantial process or operation that is economically justified was performed; this is on the understanding that this process or operation has been carried out in an undertaking equipped for this purpose, and resulting in the manufacture of a new product or representing an important stage of manufacturing (Wyatt and Dashwood, 1993).

Customs valuation

The correct application of the CCT also requires that, once the appropriate tariff classification and origin of a product have been established, the relevant customs duty should be computed properly and uniformly regardless of its point of entry into the EU. As most CCT rates are *ad valorem* duties, it is vital that there be as clear a set of rules as possible in order to ensure that the method of assessing the customs value be identical in all member states. The relevant rules are stated in Regulation 1224/80 (which replaced the original Regulation 803/68/EEC).

The basic rule contained in this Regulation is that goods are valued at their point of entry into the EU. As a result, expenses incurred within the EU, such as warehousing or transport costs, are not included in the relevant value, provided that these costs are capable of being distinguished from the price paid or payable. Expenses such as the cost of obtaining an import licence or an unused share of a quota are not taken into account when assessing the value on importation, though the cost of a certificate of authenticity showing that EU quality criteria are met is counted, as are – in part – commissions payable on purchase and payments for waiting time (Lasok, 1989, p. 170).

Competition law

It has already been mentioned above that free and fair competition is one of the basic principles of business law within the member states. Because the operation of the 'four freedoms' was expected to increase cross-border trade within the Community, it was anticipated by the Founding Fathers that fair trading would need to be safeguarded at the European level. Failure to adopt the necessary competition law measures at the Community level would have a number of undesirable consequences which could undermine the objective of the Founding Treaties. On the one hand, companies might be tempted to take advantage of both their size and the larger market to engage in restrictive practices and/or abuse monopolistic positions. On the other hand, the member states might succumb to the temptation to give their companies unfair advantages on the European market by granting subsidies and abusing state monopolies. It is this type of distortion that the relevant rules of EU competition law seek to prevent or eliminate. The rules fall under two general headings:

Competition rules applicable to the private sector

Here, the EC Treaty is concerned to curb two types of abuse. In Article 85, it penalises restrictive agreements between enterprises which affect trade between member states and have the object or effect of distorting competition. Such agreements are automatically void unless exemption has been granted by the Commission. The term 'agreements' must be understood as covering not only legally enforceable contracts, but also non-binding arrangements, which the Treaty defines as 'concerted practices', and even decisions made by associations of undertakings.

Competition is adversely affected when any kind of agreement, decision or action by firms directly affects the market and is detrimental to production or sales to consumers, because it limits freedom of choice (Wyatt and Dashwood, 1993). The Court of Justice has developed the meaning of 'distortion of competition' by adding that competition must have been prevented, restricted or distorted to an appreciable extent (Cases 56 and 58/64, p. 299). The Treaty also specifies that the prohibited distortion must take place within the common market, that is, agreements which restrict competition in a non-member state are not covered by this prohibition. Article 85(1) gives a number of specific examples of the type of agreement envisaged: price-fixing arrangements, market-sharing agreements, and the application of different conditions to equivalent transactions with other trading parties.

The Treaty is not, however, totally inflexible on this subject, and recognises that there are circumstances in which certain restrictive practices may be allowable. This is why Article 85(3) enables the Commission to grant exemption to agreements which contribute to improving the production or distribution of goods or to promoting technical or economic progress, whilst allowing consumers a fair share of the resulting benefit.

The other type of conduct by private undertakings which is caught by EU competition law is the abuse of a dominant position by an undertaking or groups of undertakings (Article 86 of the Treaty). By 'dominant position' is meant a position of economic power enjoyed by an enterprise which allows it to prevent effective competition on the relevant market by behaving to an appreciable extent independently of its competitors, customers and consumers (Case 27/76, p. 207).

The term 'abuse' has been a difficult one for the Court and the Commission to define. In general terms, it relates to any behaviour of an enterprise enjoying a dominant position which interferes with one of the basic freedoms of access to business (Mathysen, 1990). In the judicial supervision of this aspect of EU law, a key role is given not only to the Court of Justice, but also to the Commission. It is the latter which can grant exemptions, oblige undertakings to discontinue infringements, investigate the practices of undertakings and, ultimately, impose fines and penalties on enterprises. The procedures enabling the Commission to discharge its duties under this heading are laid down in Regulation 17.

One way in which companies could restrict competition is by acquiring others to the point where they enjoy an unhealthy monopolistic position. The EC found this hard to control on the basis of the EEC Treaty, but the Council of Ministers hesitated for years before introducing legislation on this subject, mainly because of a fear of offending national sensitivities. However, in September 1990 a regulation on merger control came into force – Regulation 4064/89. Under the Merger Control Regulation, any plans involving cross-frontier mergers of firms having a combined turnover amounting to at least 5000 million ECUs must be notified to the Commission for approval. However, where each of the firms concerned obtains two-thirds of its business within the EU in one and the same member state, the merger is not to be subject to EU control, but is to be regulated by the domestic authorities. The Regulation also controls lesser forms of concentration, such as partial mergers and joint ventures, which have an effect similar to mergers. Infringement of the Regulation may lead to the imposition of heavy fines.

The Merger Control Regulation has important implications for business for it has, as part of its purpose, to avoid double scrutiny of proposed mergers at the EU and at the national level. The Commission has, up to the time of writing, approved all but one of the references made to it, although conditions have been attached to some of the mergers which have been authorised.

Competition rules applicable to the public sector

Aware that the public authorities of member states were in a position where they could distort intra-Community trade, the drafters of the EEC Treaty imposed two main types of curbs on their powers of economic intervention.

First, in relation to subsidies, Article 92 prohibits any aids granted by the state to certain enterprises or favouring the production of certain goods, where these affect trade between member states. The Treaty is, however, sufficiently flexible to acknowledge that certain types of state subsidy are necessary for social and economic reasons. This is why Article 92(2) and (3) lists those state aids which are, or may be considered to be, compatible with the common market. Here again, it is the Commission which has a key role in the supervision of these competition rules. Article 93 lays down the procedural rules under which the Commission, assisted by the Court and Council, can bring defaulting member states to order.

A good example of the Court's approach towards state aids is provided by its ruling in Case 102/87. Here, the French Government challenged a Commission decision that a loan below market rate provided by the *Fonds Industriel de Modernisation* (FIM) constituted an illegal state subsidy, and as such was incompatible with the common market. FIM was financed by means of a savings scheme under which the investors obtained a lower rate of interest in return for tax exemptions. The Court ruled that the loan in question did not constitute an aid unless it raised issues not considered by the Commission. The ECJ also held that intra-EU trade could be affected even if the firm which stood to benefit did not engage in exports, provided that its products competed with imports from other member states.

Second, in relation to public undertakings, Article 90 requires that undertakings which the state can influence either directly or indirectly are kept within the Treaty rules on competition. In practice, this has proved to be a very difficult area for the Court to rule on, for the Council to legislate on, and for the Commission to police.

Corporate structures

In order to make the 'four freedoms' a more practical proposition, company law must be harmonised within the EU. Since, as has been mentioned earlier, companies have legal personality, they too must enjoy freedom of establishment. This is why Article 54(3)(g) of the EC Treaty requires the Council to enact legislation harmonising those safeguards which are expected of companies for the protection of the interests of company members and the general public. Thus far, the Council has enacted a sizeable body of legislation under this Treaty provision, notably on the disclosure of vital information, the formation of public limited companies, the division of public limited companies, consolidated accounts and statutory auditors. By mid-1993, seven directives were in place (see Table 3.1), though political differences were still preventing the enactment of legislation providing for a European company statute.

TABLE 3.1   Seven directives relating to company law

First Directive on the disclosure of vital information for the protection of shareholders and others (Directive 68/151, OJ Special Edition 1968 (I), p. 41)

This directive, which has had an important reforming function in certain member states, covers a wide range of disparate but important aspects of company law. It regulates not only the duty to disclose certain documents, but also the validity of obligations entered into on behalf of a company by its officers, and the various factors which could lead to the annulment of a company.

Second Directive on the formation of public limited liability companies and the maintenance and alteration of their capital (Directive 77/91, OJ 1977 L 26/1)

The information which a public limited company is required to have included in its articles of association as a result of this directive includes the type and name of the company, its objects, the authorised (if any) and subscribed capital at the time of incorporation, the registered office, and various items of information regarding its shares. The directive also stipulates minimum numbers of members and of capital, and contains detailed rules on the distribution of dividends and of interest relating to shares and on the maintenance, increase or reduction in the company capital.

Fourth Directive on company accounts (Directive 78/660, OJ 1978 L 222/1)

The Fourth Directive was adopted earlier than the Third. It is concerned with the preparation, presentation and publication of accounts of the type of companies envisaged in the preceding directives. It contains a great deal of technical detail necessary for the practical approximation of the member states' systems, such as the layout for the presentation and contents of the balance sheet and the profit and loss account, valuation rules, and the contents of the annual reports.

Third Directive on mergers of public limited liability companies (Directive 78/855, OJ 1978 L 295/36)

The crucial section of this directive is Chapter II, which regulates in detail mergers by acquisition. The administrative or managerial bodies of the merging companies must draw up a merger plan which must be published in accordance with Article 3 of the First Directive and approved by the general meeting of each of the companies involved. The merger plan must also contain basic information such as the type, name and registered office of each of the companies, the terms of the allotment of shares in the acquiring company, etc.

Sixth Directive on the division of public limited liability companies (Directive 82/891, OJ 1982 L 378/47)

This complements the Third Directive in that it concerns operations under which a public limited company within the same member state transfers to a number of public limited companies, which are already in existence or about to be formed, all its assets and liabilities in exchange for the issue of shares to the shareholders of the divided company. Its structure is modelled on the Third Directive, and indeed the original plan was for the two directives to be amalgamated. In view of the special problems to which the division of a company was thought to give rise, this plan was not carried into effect.

Seventh Directive on consolidated accounts (Directive 83/349)

The object of this directive is to approximate accountancy legislation relating to large economic units, i.e. the so-called groups of undertakings. It imposes on the member states the duty to require the undertakings to draw up consolidated accounts and assumes a substantial degree of control by one undertaking.

Eighth Directive on statutory auditors (Directive 84/253, OJ 1984 L 126/20)

The purpose of this directive is the standardisation of the auditing procedures of those companies which are most common in the Community. It sets out the rules for the approval of persons or bodies empowered to carry out company audits as well as laying down standards of professional integrity and independence of such persons.

Fiscal measures

In principle, trade among the member states is not totally free from distortion as long as direct and indirect taxation are subject to different rates within the EU, since both could be manipulated by national authorities in order to give their own business enterprises an advantage over their competitors. Accordingly, Article 95 of the EC Treaty provides that no member state may impose, either directly or indirectly, any internal taxation on products which discriminates in favour of domestic products. However, this Article has proved to be very difficult for the Court of Justice to unravel, and political sensitivities on the subject have resulted in the Council of Ministers being very reluctant to introduce legislation in this field to any significant extent. As is shown in Chapter 5, attempts at fiscal harmonisation have been confined to indirect taxation, and even here national authorities have been left considerable scope for action.

CONCLUDING REMARKS

Although the two main legal systems which apply within the EU – common law and codified law – reveal considerable differences in principle, business experiences relatively little difficulty arising from these differences. So many business transactions take place in an international context that the countries of Western Europe have found it expedient not to allow too many barriers to inhibit trade between them. Nevertheless, the EU has set itself the goal of reducing such barriers as still exist. In so doing, it has chosen to give priority to ensuring that the member states' governments, as well as powerful commercial concerns, are given as little opportunity as possible to distort intra-EU trade. This it has done in preference to attempting a comprehensive harmonisation programme involving the major areas of business law as it applies to the member states.

The evidence suggests that the EU has been wise in establishing its priorities in this manner. The fact that member states can not only be brought to account by the Commission and the Court of Justice, but also face defeat in their own domestic courts if they fail to adjust their discriminatory legislation, has achieved more than would, in all probability, have been realised by a massive exercise in across-the-board harmonisation of the law of contracts, company law, property law and the law of torts. Since the differences between the member states in these areas, although real, have proved to be no major obstacle to trade, it has been infinitely preferable to concentrate on those restrictions which are potentially strong weapons in the hands of the member states to restrict trade between them. The wisdom of this approach has been confirmed especially in recessionary times when the temptation to adopt pro-tectionist measures could be overwhelming for national authorities.

Therefore, the balance between national and EU business law would, at present, appear to be reasonably satisfactory. The twin objectives of securing free trade within the EU and of ensuring that businesses compete as freely and fairly as possible have largely been met by the 'four freedoms' and competition law, and most of the obstacles that remain are likely to be removed under the impulse of the Single European Market. This, in time, may well give rise to the elaboration of a common legal system which also applies to the law of contracts, property and torts.

Notes

1. In registration formalities the intervention of a person enjoying a semi-official status (such as the solicitor in the United Kingdom, or the *notaire* in France) will be required.
2. Not only do they settle cases involving EU law after having sought a preliminary ruling from the ECJ; in some cases they also apply EU law by themselves, by virtue of the *acte clair* theory.
3. On each occasion in a preliminary ruling given under Article 177 of the EEC Treaty.
4. The national court *must* refer a case to the ECJ where it is a court against whose decision no further appeal is possible.
5. This exception was further elaborated by Directive 64/221.

List of Cases before the European Court of Justice

Cases 2 and 3/62, *Commission v. Luxembourg and Belgium* (1962) European Court Reports (ECT) 423
Case 26/62, *Van Gend and Loos v. Nederlandse Administratie der Belastingen* 91963) ECR 1.
Case 6/64, *Costa v. ENEL* (1964) ECT 585.
Cases 56 and 58/64, *Consten and Grundiq v. Commission* (1966) ECR 299.
Cases 2 and 3/69, *Diamantarbeiders v. Brachfeld* (1969) ECR 211.
Case 8/74, *Procureur du Roi v. Dassonville* (1974) ECR 837.
Case 4174, *Van Duyn v. Home Office* (1974) ECR 1337.
Case 27/76, *United Brands Company v. Commission* (1978) ECR 207.
Case 120/78, *Rewe v. Bundesmonopolverwaltung für Branntwein* (1979) ECR 649.

Case 128/78, *Commission* v. *United Kingdom* (1980) ECR 417.
Cases 286/82 and 26/83, *Luisi and Carbone* v. *Ministero del Tesoro* (1984) ECR 377.
Case 1/83, *IFG* v. *Freistaat Bayern* (1984) ECT 349.
Case 357/87, *Albert Schmid* v. *Hauptzollamt Stuttgart* (1988) ECR 6239.
Cases 389 and 390/87, *GBC Echternach and A. Moritz* v. *Netherlands Minister for Education* (1990) ECT 557.
Case 145/88, *Torfaen Borough Council* v. *B and Q plc* (1989) ECR 765.

Guide to Further Reading

For a general comparative overview of the major principles of business law which apply in the member states, the *International Encyclopedia of Comparative Law*, volumes VII (Contracts) and XIII (Company Law) is recommended.

As for the business law systems of the major EU member states, the handbooks by Klunzinger (1993) for Germany, Cremades (1992) for Spain, Studio, Maisto and Miscali (1992) for Italy, Guery (1991) for France, and Schmitthoff and Sarre (1988) for the United Kingdom, will provide a thorough insight into each system.

For a *general* guide to the EU business law, the best work available is Wyatt and Dashwood (1993). The legislation and case law of the EU which is relevant to business law are set out in detail in Weatherill (1992). Other useful general guides to EU law are Kent (1992) and Mathysen (1990).

For individual areas of EU business law, the following are recommended. Lasok (1989) for customs law and the free movement of goods, Lasok (1986) for the free movement of persons, Bellamy and Child (1987) for competition law, and Gleichmann (1991) for company law.

CHAPTER 4

Labour markets and industrial relations

Martin Rhodes

INTRODUCTION

Although the labour market and labour relations have been marginal to the process of European integration, present developments, both within member states and at the European Union (EU) level, have major implications for the European business environment. The last thirty years have witnessed profound changes in the nature of European employment, with important implications for both employers and trade unions. In the 1960s, the traditional image of the worker as a full-time, securely employed male in manufacturing was still fairly close to the norm. In the 1990s, the number of workers fitting that description has declined: the growth in the proportion of women in the workforce, the expansion of service sector employment, and the proliferation of part-time and temporary work – not to mention the persistence of high levels of unemployment (especially among younger workers) – have all transformed the character of labour markets and the nature of industrial relations. At the same time, a major new force in labour market regulation has appeared in the form of supranational government, initially in the area of the freedom of movement of labour but more recently in the progressive development of new rules regarding health and safety and the harmonisation of social protection and workers rights across the EU.

This chapter will explore these changes and their implications for business in Europe and, more broadly, for the future of the European economy. One theme in particular will be central to the analysis – the importance of labour market management, by which is meant the organisation, education and deployment of the workforce, for the performance of national economies and for the capacity of the EU as a whole to respond successfully to two concurrent challenges: the need to preserve political stability and social cohesion while also coping with the intensification of competition and industrial adjustment which is following in the wake of the creation of the Single European Market (SEM).

Perhaps the most important immediate problem in this regard is the apparent inability of the EU member states to combat unemployment and non-employment: for not only have they experienced high and rising unemployment over the last two decades but they have been less successful than other countries in creating employment opportunities. In 1992, 60 per cent of the working age population in the EU were employed, compared with 70 per cent in the United States and almost 75 per cent in Japan. The employment rate in the United States, Japan and the EFTA countries was higher in 1992 than in the 1970s, but in the EU it was lower. The contrast with the US is greatest: between 1975 and 1985, an extra 6 per cent of working age people were brought into the workforce while in the EU the size of the workforce declined, even though economic growth rates were broadly comparable (Commission 1993, pp. 23–30). This problem – and the associated income disparities, social divisions, and threats to stability and cohesion – have major implications for the policy agenda at both member state and EU levels.

The discussion which follows is broken into four major sections. The first examines the changes which have occurred in the nature of employment and unemployment across the EU. As for employment, the focus will be on three interrelated developments: the growth of service sector, female and 'atypical' forms of employment. The analysis of unemployment will concentrate on the apparently intractable problems of long-term and youth unemployment and their concentration in particular regions. The second section will discuss the relationship between employment, labour market policy and industrial relations in the EU member states. Are some countries better than others in sustaining a high level of employment? After considering the debate on employment creation – which focuses on the issue of workforce 'flexibility' – this section will explore the key differences between three broad modes of labour market management in the EU. In section three the discussion shifts from the national to the supranational level (the so-called 'social dimension' of European integration) and will examine three areas of EU policy concerning the labour market: the growing role of the EU in creating a 'European' labour market through the promotion of labour mobility, intervention through the Structural Funds to assist employment in depressed and backward regions, and the attempted harmonisation of rules and workers' entitlements. The fourth section will consider the parallel project of creating a new, European level of industrial relations based on new forums for collective bargaining and new forms of workers' representation in transnational companies. The conclusion will address the issue which is now at the heart of the European labour market debate: the achievement of a desirable balance between policies to protect employment and policies to create it.

LABOUR MARKETS IN THE EUROPEAN UNION

The changing nature of employment

The three most important labour market developments across the member states of the EU over the last twenty years have been the steady increase in service sector employment and the parallel decline of both agricultural and industrial employment, the 'feminisation' of the work force as the number of women as a proportion of total employment has grown, and the increase in 'atypical' forms of work as the traditional full-time, permanent character of employment has steadily given way to a much more variegated structure, including an expansion of part-time and temporary work.

TABLE 4.1   Share of economic sector in total employment

	Agriculture		Industry		Services	
	1985	1991	1985	1991	1985	1991
Belgium	3.6	2.7	31.9	30.5	64.5	66.8
Denmark	6.7	5.7	27.9	27.6	65.4	66.7
Germany	5.2	3.5	41.9	40.1	53.8	56.4
Greece	28.9	22.2	25.7	25.7	45.4	52.1
Spain	16.2	10.9	31.9	33.0	52.0	56.1
France	8.2	6.0	32.4	30.0	59.4	63.9
Ireland	16.6	14.0	29.9	29.0	53.5	57.0
Italy	11.0	8.5	33.5	32.2	55.5	59.3
Luxembourg	4.7	3.5	31.8	28.9	62.8	67.6
Netherlands	5.3	4.4	28.3	25.6	66.3	70.1
Portugal	21.5	17.4	33.9	34.0	44.4	48.6
United Kingdom	2.4	2.3	34.6	31.2	63.0	66.5
EEC	8.3	6.2	32.8	31.3	58.9	62.3

SOURCE   Commission of the European Communities (1992).

As illustrated in Table 4.1, services now employ between 60 and 70 per cent of workers and employees in the more advanced EU countries, and industry often accounts for less than one third. Agriculture remains an important source of employment in many countries, although decreasingly so. In recent years, there has been a tendency for the rate of increase in tertiary sector employment to be greater in the less developed parts of the EU, reflecting the fact that these economies are 'catching up' with their more developed counterparts. Thus, between 1985 and 1990 – a period of employment growth in the EU – the increase in jobs occurred mainly in services although most countries also recorded some growth in industrial employment as well.

The link between the growth of service sector employment and the expansion of the female labour force is clear. Women have accounted for most of the new employment created in the EU over the last twenty-five years. Female employment in the EU grew from less than 40 million in 1965 to more than 53 million in 1991, while that of men fell from 83 to 82 million. Moreover, it is mainly women in the 25–49 age group (i.e. of child-bearing age) which account for this growth in employment. During the 1980s, the number of men employed grew by only 1 per cent (an extra 1 million), while the number of women increased by almost 16 per cent, equal to around 7 million workers, with significant growth especially in the southern countries as the importance of family work declined (Commission, 1993, p. 28). Most of this growth was in services. In 1991, more than 75 per cent of women in work were employed in services compared with around 20 per cent in industry.

TABLE 4.2   Employment, unemployment and non-employment (percentages)

	Employment (working age popn.)				Unemployment				Non-employment	
	Male		Female		Male		Female		Male	Female
	1985	1991	1985	1991	1985	1991	1985	1991	(1980s	Average)
Belgium	69.1	69.1	37.2	43.2	7.4	4.6	17.8	10.6		
Denmark	82.9	81.2	68.3	70.9	6.4	8.3	9.5	10.0		
Germany	77.2	79.2	47.9	55.1	5.8	3.6	8.5	4.8	24.0	54.1
Greece	79.0	74.7	37.4	35.9	5.7	4.8	11.7	12.9		
Spain	64.2	68.6	25.7	31.6	19.6	12.0	25.0	23.2	30.2	72.6
France	72.8	70.4	49.9	51.7	8.5	7.2	12.6	11.7	27.0	50.6
Ireland	70.1	68.8	32.2	36.1	17.4	15.4	19.1	16.6	31.9	68.0
Italy	75.0	72.8	34.1	37.8	6.4	6.8	15.4	15.8	28.4	66.0
Luxembourg	77.9	77.7	39.8	44.0	2.2	1.1	4.3	2.0		
Netherlands	68.8	76.6	36.2	48.6	9.5	5.6	12.4	10.0	25.9	56.0
Portugal	80.6	84.3	49.4	58.7	6.8	2.6	11.7	5.7	20.6	49.9
United Kingdom	77.3	79.6	55.0	61.9	11.8	9.4	11.0	7.4	23.5	42.3
EEC	74.6	75.3	42.8	48.0	9.4	7.2	12.9	11.5		

SOURCE   Commission, *Employment in Europe* 1993, OECD, *Employment Outlook*, July (1993), tables 2.7 and 4.1.

The increase in the number of women in work has gone hand in hand with higher levels of underemployment and insecurity in the workforce (Commission, 1993). Female rates of non-employment (i.e. those not just unemployed but also excluded from the labour force) remain much higher than for men (see Table 4.2) while the proportion in part-time and temporary employment also tends to be higher (see Tables 4.3 and 4.4). The subordinate position of women in the workforce is also reflected in their low rates of self-employment. The increase in the number of part-time jobs is the major reason for the growth of the female workforce. In all EU member states, part-time and temporary workers have increased in number – sometimes dramatically – over the last decade. Table 4.3 illustrates the increase in part-time employment since the 1970s and Table 4.4 the growth in fixed-term employment. A number of general features stand out in these tables.

First, EU countries converge in one respect: in all of them women make up the great majority of part-time employees. But there the similarity ends. As far as the proportion of part-timers in the total workforce is concerned, there are two camps: a northern one (Belgium, Britain, The Netherlands and Denmark) where part-timers make up between a quarter and a third of all workers; and a southern one (Greece, Italy, Portugal and Spain) where there have tradition-ally been restrictions on the use of non-standard employment contracts and where the number of part-timers is small.

Second, there is a growing correlation between the growth of employment and the increase in the number of part-time jobs. In the Netherlands especially, two-thirds of the net addition to jobs in the 1980s were part time rather than full time. Part-timers also accounted for a significant proportion of new jobs created in Germany, France and Belgium. In 1991, there was a decline in employment among full-time workers (especially in the UK and Ireland), while a high proportion of additional jobs were part time in those countries where employment increased (Belgium, Germany, The Netherlands, Portugal and Italy) (ibid.). This tendency is likely to increase as restrictions on the use of part-time employment are lifted or modified, as seems likely, in most EU countries where they currently exist (this trend is discussed in greater detail in the next section).

Third, there has also been an increase in the use of temporary contracts, although it has been much less marked. Temporary work has been restricted in certain EU countries – Greece, Italy and Spain, for example – by forbidding the use of agency work contracts. However, as illustrated in Table 4.4, the greatest recourse to temporary contracts now occurs precisely in the southern group of countries, especially Portugal and Spain. In Spain, in particular, temporary contracts have been used by employers increasingly to evade the rigid restrictions on dismissals which apply to full-time employees. This also explains the growing use of such contracts in Greece. And while there tend to be more women working on temporary contracts than men – as in the case of part-time work – it is the younger group of workers which is massively overrepresented in this category. Once again, the particular correlation between female employment and the more insecure forms of work is worth noting. A significant and growing number of women are in temporary jobs (see Table 4.4) and in 1991 some 36 per cent of women in the EU employed on fixed-term contracts also worked part time, compared with 14 per cent of men. In the UK, the figure was more than 75 per cent, in The Netherlands 60 per cent and in Ireland, Luxembourg and Italy more than 50 per cent (ibid.).

As discussed in the third section, the increase in the size of the so-called 'atypical' group of workers on non-standard contracts has led to EU proposals

TABLE 4.3 Size and composition of part-time employment, 1979–90 (percentages)

| | Part-time employment as a proportion of | | | | | | | | | Women's share in part-time employment | | |
| | Total employment | | | Male employment | | | Female employment | | | | | |
	1979	1983	1990	1979	1983	1990	1979	1983	1990	1979	1983	1990
Belgium	6.0	17.5	21.3	1.0	2.0	1.7[a]	16.5	19.7	25.0	88.9	84.0	89.6[a]
Denmark	22.7	23.8	23.7[b]	5.2	6.6	9.0[b]	46.3	44.7	41.5[b]	86.9	84.7	79.4[b]
France[c]	8.2	9.7	12.0	2.4	2.6	3.5	16.9	20.0	23.8	82.2	84.4	83.1
Germany	11.4	12.6	13.2[b]	1.5	1.7	2.1	27.6	30.0	30.6[b]	91.6	91.9	90.5[b]
Netherlands[d]	16.6	21.4	33.2	5.5	7.2	15.8	44.0	50.1	61.7	76.4	77.3	70.4
United Kingdom	16.4	19.4	21.8[a]	1.9	3.3	5.0[a]	39.0	42.4	43.8[a]	92.8	89.8	87.0[a]
Ireland	5.1	6.6	8.1[b]	2.1	2.7	3.8[b]	13.1	15.5	17.1[b]	71.2	71.6	68.2[b]
Greece	—	6.5	5.5[b]	—	3.7	2.9[b]	—	12.1	10.3[b]	—	61.2	65.7[b]
Italy	5.3	4.6	5.7[a]	3.0	2.4	3.1[a]	10.6	9.4	10.9[a]	61.4	64.8	64.7[a]
Portugal	7.8	—	5.9[a]	2.5	—	3.1[a]	16.5	—	10.0[a]	80.4	—	69.8[a]
Spain	—	—	4.8[a]	—	—	1.6[a]	—	—	11.9[a]	—	—	77.2[a]

NOTES

[a] 1989.

[b] 1988.

[c] 1990 data for male employment include conscripts, contrary to the situation for earlier years.

[d] Break in data in 1985.

SOURCE   OECD, *Employment Outlook*, July (1991), table 2.9.

TABLE 4.4   Temporary employment in the EC by age and sex, 1983–91
(percentages)

	Temporary jobs as a proportion of total wage and salary employment[a]			Employees with temporary contracts by age and sex (distribution) 1991				
	1983	1987	1991	Men	Women	Under 25	25–54	55–64
Belgium	5.4	5.6	5.1	35.9	64.1	35.8	62.6	1.6
Denmark	12.3[b]	11.2	11.9	47.4	52.1	56.6	39.7	3.8
France	3.3	7.1	10.2	47.4	52.6	44.5	53.4	2.1
Netherlands	5.7	9.2	7.6	46.9	53.1	45.5	53.0	1.5
Germany	10.0	11.6	9.5	54.9	45.1	58.3	39.0	2.7
United Kingdom	5.5	6.3	5.3	37.5	62.5	39.1	52.1	8.8
Ireland	6.2	8.6	8.2	44.8	55.2	39.2	56.5	4.2
Greece	16.3	16.6	14.7	65.3	34.7	25.8	66.7	7.5
Italy	6.6	5.4	5.4	62.4	37.6	33.8	59.2	7.0
Portugal	—	17.0	16.5	57.2	42.8	49.2	47.7	3.1
Spain	—	15.6	32.2	66.2	33.8	24.1	66.9	8.9
EEC	—	9.5	11.5	51.4	48.5	41.0	54.3	4.5

NOTES
[a] Wage and salary workers only, persons with a non-declared status excluded.
[b] 1985.

SOURCE   OECD, *Employment Outlook*, July (1991), table 2.11 and July 1993, table 1.13; and Eurostat, *A Social Portrait of Europe*, 1991, tables 5.13 and 5.14.

for a harmonisation of working conditions and rights for part-time and temporary workers – currently, conditions and rights differ substantially across the member states. Suffice it to say at this point that fixed-term and part-time contracts are less secure and those working on them are less well protected in some countries than in others. At present there is legislation covering the use of temporary contracts in all EU countries except Denmark, Ireland and the United Kingdom. As far as part-time contracts are concerned, in most member states part-time workers receive equal treatment to full-time workers in terms of basic conditions, minimum notice periods and redundancy payments. However, in Ireland part-timers must work a certain number of hours to qualify for annual leave and in Britain there is a minimum ceiling on working hours for cover by dismissals legislation as well as an earnings threshold for inclusion under national insurance cover. In The Netherlands, the statutory minimum wage only applies if the part-timer works more than a third of the standard working week (Commission, 1989).

The changing character of unemployment

Following an improvement in the state of the EU labour market in the late 1980s, the early 1990s saw a return to much higher levels of unemployment in many EU countries as economic growth slowed. By 1992, seven EU countries experienced higher rates of unemployment than their average for the 1980s (see Table 4.5). By mid–1993, unemployment in all of them was higher than a year earlier, while in five – Denmark, France, Ireland, Italy and the United Kingdom – the rate of unemployment had climbed to a similar or higher level to that of 1985, a year in which EU unemployment as a whole was at its most recent peak (Commission, 1993, p. 41). Nevertheless, three groups of countries can be distinguished, whose employment performance has been more or less consistent in recent years: the first, and most successful group, is composed of Germany, Denmark, The Netherlands and Belgium – where unemployment in 1992 was less than 10 per cent; the second – middle-ranking group – consists

TABLE 4.5   Unemployment and long-term unemployment (percentages)

	Unemployment rate[a]				Incidence of long-term unemployment[b]			
	Average 1974–79	1979	Average 1980–89	1992	Average 1975–80	1980	Average 1980–89[c]	1991
Belgium	6.3	8.2	10.8	8.2	—	61.5[d]	70.9	61.6
France	4.5	5.9	9.0	10.0	27.1	32.6	43.6	37.2
Germany	3.2	3.2	5.9	4.5	—	28.7[d]	45.0	45.5
Netherlands	4.9	5.4	9.7	6.7	—	35.9[d]	51.0	43.0
Denmark	5.8	5.8	8.9	9.5	—	36.2	31.6	31.2
United Kingdom	5.0	5.0	10.0	10.8	—	29.5[d]	44.4	28.1
Ireland	8.4	7.3	15.2	17.8	—	38.2	62.7	60.3
Greece[e]	—	—	2.9	7.7	—	—	43.0	47.0
Italy	6.6	7.6	9.5	10.3	—	51.2[d]	64.6	67.1
Portugal	—	—	7.3	4.8	—	—	53.7	38.3
Spain	5.2	8.4	17.5	18.0	28.4	32.8	55.4	51.1
EEC	4.8	5.7	9.2	9.5	—	32.7	52.8	46.4

NOTES

[a] Standardised rates, except for Denmark and Greece where registration data are used.

[b] Unemployed for twelve months and over.

[c] Or adjacent years.

[d] 1979.

[e] Greek figures are a poor indicator of actual rates: the actual rate may be two to three times higher.

SOURCE   OECD, *Employment Outlook*, July (1991), table 2.7; OECD, *Employment Outlook*, July (1992), table 2.10; Eurostat, *A Social Portrait of Europe* (1991), table 4.21; Eurostat, *Eurostatistics*, 7 (1993).

of France, Italy and the United Kingdom, where unemployment in 1992 was over 10 per cent; and the third group comprised of Spain and Ireland, where unemployment in 1992 was substantially higher, at around the 18 per cent level. Greece and Portugal are special cases which benefit from continuing net migration and whose official unemployment rates conceal considerable rural unemployment.

Long-term unemployment has been particularly high in the EU and has proven resistant to considerable policy efforts: between 1985 and 1990, 9 million new jobs were created in the EU but less than one third went to the registered unemployed and even less – only around 1 million – to the long-term unemployed. Long-term unemployment is especially a problem in the less developed regions of the EU where it is concentrated in much the same areas as youth unemployment (see Table 4.5). Once again, women occupy a special place in the unemployment statistics. Overall, female unemployment tended to rise relative to that of men in the less developed parts of the EU and to fall in the more developed parts between 1985 and 1993 (Commission, 1993, p. 43). But unemployment rates for women are generally higher, as is average long-term unemployment. A higher proportion of women also figure among the high youth unemployment statistics).

Apart from Germany, unemployment among young people under 25 is higher than for older people, especially in the less developed parts of the EU (Table 4.6). Regionally, youth unemployment is concentrated in those less developed areas where agriculture is still important and high rates of youth unemployment tend to coincide with high general unemployment rates. The southern member states have experienced the most serious problems in this area, reflecting the decline of agricultural employment and serious deficiencies in education and training systems. In Greece, Italy and Spain around a quarter of all males under 25 are long-term unemployed, as are more than a third of women in the same age group. The members of this age group are destined to remain marginalised from the labour market for long periods of time. They are the victims of a combination of factors: a mismatch between the supply and demand for skills, poor levels of education and vocational training, and recruitment and dismissals regulations which favour full-time employed workers at the expense of labour market 'outsiders' (see the next section).

During the 1980s there was actually some improvement in this area of the labour market. Until 1990, the rate of youth unemployment (both male and female) fell in relation to other age groups. Four countries – Spain, Portugal, the Netherlands and Germany – were especially successful in reducing youth unemployment due to a combination of special measures and favourable demographic trends. Measures taken in the 1980s included an increased recourse to fixed-term contracts (especially in Spain and Portugal), a major new effort to improve skills (an increase in training provision was assisted by greater financial support from the European Social Fund) and encouraging young people to stay in education. However, some of these policies have had the

TABLE 4.6 **Youth unemployment and young adult non-employment**

| | Youth unemployment (%) (under 25) | | Young adult non-employment (20–24)[a] | |
| | 1992 | | 1989 | |
	Male	Female	Male	Female
Belgium	14.8	20.6	11.1	24.0
France	19.1	24.7	13.6	25.8
Germany	4.1	3.8	8.1	16.8
Netherlands	10.9	10.3	9.8	17.9
Denmark	10.4	12.4	12.8	17.7
United Kingdom	19.5	14.1	12.0	25.3
Ireland	29.4	25.8	21.7	23.4
Greece	17.1	33.5	16.9	42.7
Italy	24.0	33.2	21.0	40.8
Portugal	8.0	13.0	9.3	24.5
Spain	27.9	38.5	21.4	40.0
EEC	17.4	19.7	14.3	27.1

NOTE
[a] These are net non-employment figures, i.e. the inactive less those in education plus the unemployed divided by the working age population.

SOURCE   OECD, *Employment Outlook*, July (1991), table 2.7; OECD, *Employment Outlook*, July (1992), table 2.10; Eurostat, *Eurostatistics*, 7 (1993).

effect of removing young people from the unemployment figures altogether, thereby reducing the official size of the workforce aged between 15 and 24 by 9 per cent between 1985 and 1991. In Belgium it fell by 23 per cent, in France by 20 per cent and in Germany by 16 per cent. Only the four southern countries plus The Netherlands saw an increase in youth employment during this period (Commission, 1993). For this reason, non-employment figures give a better indication of the plight of this age group (see Table 4.6).

There is a clear coincidence between high levels of youth unemployment and high levels of long-term unemployment in parts of the EU. The persistence of these structural forms of unemployment – regardless of policy measures to attenuate them – are closely related to the way in which the workforce is educated and trained and the way in which labour markets are organised. It is to these matters that attention is now turned.

TABLE 4.7   Modes of labour market management in the EU

	State intervention	Labour organisation	Workers participation	Education and training	Labour market flexibility
Northern	Traditionally limited; bargaining important in setting rules; high level of spending on active labour market policy.	Low level of hierarchy in firms; union membership density high, little change in the 1980s.	Important influence over decisions which affect organisation of work and training.	High level of participation in vocational, professional, and continuing training.	High level of skills allows organisational flexibility; restricted external flexibility.
Mediterranean	Strong state role through legal system; bargaining also important; low level of active labour market spending.	High level of hierarchy in firms; union density lower, significant decline in the 1980s.	Traditionally weak; of greater importance since 1980s, with shift towards Northern model in France and expansion of quality circles.	Lower level of participation in higher levels of education and training; poorer skills provision.	Lower skills level restricts organisational flexibility; restricted eternal flexibility.
Anglo-Saxon	State role traditionally weak; little legal regulation until the 1980s in the UK; decline in UK bargaining but not in Ireland; low active labour market spending in UK, higher in Ireland.	High level of hierarchy; union density traditionally high, but significant decline in the 1980s.	No formal mode of participation; traditional defence of craft organisation/demarcation significantly weakened since the early 1980s.	Low levels of participation in higher levels of education and training; poor levels of skills provision.	Collapse of apprenticeship system adds to deficiency in skills, reducing organisational flexibility and exacerbating employment problems; few restrictions on external flexibility in the UK.

SOURCE   Adapted from Hellier and Redor (1991), pp. 114–24.

LABOUR MARKET POLICY AND INDUSTRIAL RELATIONS

There is a good reason for discussing labour market policy and industrial relations together, for in combination they provide the principal elements of national systems of labour market management. Although national systems of labour market management differ enormously across the EU, it is possible to distinguish three broad types: the so-called 'Northern' mode of Germany, Denmark, The Netherlands and Belgium; the 'Mediterranean' mode of France, Portugal, Spain, Italy and Greece; and the 'Anglo-Saxon' mode which includes the United Kingdom and, with some important qualifications, the Irish Republic. Table 4.7 illustrates the principal differences between these modes.

There are obviously major differences within each of these three groups. Within the Northern group, for example, the system of training and skills provision is more advanced in Germany than among its other members; within the Mediterranean group, levels of education and training in France are lower and less adapted to the needs of employers than, for example, in the Northern group but higher than in the countries of the EU's southern periphery; and within the Anglo-Saxon group, Britain has proceeded further in the direction of a deregulated labour market than Ireland: in the latter, relations between government and trade unions remain far more positive and productive than in the UK where the role of organised labour has been substantially diminished. Nevertheless, this categorisation does allow some key systematic contrasts to be identified which have important implications for both employment and the capacity of countries for industrial adjustment.

The industrial relations context

Beginning with the role of the state, the Northern group tends to have a low level of *state* regulation of the labour market (although government intervention has been important in Belgium and the Netherlands), but regulation by law – including individual rights and entitlements – or by collective bargaining is extensive. Denmark stands out from the group as a country with a strong tradition of 'voluntarism' (where rights and entitlements depend on collective agreement rather than legislation). The countries of the Anglo-Saxon group are closer to Denmark in this respect, with an important but more limited range of individual rights set down by legislation and an emphasis on regulation via collective bargaining.

A second major difference lies in the nature of the trade union movement – its organisation and membership – the importance of workers' participation, and the extent to which relations between unions and employers have been characterised by conflict or cooperation. Union organisation in the Northern group tends to be more centralised than in either the Anglo-Saxon or Mediterranean groups and union membership – a key measure of union strength –

was largely sustained during the 1980s when elsewhere in Europe it declined. The only exception was The Netherlands, where membership fell sharply. As shown in Table 4.8, while union density (membership as a proportion of the workforce) fell in most EU member states except for Belgium and Italy, the decline was precipitous in France, Portugal, Spain and the United Kingdom.

However, it must be stressed that membership figures require cautious interpretation, for they are just one indicator of trade union strength, and an imperfect one at that. In France, for example, low membership has not traditionally deprived unions of influence, for French unions also derive their strength and legitimacy from workers support in *prud'homme* (labour 'court') elections and from the militancy of their rank and file. Nor does low membership necessarily reflect a lack of involvement in collective bargaining, for, to take the case of France again, some 80 per cent of the workforce is covered by collective agreements. However, the unions in France have clearly lost ground during the last decade, and, as in other countries, the decline in union membership can be seen as both cause and consequence of this loss of influence.

As far as the balance between conflict and cooperation is concerned, strike figures show that the countries of the Northern group – and especially Germany, Belgium and the Netherlands – have experienced a lower level of industrial conflict than the Anglo-Saxon and southern countries, a distinction which continues regardless of an overall decline in militancy since the early 1980s. It is less easy to generalise about forms of workers' representation and collective bargaining, but a number of observations can be made. First, in the countries of the Northern group – especially Germany, Denmark and Belgium – not only have unions been able to resist the general tendency for membership to decline over the 1980s, but they have also retained a key role in the national policy arena as well as in the firm, even if, as in other EU countries, there has been a shift away from centralised to decentralised forms of collective bargaining.

This decentralisation of collective bargaining has resulted from a concern by employers in all EU countries to shift the locus of bargaining on wages and conditions of work much closer to the workplace in line with their quest for greater flexibility on pay and workplace issues. In general, one can say that the *solidity* of collective bargaining – the recognition of unions as actors, the bargaining power of unions, and the scope and depth of collective bargaining cover – has been weakened most in those countries where it has never been especially strong (Baglioni, 1990, p. 22). An extensive union and bargaining presence remains important in the four Northern countries. But while France has seen an affirmation of the importance of collective bargaining since the 1980s because of Socialist government legislation, in Spain and Portugal it remains weak. The two Anglo-Saxon countries have followed different paths: while the United Kingdom has seen both the presence of unions and bargaining decline dramatically, Ireland has moved in the opposite direction, seeking corporatist (i.e. bargained) solutions to its economic problems.

TABLE 4.8 Union membership and union density in the EC, 1970–89

	Union membership (thousands)[a]			Change in membership (%)		Union density (%)			Change in density (%)	
	1970	1980	1989	1970–79	1980–89	1970	1980	1988	1970–80	1980–88
Belgium	1 606.0	2 310.0	2 291.4[b]	43.8	-0.8	54.9	75.7	77.5	37.9	2.4
Denmark	1 143.4	1 795.8	2 033.6[b]	57.1	13.2	62.2	91.4	86.0	46.9	-5.9
France[c]	3 549.0	3 374.0	1 970.0	-4.9	-41.6	22.3	19.0	12.0	-14.8	-36.8
Germany	8 251.2	9 645.5	9 637.0	16.9	0.0	37.9	42.9	40.1	13.2	-6.5
United Kingdom	11 178.0	12 947.0	9 214.2	15.8	-20.9	49.7	56.3	46.1	13.3	-18.1
Greece	—	556.6[d]	650.0[e]	—	—	35.8[d]	36.7[e]	25.0	—	-8.2
Ireland	422.9	544.5	474.0[f]	28.7	-12.9	59.0	63.4	58.4[f]	7.5	3.6
Italy	5 224.5	8 772.0	9 568.2	67.9	9.1	40.8	60.5	62.7	48.3	-4.8
Luxembourg	52.4	72.0[g]	75.0	37.5	4.2	46.8	52.2[g]	49.7[h]	11.5	-24.3
Netherlands	1 585.4	1 740.8	1 635.9	9.8	-6.0	40.5	39.9	30.2	-1.5	-12.2
Portugal	730.9[i]	1 669.7[k]	1 463.0[k]	128.4	-12.4	59.0[i]	58.8[g]	30.0	0.3	-27.3
Spain	—	1 703.0[g]	1 163.0[d]	—	-31.7	30.4[l]	22.0[g]	16.0[e]	—	—

NOTES
a Recorded membership.
b March 1990.
c Employed membership.
d 1977.
e 1985.
f 1987.
g 1981
h 1989.
i 1969.
j Average 1979–84.
k Average 1985–6.
l Average 1974–9.

SOURCE OECD, *Employment Outlook*, July (1991), table 4.1.

At the level of the firm, the distinctions between the groups in terms of workers' participation are even less clear. In eight of the EU member states – Belgium, France, Luxembourg, Greece, Germany, The Netherlands, Portugal and Spain – there are mandatory systems of participation which are either composed of workers only (as in the first three countries) or workers and management together (in the rest). Legislation also provides for industrial group level councils in France, Germany, Luxembourg and The Netherlands. The number of workers required in a firm for a works council to be created varies from country to country, as do the entitlements of the council. However, Germany, Denmark and Spain differ from the rest in that their works councils have negotiating rights, while elsewhere their role is largely consultative.

Actual participation by workers in company decision-making is rare, although Denmark, Germany and France all have statutory provision for worker (and in Germany union) representation on management (or, in Germany, supervisory) boards in companies over a certain size (50 employees in Denmark, 50 employees in France, and 500, 1000 or 2000 in Germany, depending on different models of codetermination). Despite the diversity of these arrangements, Germany and Denmark stand out, both for the degree of actual participation in decision-making (in France workers' representatives have a consultative role only) and the range of issues they can influence. In Germany, works councils can conclude agreements on issues not covered by collective agreement (and since 1987 can also interpret and negotiate sectoral agreements on working hours), while in Denmark firms with thirty-five or more employees have been required to create Cooperation Committees under the national Technology/Cooperation Agreement of 1986, to improve information on the introduction of new technology. In both countries, cooperation within the firm mirrors that which generally prevails between unions and employers in the wider economy.

The industrial relations context is therefore important for understanding the nature of labour market management. With the possible exception of the Netherlands – where unions have been weakened and bargaining decentralised – the collective and strongly institutionalised nature of industrial relations in the countries of the Northern group provides a conducive environment for the firm, one in which an emphasis on consensus and joint responsibility outside the enterprise corresponds to a similar ordering of priorities within it. The next section looks in greater detail at the relationship between the firm and the industrial relations and labour policy context.

Labour market management and 'flexibility'

At this point the concept of 'flexibility' becomes important. Since the early 1980s there has been a widespread debate on the appropriate balance between measures to protect workers who already have jobs and measures to promote new employment. In all EU countries, employers have called for fewer constraints on their freedom to manage, in particular on their ability to hire and fire without restriction and their use of diverse types of contract. Much of the debate about employment protection and creation is conducted in terms of labour market flexibility.

Labour market flexibility

Broadly speaking, labour market flexibility can take two general (ideal type) forms: 'competitive' flexibility (where firms operate in a largely unregulated labour market) and 'constructive' flexibility (where firms operate in a labour market heavily regulated by rules and contracts). The form taken by flexibility in a 'competitive' labour market derives from the ease with which firms can hire, fire and remunerate their employees. 'Constructive' flexibility, on the other hand, derives from the establishment of a degree of trust between employers and their employees (or their representatives) and from a collective investment (and institutional involvement) in the provision of public goods such as vocational training. The concept of flexibility can be further broken down into *external flexibility* (the ability to recruit, dismiss and rotate manpower with few impediments), *internal qualitative flexibility* (the ability to deploy workers within the firm – which depends both on levels of multi-skilling and the good will and cooperation of the workers themselves), *internal quantitative flexibility* (the ability to vary the hours and duration of workers through the use of a combination of part-time, fixed-term and full-time, permanent contracts) and *pay flexibility* (the ability to alter pay rates in line with changes in demand, the fortunes of the firm or the performance of the worker).

How do each of the three groups of countries compare in terms of flexibility? The first step is to establish how employers perceive their environment in terms of freedom and constraint. Table 4.9 compares these perceptions across four areas of internal and external *quantitative* flexibility.

TABLE 4.9   Employers perceptions of flexibility

Degree of flexibility	Hiring and firing	Termination of contracts	Redundancy payments	Temporary contracts
High	UK	UK	Netherlands	UK
	Netherlands	Denmark	France	Spain
	Germany	Ireland	UK	Portugal
	Luxembourg	Belgium	Ireland	Ireland
	Ireland	Spain	Germany	Denmark
	Greece	Portugal	Luxembourg	Luxembourg
	Belgium	Netherlands	Greece	Germany
	France	Italy	Belgium	France
	Italy	Germany	Italy	Netherlands
		France		Italy
Low				Belgium

SOURCE   Adapted from Emerson (1988), pp. 783–90.

According to these perceptions, Italy is the EU's most heavily regulated labour market and the United Kingdom its least, with the remainder falling somewhere in between. This roughly accords with the importance of labour market legislation and collective agreements in these countries. Thus, as far as unfair dismissals are concerned, while all member states require some form of monetary compensation and a written statement of reasons, only Denmark, Portugal, Spain, Italy and Germany require consultation with worker representatives – often producing onerous delays – and only The Netherlands requires prior administrative (official) authorisation. Italy is the only country with measures to regulate *recruitment* as well: the public employment administration has attempted to make firms observe priority lists, in which ranking has been determined by social criteria such as the duration of unemployment or family commitments, although the application of this system has been relaxed in recent years. There is more uniformity with regard to collective redundancies since this is one area where the EU has managed to require certain common consultation procedures (via Directive 75/129 of 17 February 1975), and all member states (apart from Germany which has its own company 'social plan' system) provide statutory redundancy payments. As for notice and severance payments, costs are much higher in Belgium, Denmark, Germany, Greece and Italy due to high levels of protection for white collar employees, while temporary employment is least restricted in Denmark, the United Kingdom and Ireland. The remainder restrict the use of such contracts by legislation, except for Belgium and The Netherlands where rules are set by collective bargaining. Italy goes furthest by prohibiting private sector temporary work agencies (Emerson, 1988a; Commission 1993).

Although these degrees of flexibility by country do not fit neatly into the categories of labour market management, employers in the 'Northern' countries – and, even more so in the 'Mediterranean' countries – generally experience less flexibility in hiring and firing and the use of 'atypical' labour than their 'Anglo Saxon' counterparts. If we combine the results of this analysis with the degree of *qualitative* flexibility in these countries, we begin to have a more complete picture of the role of the firm and collective organisation in labour market management.

Education, training and skills

The most important contribution to *qualitative* flexibility is made by the system of vocational education and training and the degree of consensus over matters which affect the functioning of the labour market both within and beyond the firm. As far as education and training are concerned, there is a clear link between general education and post-school training: less formal schooling seems to lead to more limited training opportunities, while an absence of widespread vocational training opportunities exacerbates disparities in earnings and income, producing greater inequalities among workers and increasing the likelihood of unemployment among disadvantaged groups (OECD, 1991,

p. 152). Table 4.10 illustrates differences between the EU member states in terms of general and vocationally oriented upper secondary level education. The principal distinction to emerge is the much higher rate of participation in general and, especially, vocational, education in the countries of the 'Northern' group compared with both the 'Anglo-Saxon' and 'Mediterranean' groups. Continuing (in work) training also tends to be much more developed in the 'Northern' group, especially in Germany and Denmark.

TABLE 4.10   Participation rates in education: national data (percentage of age group in relevant sector)

	Sec I- education	Sec II- general	Sec II- training	Total Sec I & Sec II	Tertiary education (to 19)
Belgium	—	—	—	77.4	11.4
Denmark	34.9	18.1	34.1	87.1	1.3
FRG	15.9	22.2	55.9	94.0	0.8
France	16.5	23.1	33.9	73.5	5.0
Greece	1.3	33.7	13.2	48.2	10.1
Ireland	15.1	31.7	6.7	53.5	8.4
Italy	1.5	19.4	36.8	57.7	—
Netherlands	—35.2—		65.8	92.0	5.0
Portugal	17.0	25.3	3.4	45.7	1.2
Spain	2.1	35.6	22.7	60.4	6.1
United Kingdom	—30.0—		25.7	55.7	5.4

SOURCE   R. Derenbach (1990), table 4.2.

The most prosperous countries also dedicate the most money to education. While Belgium, France, Denmark and the Netherlands all devote close to 6 per cent of the GDP to education, Greece, Spain and Portugal devote less than 4 per cent (Hellier and Redor, 1991, pp. 90–100). This is reflected in rates of participation in higher education: while in Germany, Denmark, Belgium and The Netherlands more than 20 per cent of those aged over 25 in the workforce in 1991 had completed a university degree or equivalent, in Portugal, Italy and Spain it was less than 15 per cent. The differences in post-compulsory education are greater still. In Germany – where professional training is carried out jointly by the school and the firm via a highly developed apprenticeship system, following an early separation of students into general, technical and pro- fessional streams – more than 80 per cent (and in Denmark more than 70 per cent) of the labour force aged 25 and over had completed a post-compulsory education or vocational training course. This compared with 65 per cent in the Netherlands, 40 per cent in the United Kingdom, less than 30 per cent in Spain and Luxembourg, and around 15 per cent in Portugal. In engineering, the number of workers with post-compulsory education and vocational training in 1991 ranged from more than 80 per cent in Germany and 70 per cent in

Denmark to less than 30 per cent in Spain, less than 25 per cent in Italy, and around 10 per cent in Portugal. Except for Greece – where insufficient jobs are being created for skilled and professional workers – employment prospects improve across the EU the longer the duration of education or training (Commission, 1993).

The Northern group, and especially Germany, is distinctive for the creation of a virtuous circle linking high participation rates in education and a high level of qualifications with high productivity, high pay, less income inequality than in other member states and relatively low rates of unemployment and non-employment. The Danish and Dutch systems are similar to that of Germany but less effective. Continuing (in work) training is also important in this group, especially in Germany and Denmark (Auer, 1992).

Other member states have rather different systems linking education with vocational training and the firm. France and Italy have relatively similar training systems, with three streams after the first stage of secondary schooling: general, technical and professional. Among 16–18 year olds, the proportion in full-time education is around 60 per cent, but apprenticeships are much less important than in the German model and the number without any training – at just under a third – is relatively high. In the United Kingdom, the apprenticeship system has collapsed in recent years (with the disappearance of large swathes of manufacturing industry) and the market-oriented system created by the government (based on privately run Training Enterprise Councils) has failed to compensate for the low level of investment in vocational training in both schools and firms and to counter the erosion of the country's skills base (Hellier and Redor, 1991, pp. 95–101; Lindley, 1991). Recent measures concentrate overwhelmingly on the young unemployed. In the southern member states vocational training is underdeveloped: in Spain, Portugal and Greece it has been marginalised by an emphasis on academic secondary education, and where it exists it is underfunded and poorly administered (Rhodes, 1992b).

The role of state policy to train and reintegrate the unemployed into the workforce is also important, and here the differences tend to mirror those already discussed above. Table 4.11 illustrates the disparities within the EU by comparing the number of participants in training programmes with the number of unemployed. Compared with the best performing member states (Denmark, France, Germany and The Netherlands), not only do Spain, Italy, Portugal and Greece fare badly, but the inadequacies of Britain's investment in training are also revealed. Figures on the percentages of GDP spent on active labour market policy to retrain and redeploy workers on the labour market tell a similar story: while the countries of the 'Northern' group spend between 1.0 and 1.2 per cent of GDP on such measures, those in the 'Mediterranean' group spend between 0.6 and 0.8 per cent, while the UK spends 0.7 per cent (OECD, 1990).

The nature of employment administrations also appears to play a role in counteracting unemployment, according to research by the OECD. The pro-

TABLE 4.11   Participation in targeted programmes aiming at regular employment compared with the level of unemployment, 1988 (000')

	Participants starting per year (1)	Unemployed persons (2)	Ratio of (1) to (2) in per cent (3)
Belgium	71	424	17
Denmark	129	172	75
France	998	2 443	41
Germany	779	2 242	35
Netherlands	170	558	31
United Kingdom	505	2 341	22
Ireland	55	220	25
Greece	55	302	18
Italy	200[a]	2 885	5–10
Portugal	32	258	12
Spain	520	2 853	18
Total	3 514	14 689	24

NOTE
[a] Estimate.

SOURCE   OECD, *Labour Market Policies for the 1990s*, Paris: OECD (1990), table 17.

vision of employment services (information and counselling, etc.) clearly depends for its efficiency and effectiveness on the structure of employment office networks, the size of staff and other resources, and in particular on the proportion of staff actively engaged in directly employment-related services such as placement operations. EU member states differ considerably along these lines, with the most inadequate services provided in precisely those countries with the worst rates of unemployment. The frequency and timing of contact between staff and the unemployed appears to be of crucial importance, and this requires both a high level of investment in such schemes and a high level of organisation (OECD, 1991, pp. 213–20).

Other labour market policies

It also important to take into account the influence of other elements in a country's general policy environment on employment, and in this respect different forms of labour market flexibility clearly play a role. Those countries which experience the most severe problems of unemployment do not simply suffer from inadequate training and education systems: often there are other sources of labour market *in*flexibility as well. For example, Italy, Greece, Portugal and Spain – countries with either high national or regional rates of unemployment – all have labour market policies which exacerbate their problems. In Italy, restrictions on dismissals translate into a lack of employment opportunities, especially for young people: consequently, Italy has one of the highest proportion of first job seekers among its unemployed in the EU (Emerson, 1988a, pp. 782–3). This problem is compounded by restrictions on the use of fixed-term contracts. In Portugal and Greece, a high minimum wage relative to the average seems to dissuade employers from recruiting young workers, while in both Portugal and Spain, restrictions on, and the high costs of (in terms of redundancy payments), dismissing permanent workers has encouraged a massive recourse to fixed-term contracts. This has created a more flexible labour market but also a *dual* one, dividing the 'insiders' – who are permanently employed – from the 'outsiders' who have to make do with insecure jobs. In Greece, insiders are similarly protected, while restrictions on part-time and temporary employment also prevent firms from hiring new workers (Rhodes, 1992b).

Throughout the 1980s, the issue of flexibility has been at the heart of the debate on improving the performance of labour markets and, more generally, the economies of the EU member states. Initially triggered by the contrast between the poor job-creating capacity of the EU countries and the relative success of the United States in the early 1980s, it has been revived by the worsening employment figures produced by the recession of the early 1990s. But how has this debate translated into policies?

By and large, despite numerous policy innovations in many European countries, the basic character of labour market management in the three 'parts' of the EU remains unchanged. Labour market *re*regulation has occurred in seven of the twelve EU member states – the United Kingdom, France, Germany, Italy, Spain, Portugal and Ireland – but there is no clear, uniform pattern. Thus, while in some countries employment protection has been weakened, in others it has been strengthened or extended to workers who were previously uncovered. Official authorisation for redundancies, for example, has been eliminated in France, while Portugal now permits dismissals for 'economic' (restructuring) reasons. The UK has removed certain categories of the workforce (younger workers) from some forms of employment protection, principally concerning pay, while the qualifying period for unfair dismissal has been extended from 26 to 105 weeks of continual employment. In Germany, the 1985 Employment Promotion Act exempted firms with five or fewer workers from the Protection Against Dismissals Act but the vast majority of the workforce remains unaffected. Elsewhere, however, protective legislation on unfair dismissals has been extended to smaller firms (Italy), to part-time workers (France and Ireland), and, in Spain, sanctions on employers who fail to conform with protective rules have been increased, while the already high cost of unfair dismissals was increased in 1990 from forty-two to fifty-four months of pay. In France, regulation has moved in a 'Northern' direction by requiring firms with fifty or more employees to formulate 'social plans' (along German lines) when ten or more employees are being made redundant.

The most important common trend has been in the relaxation of regulations governing the use of temporary contracts. Temporary and 'atypical' forms of employment have never been restricted in the United Kingdom and other countries seem to be moving towards at least a less constraining form of regulation, if not deregulation, on UK lines. Among the northern countries with a high degree of regulations in this area, Germany has allowed the use of fixed-term employment contracts without special authorisation since the 1985 Employment Promotion Act, but the impact on the labour market has not been great and recourse to fixed-term contracts remains far more limited than elsewhere. The most significant changes have occurred in the southern group of countries. In 1986, the new right-wing government in France eliminated restrictions on the use of temporary employment and extended the duration of such contracts to two years. However, the change in government once again in 1988 led to a reimposition of the need to justify the use of fixed-term employment. But, as in Spain and Portugal – where restrictions on the use of fixed-term contracts were also relaxed during the 1980s – a significant increase in the proportion of employees recruited in this fashion has occurred, with more than 10 per cent of employees now employed on temporary contracts compared with only 3 per cent in 1983 (see Table 4.4 above). In Spain this proportion increased from 16 per cent in 1987 to 32 per cent in 1991, while in Portugal it grew from 13 per cent in 1986 to 16 per cent in 1991. In all three of these countries, fixed-term contracts account for the vast majority of new recruits.

Four general conclusions emerge from the above analysis:

- First, employers in the 'Northern' countries are more constrained by rules and regulations regarding external flexibility (set by collective bargaining or law) but are compensated in part by greater flexibility deriving from a high level of skills, a highly educated workforce, a lower level of hierarchy within the firm, and a consensual treatment of issues such as the introduction of new technology or the restructuring of production. An active labour market policy – one which is based on measures to reintegrate the unemployed into the workforce rather than merely provide 'passive', compensatory support (through benefits) – helps ensure low levels of structural (i.e. entrenched, long-term) unemployment.
- Second, employers in the 'Anglo-Saxon' group enjoy a high degree of external flexibility (there are far fewer constraints on recruitments and dismissals and the use of fixed-term or temporary contracts), but due to a deficit in skills and, especially in the United Kingdom, a tradition of adversarial industrial relations (excluding meaningful worker participation), their internal or organisational flexibility has been low, and their capacity for adjustment to new market conditions weak. Ireland has moved steadily away from this model by sustaining the role of trade unions in bargaining and by extending rather than reducing the protection of the workforce.
- Third, employers in the 'Mediterranean' countries have traditionally

suffered from rigidities in both respects: if, on the one hand, there have been strict limitations on their freedom to hire, fire and recruit on part-time or fixed-term contracts, on the other hand, a low level of skills provision and inadequate training systems, combined with an adversarial relationship between management and labour, have given them only a low degree of organisational flexibility, unless – as has frequently been the case in Italy, for example – employers have found ways of evading these constraints. More recently, the expanded use of fixed-term contracts in these countries has compensated for labour market inflexibility elsewhere in the system, but at the risk of creating a dual labour market, dividing the privileged full-time, permanent, older workers from a younger workforce restricted to insecure jobs.

- And fourth, in both the 'Anglo-Saxon' and 'Mediterranean' groups, inadequate training and a low level of spending on active labour market policies contribute to the persistence of long-term, structural unemployment and a mismatch between the demand for and supply of qualified labour.

The future direction to be taken by labour market policy is still uncertain. There is growing pressure, however, for a further shift towards greater employer freedom in recruitment and dismissals and in the use of 'atypical' (part-time, fixed-term) contracts. How far this will begin to undermine traditional forms of regulation in those countries where an emphasis has been placed on industrial relations consensus and *constructive* flexibility (the Northern group and, increasingly, Ireland) remains to be seen. What is certain is that the EU will play an important role in determining the outcome.

THE EUROPEAN UNION AND THE LABOUR MARKET

The hesitant beginnings

Although the idea of a European 'social dimension' – covering social and labour market issues – is not new, few major advances were made until the 1980s. Early theorists of European integration imagined that the construction of a new supranational locus of decision-making in Brussels would have a 'spillover effect' and lead European interest groups – including employers, unions and consumers – to follow suit. As market integration proceeded, the integration of systems of social security and labour market organisation was expected to follow. In fact, little progress in any of these areas occurred until the late 1980s. A European employers' organisation (UNICE) was created as early as 1958 and a European Trade Union Confederation (ETUC) in 1973, but only modest advances were made in EC labour legislation. Such legislation as there was included directives on equal pay and equal treatment for men and women, on rules for collective redundancies, on employees' rights in the case of transfer of undertakings or employer insolvency, plus several covering health and safety at work issues (Eberlie, 1990). Other initiatives – most notably the Vredeling proposal of 1980 on employees' rights to information and consultation in multinational companies (MNCs) and the Fifth Company Law Directive on board level employee participation – were defeated by a campaign conducted by European employers, multinational companies, and certain member states (Barnouin, 1986). The British veto constituted a major obstacle to progress during the first half of the 1980s.

More market-oriented initiatives encountered far less resistance from employers and member state governments. Thus, EC policies to increase the freedom of movement of labour, and the use of the Structural Funds (especially the European Social Fund) to assist training in less developed regions, were widely supported by unions, employers and governments alike. By the late 1960s, most legal discriminations against migrant workers had been removed by Regulation 16/2/66 and Directive 68/360/EEC and workers were allowed to apply for jobs in any member state, enjoy the same rights and entitlements as national workers, and settle there with their families. The EC also tried to encourage mobility by establishing the principle of mutual recognition of diplomas and qualifications from 1975. The European Structural Funds – the European Regional Development Fund (ERDF), the European Agricultural Guidance and Guarantee Fund (EAGGF) and especially the European Social Fund (ESF) – made an important contribution to the promotion of vocational training in the poorer member states. However, a lack of 'additionality' (ensuring that EC funds did not simply fund measures already in place) and limits on the extent to which the EC could influence the *quality* of national training systems reduced their impact (Cutler *et al.*, 1989; Steinle, 1988).

From 1986 to the present: the 'social dimension'

The early to mid-1980s saw growing support for a reform of existing forms of intervention (the promotion of mobility and the use of the Structural Funds) and – more controversially – for a strengthened system of EC labour market regulation. Thus, support came from the European unions (which were slowly overcoming their own internal differences of ideology and policy), the European Commission, and the European Parliament, as well as from the government of many member states. But support for a greater role for the EC in labour market regulation also met with strident opposition from others, including the British Conservative government and Europe's employers whose traditional opposition to European-level regulation was bolstered by their new-found credo of labour market flexibility. From this clash of interests and philosophies has emerged a complex debate on the desirability of a 'social dimension'.

The 'social dimension' debate

The most popular argument for harmonising labour market measures across the EU claims that disparities in social security and labour protection – the source, in part, of differences in labour costs – distorts competition and tempts companies to shift to lower cost regions. Companies from low cost countries can also, it is claimed, export their poorly protected workers and outbid higher cost competitors in the EU's liberalised market for public sector contracts. Variations on this, the so-called 'social dumping' argument, have been invoked by the Commission in support of its new social action programme measures (see p. 147). It has also been argued that only a flexible form of corporatism (i.e. joint decision-making on employment-related issues by employers, unions and governments) in the EU member states can encourage a consensus on major social priorities and ensure the convergence, rather than continued or greater *divergence*, of protective labour regulations and wages (Rhodes, 1992a, pp. 277ff).

Employers and the British government have replied that neither a uniform upward alignment of social protection nor corporatist policy-making is appropriate for the single market: only an unfettered European economy can be truly dynamic, and more regulation will lead to less employment creation rather than more. They are supported by mainstream economic orthodoxy: given the projected removal of exchange rate flexibility under EMU – and thus of the use of currency depreciation by certain member states to compensate for higher labour costs – *increasing* the costs of employers in the poorer EU countries may either drive them out of business altogether or into the shadows of the hidden economy. At the very least higher levels of workforce protection will, it is claimed, lead them to reduce the numbers they employ – especially at a time when the liberalisation of the European market for goods and services will expose them to greater competition. This argument suggests that an upward alignment of EU labour legislation and wages in the poorer member states should follow rather than precede their achievement of higher productivity (Kay and Posner, 1989).

The 'social dumping' argument may be flawed in at least one important respect, for it underestimates the dependence of capital productivity on the quality (in other words, the skill level) of labour. Thus, if companies are tempted to relocate in lower labour cost regions, they are likely only to shift the less skill-intensive parts of their operations. However, given the increasing dependency of manufacturing on high levels of skills, industry is most likely to relocate to where skills provision is greatest – implying a concentration of production in those regions which are best endowed with education and training, rather than a dispersion to low wage/low productivity areas. From this argument it follows that an excessive concentration on labour market harmonisation by the EU may be misguided: the major focus of EU policy should seemingly be in the area of vocational training and skills acquisition, for it is here that both the poorer and richer EU countries face their greatest challenge.

The Single European Act and the Social Charter

Notwithstanding the observations that have just been made, the arguments for a harmonisation of European labour legislation have prevailed in recent years. Following the Belgian Presidency's proposal for a floor of minimum social rights in 1987, support for new EC social legislation – based on a charter or constitution – gathered growing support. Ostensibly, the 1986 Single European Act (SEA) should have helped this project by amending the EEC Treaty in such a way as to make it easier for the Commission to act in the social arena. A new Article 118A of the EEC Treaty gave the Commission greater powers, specifically the power of proposition (after consulting the Economic and Social Committee and in cooperation with the Parliament), and a new Article 100A provided for measures essential for the completion of the SEM to be introduced by a so-called 'qualified majority', that is, a minimum of fifty-four votes out of a possible seventy-six in the Council of Ministers. But, as well as easing the way for the development of EC social policy, the SEA also introduced new restrictions. Paragraph 2 of Article 118A prevented directives from imposing legal, financial and administrative burdens on small- and medium-sized firms, and Article 100A specifically excluded measures relating to the free movement of persons and the rights and interests of employees. Only health and safety measures fell unambiguously under the new majority voting system, and it is in this area that the greatest progress has been made. More generally, by the second half of 1989 it was clear, in the face especially of British opposition, that an *exemplary* charter of social rights – rather than a set of binding obligations – was the most that could be achieved. Thus, backed by eleven of the EC twelve (the UK excepted), the *Community Charter of Fundamental Social Rights of Workers* (the Social Charter) emerged as a 'solemn declaration' – a document with no legal status as an instrument of EC policy-making (Rhodes, 1991).

However, some advances were made. Most of the opponents of the Social Charter and of the Commission's new initiatives in other areas were willing to accept and comply with the EC's health and safety legislation since – apart from their requirement to consult workers on related issues – such initiatives pose little threat to the balance of power within the workplace. Moreover, Britain – the Commission's principal antagonist on social policy – already had substantial health and safety legislation in place and was obviously keen for health and safety standards in other countries to be upgraded, lest they derive any competitive advantage from a lower level of regulation. In March 1989, a Framework Directive for the *Introduction of Measures to Encourage Improvements in the Safety and Health of Workers* was approved, followed by a series of daughter directives to cover specific risks: the first laid down minimum health and safety requirements for the workplace, the second prescribed minimum health and safety requirements for the use by workers of machines and equipment, while the third established minimum health and safety requirements for the use by workers of personal protective equipment. Two further directives on the use of visual display units and on the handling of heavy loads where there is a risk of back injury have followed (Eberlie, 1990).

Advances have also been made in other areas which neither challenge established industrial relations practice nor work against market principles. Thus, a Council resolution on the compatibility of vocational training qualifications issued in 1985 sought to increase worker mobility across the EC by encouraging mutual recognition. The member states were asked to investigate the revisions required to make other member states' qualifications comparable with their own. Mutually agreed descriptions of professional qualifications have been drawn up for hotels and catering, motor vehicle repair and construction, while work is progressing on agriculture, forestry and the electrical industry. Two other schemes – ERASMUS and COMETT – also aim to increase mobility, the first by encouraging inter-university exchanges and the second by promoting EU-level cooperation between businesses and universities. Eventually, schemes like ERASMUS and COMETT could help close the gap between the northern and southern member states in terms of educational opportunities and the provision of technical and professional qualifications. Similarly, important changes have been introduced in the use of the Structural Funds since the late 1980s. The main innovation has been an expansion of funding and the concentration of expenditure (60 per cent) on combating unemployment in the least developed regions of the most disadvantaged member states.

Controversial areas of EU intervention

By contrast with these market-orientated initiatives, innovations in areas which affect the balance of power between employers and employees, impose higher costs on employers or, more generally, seek to modify the operation of the labour market with new rules, have all faced opposition. The Commission's Social Action Programme – which contains proposals for implementing the Social Charter – already anticipated the problems which would follow. Thus, binding legal instruments (directives and regulations) were restricted to living and working conditions, health and safety issues, and the protection of adolescents and children. As for the rest – including minimum pay, collective bargaining, and the consultation and participation of workers – unspecified instruments or 'opinions' were proposed.

However, as was clear from the draft legislation produced between 1990 and 1992, the Commission hoped to play a more pro-active role and go further in practice than its Action Programme suggested. It sought to do this by pushing its legal competence to the limit. By playing the so-called 'treaty base game' – attempting, that is, to link as much of its new legislation as possible to treaty articles which allowed for majority voting – it sought to evade the predictable British veto and provoked much controversy in the process. Some of the Commission's new social legislation has been linked directly to Article 118A (allowing qualified majority voting on health and safety legislation) and has consequently enjoyed a fairly free passage through the Council of Ministers. This is the case, for example, for the *Third Draft Directive on Atypical Work* which aims to improve the health and safety protection of temporary workers. It was less clearly so, however, for the *Draft Working Time Directive* (the so-called 48-hour-week law) which lay down minimum requirements on daily and weekly rest periods and on night and shift work. This was because the British Conservative government challenged its legal basis, arguing that it placed financial and other burdens on employers – which paragraph 2 of Article 118A seeks explicitly to prevent. The *Draft Directive on Pregnant Women in the Work Place* also provoked the opposition of the British, for, in seeking to combine contractual rights (maternity leave of fourteen weeks linked to full pay) with health and safety measures (exposure to toxins, etc.), it also contravened the strict letter of the Article. The passage of both the above directives required concessions to the British government which either modified their content or delayed their implementation in the United Kingdom.

The Commission has similarly tried to play the 'treaty base game' in respect of the *Second Draft Directive on Atypical Work*. This covers workers entitlements which involve variable costs to employers (including social protection, holidays and dismissals procedures for part-time and temporary workers), and the Commission argues that harmonisation is needed to prevent a distortion of competition. Thus, it maintains, the appropriate Article is 100A. However, this article also specifically excludes workers' rights, suggesting that as far as this Directive is concerned, the Commission has lost the game. It has tried a similar ruse with regard to the European Company Act (discussed on p. 152) by invoking Article 54 (3) (g) of the EEC Treaty, (now EC Treaty – see Chapter 1) as amended by the SEA. This provides for qualified majority voting to coordinate safeguards required by member states or companies or firms, and the Commission wants to use it for the Company Act's employment provisions. Its company law provisions will be linked to Article 100A. But the British Conservative government has opposed the use of both legal bases. Finally, there are three draft directives whose passage can only be carried under Article 100 of the EC Treaty, and therefore demand unanimous support: the *Directive on a European Works Council* discussed on p. 152, the *Proof of Employment Directive* (giving all workers the right to a written contract) and the *First Atypical Work Directive* which seeks to extend full-time employment conditions to part-time and temporary employees – a most important initiative designed to preserve social cohesion by preventing the emergence of a large number of exploited, 'second-class' workers in the EU.

Maastricht and the Social Agreement

With the entry into force (in November 1993) of the Treaty on European Union (TEU), some of the obstacles to the development of the EU's 'social dimension' were removed. In order to prevent outright failure in the negotiations at Maastricht in December 1991, British opposition to the proposed 'Social Chapter' of the TEU was circumvented by a separate Social Agreement for the other eleven member states *outside* the new Treaty. Under the Agreement (which is preceded by a Protocol excluding the United Kingdom from its provisions) qualified majority voting is extended from health and safety legislation to include working conditions, the information and consultation of workers, equality between men and women with regard to labour market opportunities and treatment at work, and the integration of persons excluded from the labour market. British opposition to most of the sensitive directives mentioned above can now, therefore, be avoided by the other eleven member states.

However, as before Maastricht, directives should not impose 'administrative, financial and legal constraints' on small- and medium-sized firms (suggesting that, even without the British veto, introducing new legislation will be far from straightforward) and they will have no legal impact on Britain. Unanimity will still be required for action over social security and social protection, the protection of workers where their contract is terminated, the representation and collective defence of workers and employees, conditions of employment for immigrant workers, and financial contributions for employment promotion. It should be noted that pre-Maastricht Treaty provisions for social policy-making have been included in the new Treaty, which means that Britain is still subject to existing and future legislation which flow from it. This will ensure that manoeuvres over the new draft legislation discussed above will continue to be a feature of EU social policy-making, although, as mentioned, in certain areas a single member state veto can now be avoided under the new Agreement's arrangements.

The 'Social Chapter' may result in the creation of a 'European Social Community' in the eleven countries covered by the Agreement, and a lower level of employment protection and statutory rights in Britain. However, certain new laws made under the provisions of the Agreement will gradually affect practice in Britain anyway, as in the case of the *Directive on a European Works Council* (discussed on p. 152) which will require transnational companies – including British ones – to create new structures for workers' consultation in the eleven states. More generally, given the concern of the EU member states with the new rules and deadlines for inclusion in full Economic and Monetary Union, it is unlikely that the 'Social Agreement Eleven' will proceed with a radical reform of social policy and labour market protection in the foreseeable future: levels of inflation, interest rates and budget deficits will take priority as, increasingly, will policies to help create *new* employment, including in many member states measures to enhance labour market flexibility.

THE EUROPEAN UNION AND INDUSTRIAL RELATIONS

Relations between European employers and trade unions

Progress in EU-level industrial relations is likely to be just as *ad hoc* and piecemeal as in the area of labour market harmonisation. For in this area of policy, more so than in any other, the opposition of employers is a major stumbling block. Their position has been consistent: they are opposed both to supranational collective bargaining and to any enhancement of workers' participation rights *by legislation* in transnational companies. Thus, while discussions between UNICE and ETUC have been promoted by the Commission in the framework of the 'social dialogue' (the *Val Duchesse* discussions launched in 1985), employers have refused to be party to any statement which might be used by the Commission as the basis for legislation. European employers have refused and are still opposed to making UNICE an effective bargaining authority: by keeping UNICE institutionally weak they can avoid its cooption into the EU social policy-making process, and ensure that the 'social dialogue' remains consultative and, for the most part, inconsequential (Rhodes, 1992a, pp. 40–6; Streeck and Schimitter, 1991).

Trade unions, by contrast, are interested in making EU collective agreements an integral part of what they regard as an emerging European system of industrial relations: national union confederations are no longer opposed (as in the 1970s) to ETUC playing a major role in advancing the collective rights of European workers, and collective bargaining at the EU level is now deemed necessary for giving regulatory force to new social legislation. Potentially, ETUC could become a negotiating partner with delegated authority. But at present, like UNICE, ETUC does not hold a valid mandate for negotiating agreements and nor does it have the organisational strength that is necessary to become a major industrial relations actor, performing the role of its national level counterparts on the European stage. It should be said that the Commission has had some success in promoting social dialogue in particular sectors: working parties have been established in retailing and construction, for example, focusing on vocational training, workers' mobility, and labour market efficiency. But, as in the *Val Duchesse* discussions, these talks fall well short of union aspirations for European collective bargaining.

Substantial advances seem unlikely unless there is a transformation of the position of employers. During 1990 there were signs that some national employers' confederations – the Italian, Belgian and Dutch – were taking a much less hostile position, arguing that negotiation might have more effect on new EU labour market policy than outright opposition. Whether that will become a majority view in the employers' camp remains to be seen. The British Confederation of British Industry (CBI) is especially hostile to such initiatives and Europe's employers are happy for UNICE to remain a weak representative body: for as long as it is deprived of a real negotiating capacity, there is little danger of its cooption into the sort of corporatist EU policy framework that Europe's unions have been calling for.

However, an important step forward was taken by UNICE and ETUC prior to the Maastricht summit when they agreed to make a joint proposal for inclusion in the TEU. Under the proposal, the European employer and employee representatives would be consulted on the content of draft EU social and employment legislation and would reach agreement on it before passing it back to the Commission. The British predictably opposed this initiative, and it became one of its justifications for blocking the entire 'Social Chapter' at Maastricht, but the new procedure for consulting the European social partners may, none the less, now be used under Article Four of the Social Agreement, which was adopted by the other eleven member states. The greatest significance of the proposal may lie in UNICE's concession to negotiate, for this could be the breach in the employers' defences the unions have long been seeking. However, Europe's employer organisations are just as likely to use this process to block wherever possible those items of social legislation which they still oppose.

Workers' representation in multinational companies

Do developments in multinational companies (MNCs) hold out any more hope for a new type of European industrial relations? Europe's unions certainly hope so, and, having been divided in the past on the desirability of co-management or workers' participation in transnational companies, they now broadly support the Commission's latest initiatives in these areas. But legislating for MNCs remains as difficult today as it was in the 1970s when the harmonisation of European company law – including the workers' information rights – was initially broached. Since then, certain MNCs have introduced experimental forms of workers participation, through pan-European committees or works councils. French companies – under the influence of national legislation (the French Socialist government's Auroux law provisions for group-level representation) – have led the way, and BSN, Saint-Gobain, Thomson and Groupe Bull have all engaged in new consultation procedures with workers. Furthermore, although there is still opposition to the inclusion of international unions in these experiments (as at BSN), others have involved the European Metalworker's Federation and the International Union of Foodworkers. BSN even called for European legislation to create an EU statute for its pan-European consultations. But while a number of large German companies have also established European works councils, most European MNCs remain opposed to such arrangements, and especially to any legal obligations (Ramsay, 1990; Rhodes, 1992a, pp. 40–4).

It is their hostility towards legal regulation and transnational collective bargaining which explains employers' opposition to the most recent EU initiatives in this area: the European Company Statute's workers' consultation provisions and the Commission's draft Directive on a European Works' Council. In order to pre-empt the degree of opposition which met the last attempt by the Commission to submit MNCs to common European legal rules – the draft Vredeling Directive of 1980 – the consultation provisions of the European Company Statute (which, as discussed on p. 148, the Commission has attempted to pass under qualified majority voting) are highly flexible, offering three types of worker involvement: German-style codetermination (with workers representation on supervisory boards), internal workers' committees (as in Belgium, France or Italy) or, the softest option, a model established by way of agreement between management and workers' representatives. All companies using the option of the statute would also have to observe existing national laws on workers' rights. But Europe's employers' organisations are still opposed, in part because the form and functioning of the chosen system of representation would require some form of collective bargaining – from which it would be difficult to exclude trade union influence – and because it would overlap with, and add to the complexity of, existing national arrangements.

The employers' organisations are also opposed to the draft Directive on the establishment of a European Works Council issued by the Commission in January 1991 – despite its minimal and rather innocuous provisions. Under this proposal, European-wide companies (those with at least 1000 employees in the EU, and at least two establishments in different member states, each with at least 100 employees) would be obliged to negotiate the creation of a company or group works council for the purposes of information and consultation on job reductions, new working practices, and the introduction of new technology. Agreement not to create a works council is also possible, although if workers do seek one and management fails to respond, there is provision for certain minimum legal requirements to be laid down by the member states – a major reason for employer opposition. Other requirements are minimal, and the procedures are close to those already used in the French MNCs mentioned above: the works council is to have up to thirty members (drawn from existing representatives or elected for the purpose if there are none) and has a right to one annual meeting with management unless there are exceptional circumstances, in which case a second meeting could be called. These requirements could also be met without formal constitution of a works council as such (EIRR, 1992, pp. 23–7). The adoption of this Directive – which is fiercely opposed by Britain – is now possible by qualified majority voting under the Maastricht Social Agreement, and although only applicable in the eleven signatory states, it will, if adopted, clearly affect British companies operating on the Continent.

CONCLUSIONS

As the first section of this chapter showed, there are major differences in national labour markets and industrial relations institutions in the EU member states. While there may be some indications of convergence in labour market trends – most notably in the expansion of the 'atypical' workforce and in the shift towards lower levels of collective bargaining – there remains a substantial degree of divergence even in these developments, conditioned as they are by nationally specific structures and traditions. The attempt to harmonise labour market regulation across EU member states, or to create some form of 'level playing field', has therefore encountered resistance.

It is, however, to be emphasised that although the extent of variety in labour relations and labour market regulation places perhaps the most important constraint on the ambitions of 'integrationists', there are many other impediments in the path of a pan-European system of labour market rules. Prominent amongst these is the resistance of employers and the absence of sufficient institutional foundations for a European system of industrial relations. Until the self-interest of labour market actors coincides with perceived collective interest in regulating the labour market supranationally, long-established national arrangements will prevail. Indeed, the principle of subsidiarity – which was strengthened in the TEU – requires that such diversity is respected. If it is to exist at all, the 'Social Dimension' will be created within national systems via influence, rather than by interference from supranational institutions and policy-making processes.

However, there have been recent signs that the Commission's priorities are changing from an overwhelming concern with employment protection to a new interest in creating employment – if necessary through a recourse to greater labour market flexibility, although not, the Commission hopes, at the expense of the draft social legislation already in place and in the pipeline. This reassessment of priorities has been triggered by the recent increase in unemployment across the EU. In mid 1993 there were some 17 million people out of work in the EU, with 1.4 million jobs having been lost since 1990. This presents a difficult policy challenge to the Commission and the EU member states because of the lack of any clear relationship between economic growth and employment creation in much of the EU during the 1980s. Given that the proportion of women in work is still growing, reducing the EU unemployment from 11 per cent to, say, 7 per cent before the end of this decade would require the creation of 10 million new jobs – more than were created during the growth period of 1985–90.

Consequently, there is now a focus at the EU level, for the first time, on the possible impediments to employment creation. These include: the costs of dismissals and restrictions on part-time and temporary work; relatively high labour costs in some parts of the EU, and in particular the burden of high payroll taxes on employers in those countries where social security systems are financed from employer and employee contributions rather than from general taxation; and the low labour-intensity of the service sector in many EU member states. Amongst measures to promote employment is a more efficient deployment of state spending on the labour market, by shifting more resources from 'passive' policies such as unemployment benefit to more 'active' measures to ensure the reintegration of the unemployed into work. This reassessment of priorities may eventually facilitate a greater consensus on labour market issues across the EU. However, in the short term it is more likely to intensify the debate on the appropriate balance between flexibility and protection in labour market management.

Guide to Further Reading

Labour markets: Current developments in employment, unemployment and labour market policies in the EU are best covered by the OECD's *Employment Outlook* and the European Commission's *Employment in Europe*, both of which are published annually. Analyses of aspects of EU employment policy constitute the focus of the edited volume by Gold (1993). For individual countries, the annual OECD *Economic Surveys* are extremely useful. On labour market policy and the debate on flexibility, see M. Emerson, (1988a and 1988b) and OECD (1990). For a comparison of three national systems of labour market management in the EU, see C. Lane (1989), and J. Grahl and P. Teague (1989)

Industrial relations: There are a large number of sources on industrial relations in West European countries. The best recent collections are G. Baglioni and C. Crouch (eds) (1990), and A. Ferner and R. Hyman (eds) (1992). For comparative and historical overviews, see R. Hyman (1991), and C. Crouch (1993).

EC 'social dimension': The evolution of the EU's 'social dimension' is analysed in P. Teague (1989a, 1989b and 1989c). For more recent analyses, see M. Rhodes (1991 and 1992a), and P. Teague and J. Grahl (1992).

CHAPTER 5

The financial environment

Peter A. Vipond

INTRODUCTION

Capital is fundamental to economic activity and its provision directly affects the performance of businesses. The cost of capital, its availability and the regulations affecting it are all of immediate concern to business. Recognising this fact, the European Union (EU) continues to lay great stress on creating a propitious financial environment for all firms within the internal market.

From the perspective of a firm there are three main components to the financial, as distinct from the general economic, environment it faces in Europe:

- The first of these concerns the financial services that all firms require, from the basic provision of banking services to the crucial issue of raising capital through debt or equity issues. At a European Union level the creation of a single market for capital has involved the creation of a European Financial Area (EFA).
- The second component concerns the accounting standards which determine the financial reporting of the firm's business which all companies, private and public, are subject to in some measure.
- The third component concerns the fiscal or tax rules to which the firm's business is subject. These include a variety of taxes on such things as turnover (Value Added Tax) and profits (Corporation Tax).

These three components collectively constitute the European Financial Environment (EFE). They are connected to the general economic environment of Europe in various ways. For example, the central bank monetary policies of member states have a causal effect on the interest rates charged to businesses by banks. This has meant that firms in some member states have very different financial environments because of governmental and monetary authority decisions as distinct from factors specific to the financial environment. Somewhat paradoxically, therefore, the financial environment is distinct from, but is also greatly affected by, broader economic policy considerations.

Finance is, above all, about the cost and regulation of capital. Although it is intuitively simple to think of capital in terms of money, any financial obligation which involves the transfer of current purchasing power in return for a stream of future payments involve the allocation of capital. In so far as banks, insurance and investment firms come between those who have capital surplus to current needs (surplus spending units) and those who have need of more capital than they currently possess (deficit spending units), they are engaged in the activity of financial intermediation.

Even within a market economy, the activity of financial intermediation is heavily regulated for a number of good reasons. Further, as we shall see in the European context, the process of deregulation, which has been a key element of the Single European Market (SEM) programme, has not, for the most part, involved scrapping those regulations surrounding finance, but rather reregulating the financial systems of member states in order to promote more efficient and competitive financial markets.

In order to make sense of the idea of a EFE it is important to contrast it with both national and international financial environments. The situation for a firm, for example the German Dresdner bank, is that on many issues it faces national regulations on its activities such as the drawing up of accounts, EU wide regulations on such issues as the establishment of new branches, and international regulations on a range of technical issues to do with capital adequacy. From the outset, then, the European environment is but one of three, and the notion of an interlocking venn diagram with three overlapping circles is most helpful. Some things belong in one circle only, while others overlap in various permutations. However, unlike set theory, but very much like the real world of policy-making, the areas of overlap contain matters of conflict (such as in the definition of capital) and generally reflect an open-ended process whereby legitimacy and power are subject to change. An area of shared responsibility, such as the definition of capital, creates the possibility of national and European policies being incompatible. Such situations, as this chapter will show, do exist and it is business that has to operate within the resultant environment.

Within this complex and changing regulatory order, financial firms provide financial intermediation. The different regulatory environments clearly affect the price of financial services, and indeed which services are available. While all EU states have encouraged the provision of basic banking, insurance and investment products by firms, many have traditionally used state controls and public ownership to control and channel the flow of capital rather than leaving it to market forces. Traditionally, many member states have exercised vigorous controls over cross-border flows of capital and prevented financial firms, even from other EU states, from competing in domestic markets. It is against this background that the EU has attempted to create a new financial environment for Europe.

The interlocking national, European, and global environments that firms face will be explored in this chapter, with particular emphasis on European issues. This differentiation of the financial environment needs to be complemented, however, by an awareness of differences between types of firms. Much of the debate about European integration has tended to focus on large firms, especially those with production and distribution facilities in more than one EU state. Such firms figured strongly in Commission sponsored studies of the 1980s which focused on restructuring and reducing the number of firms to gain economies of scale and scope (Emerson *et al.*, 1988). In addition, it was argued that an open and competitive market would lead to the more efficient use of capital in investment and in research. In such a market, large firms would clearly benefit from a common financial environment by facing similar company tax and accounting rules. Integrated capital markets and a highly competitive Europe-wide financial services industry would allow them to achieve the lowest cost for new capital.

There are 12 000 large firms in the EU (i.e. firms employing over 500 people) and 15.7 million small and medium enterprises (SMEs) (European SME Observatory, DG XXIII, quoted in Robinson, 1993). The SMEs are the fastest growing part of the EU economy and the part that makes the greatest contribution to job creation. Yet they face a financial environment that is different from large firms. They are, for example, unlikely to have access to capital markets and therefore are more dependent on banks. On average they are charged more pro rata for financial services than well-known large firms. Compliance with tax and accounting rules costs them more as a percentage of turnover, yet they benefit less from European rules as they are much less likely to engage in cross-border sales. This does not mean that they have not benefited from the SEM: as national markets have become more open and contestable through EU-led deregulation, national banking systems have been galvanised into becoming more efficient and more competitive. This has benefited SME's, though the extent of this benefit, as a recent Bank of England study makes clear, is 'yet to be fully realised' (Bank of England, 1993a, p. 378).

Thus although financial companies operate within the same financial environment as manufacturing firms, their position in it is somewhat different. There are some activities on which financial firms only do well when the economy prospers. For example, it is very difficult for a bank which is heavily involved in corporate lending to make profits in a recession when many of its customers are not investing in new capital equipment and some are going bankrupt. There are other activities, however, where financial and non-financial firms are in a zero-sum relationship to some degree. For example, a recent European Commission report points out that the savings in transaction costs within the EU economy, if a single currency existed, would be up to 13 billion ECU (*European Economy*, no. 44, 1990). These would be savings to all firms that buy foreign exchange services, but they would be lost revenue to those financial firms which provide such services. In consequence, there is only a partial identity of interest between some financial firms and the rest of the economy as regards changes to the financial environment. The EFE, therefore, is both internally complex and also differentiated by the type of firms being considered, as the examples of SMEs and foreign exchange indicate. These two points are worth bearing in mind throughout this chapter.

The next section analyses the creation of a single financial area in the EU – the EFA – from a regulatory perspective and situates it in the context of globalisation in the world economy. Following that, the continuing significance of different national systems for providing finance to industry is examined in a section which compares a number of EU states, both in terms of the traditional differences between the systems and in terms of how those national systems are subject to new pressures under the SEM. The next two sections deal with financial reporting and tax issues respectively. Although these may seem specialised and somewhat tangential areas, they are, in practice, areas of great importance. At a generic level, they concern the regulation of capital, and can, therefore, affect the entire processes and allocation of capital through financial intermediation, even when the markets for capital are otherwise efficient. The creation of a EFA is important but unless these two additional areas – of financial reporting and taxation – are addressed the EFE will remain fundamentally incomplete. In other words, financial reporting and taxation are covered because they matter. The final section reviews the arguments provided in the chapter with a view to considering where the processes of change currently at work are leading, as regards the European Financial Environment.

FINANCE: TOWARDS A EUROPEAN FINANCIAL AREA

The importance of finance in the EU derives from the fact that freedom of capital is one of the four basic freedoms of the common market. As a factor of production, capital is profoundly important in contemporary business. Research undertaken by the Commission shows that over 50 per cent of the output produced by the financial services industry is for intermediate purposes, that is to say it is consumed by other manufacturing and services industries as they generate added value (Emerson *et al.*, 1988, p. 98).

From the outset of the SEM programme the importance of creating a EFA for industry was recognised. It was clear that creating the right financial environment would have wide ranging and positive effects on the entire European economy. Although many of the figures produced by the Commission sponsored Cecchini research of the mid–1980s on the likely benefits of the SEM are now treated with considerable caution as to the margin of error, the gains from a single market in finance were very considerable. Indeed, they were calculated to be greater than the gains associated with the abolition of frontier controls (Vipond, 1991).

This kind of argument carried considerable weight with policy-makers in Brussels, but it was reinforced by three further factors. First, as Sandholtz and

Zysman (1989) have argued, there were powerful business elites pushing for a single market in Europe. These groups wanted a more integrated market so that European firms could gain from economies of scale and scope, thereby becoming more effective competitors in the global economy. Second, the 1980s saw a growing convergence of views amongst the governments of the main EU member states regarding economic convergence. There is strong evidence for what has been called the 'preference convergence hypothesis' in economic management (Keohane and Hoffman, 1991), whereby policies inclined towards nationalism and state planning were abandoned in favour of deregulation and the benefits of competition. In this context the financial sector was seen as having particular importance, both as a retail industry in its own right and as the supplier of capital to other firms. Third, the nature of the financial services business was changing due to such factors as new technology and the deregulation of key international markets for funds. Firms were seeking to break out of the geographical and functional constraints which restricted their right to compete. Collectively, these factors meant that the White Paper proposals of 1985 were essentially well received and acted on. In fact, there have been areas of financial intermediation, such as the provision of life insurance, where the progress of new policy has exceeded general expectations – a rare event in the EU context!

Capital movements

It is not surprising, in the light of the above analysis, that the main proposals for creating a single market for capital have generally been agreed at the EU level and that considerable progress has been made on their implementation.

The most basic deregulation of capital is contained in the Capital Movement Directive (88/361) which boldly announces in Article 1: 'Member states shall abolish restrictions on movements of capital taking place between persons resident in member states' (88/361). Of course, movements of capital between firms in different member states are not new phenomena, but they were usually for the purchase of capital goods or transfers to buy subsidiary firms, or to purchase wholesale products for retail distribution. The Capital Movements Directive extends those movements and the 'critical factor is that the transfer must be an independent transaction in its own right, and not the corollary of another effected for other purposes' (Servais, 1988, p. 25). Although relatively short, the Directive has caused a major change in financial markets in Europe and in the behaviour of governments. It is a rare example of the removing of restrictions on the behaviour of firms and individuals without imposing new and equally complex restrictions upon them. It remains an important measure, not least because it allows capital to be moved out of national jurisdictions where the controls or taxes on that capital are perceived to be onerous. In consequence, member states have had to review many issues such as the withholding taxes they charge on savings accounts. It allows a more efficient allocation of capital within Europe as more of it can be moved into those markets or projects which deliver a better return.

Given that countries such as Germany, Holland, Luxembourg and the UK had generally removed controls on capital movements during the late 1970s and early 1980s, the Capital Movements Directive also allowed European capital to be better integrated into the capital markets of North America and the Far East. As a measure, it embodies the move towards deregulation and a recognition of interdependency within Europe that was discussed earlier.

There are a number of unresolved issues that arise out of the Directive. One concerns the continuing national controls on capital allocation decisions that governments still have through controls of financial institutions such as pension funds. Traditionally, their assets have been overwhelmingly invested in the country of their domicile and only now is a new Directive being considered to remove these constraints. As this example shows, a broad deregulatory measure in finance can still be blunted in impact because of second tier national rules.

Another issue that has become more prominent because of deregulation is the effect of this Directive on macroeconomic stability, and in particular on the ERM. The Directive allows countries to reimpose capital controls and keep them in place for up to six months subject to Commission support (Article 3). While this measure is aimed at currency speculation, it creates uncertainty, which in turn affects capital allocation decisions. Both Spain and Ireland have had recourse to reintroduce controls, and the general uncertainty of the EMU process means this is an area where other states may engage in repeated bouts of capital controls.

It is also worth stressing that the theory of deregulation is based on a model of capital markets which conceives them as inherently very efficient (see Balling, 1993, especially chapter 8 for further discussion of this point). This view is at least contestable. Historically, many European governments introduced state involvement in their domestic banks and capital markets because of their failure to provide funds for industry or a stable financial environment. Further, since World War II, the European state with the most developed capital markets system (the UK) has not enjoyed the most successful economic growth, and has had a particularly bad record in terms of its manufacturing sector. Further, most EU politicians and business leaders recognise that there are many worthwhile infrastructure and commercial projects in the EU and Eastern Europe that private sector capital markets, or other financial intermediaries, fail to finance. This can be seen in the need to maintain the long-standing European Investment Bank (EIB), and in the decision to establish, for the purpose of assisting economic reconstruction in Eastern Europe, the European Bank for Reconstruction and Development (EBRD). The EBRD had made nearly 1.5 ECU billion of loans at the end of 1992 (EBRD, 1993). These loans, as well as the equity stakes in firms which it has taken, have generally been made because capital markets would not have provided the funds within an appropriate time frame, or at an acceptable cost. In this light, the importance of capital movements can be put in the context of realising the weaknesses of such markets as well as the strengths. Many member states, and to a degree the EU as a whole, will continue to supplement capital market decisions in various parts of Europe. Trying to improve on market outcomes in this way is widely accepted as a general principle, but the point at which to draw the line between market outcomes and government interventions remains a very live policy issue in Europe.

Overall, however, it cannot be denied that the creation of a single market in financial services has been greatly aided by the free movement of capital. It has facilitated the cross-border selling of financial products, and, more importantly, forced national regulators to make domestically available products more attractive or risk the possibility of capital flight.

From the case of capital movements it is possible to argue that much of what is involved in the creation of a EFE is not so much a distinctive European regulation of capital, but is rather the opening up of the member states' domestic financial markets to external competitive pressures from firms in other states of the EU.

Financial services

Firms need financial services because they require capital, either in the forms of loans or equity. Interestingly, although EU states have long supported free trade as a collective goal, financial services were not actively included in this during much of the period prior to the single market. There had long been international banks specialising in areas such as trade finance and some foreign exchange dealing. Equally there were products, such as reinsurance, which had been traded on an international level for some time. Yet national markets for financial services were found to be closed to outside firms in many respects (Cecchini, 1988; Emerson *et al.*, 1988). This was compounded by the fact that in many countries ownership of financial institutions was in the hands of the state: for example, forty-four of Europe's top 100 banks were in public (i.e. state) ownership as recently as 1987 (Bisignano, 1992).

In this context the SEM programme had the task of promoting competition and bringing down national barriers to new market entrants. Although the term 'single' market is widely used, the existence of very different national systems, the significance of state involvement, and the importance of financial systems for all EU states meant that the single market was never going to be a 'unitary' market, at least not for a generation. The SEM programme acknowledges that some national difference will remain, and that mature competitive national markets are likely to stay relatively unattractive to new entrants, particularly when, as in the case of retail banking, there are high sunk costs involved in market entry (Bank of England, 1993a).

In response to this situation the EU has achieved substantial progress towards the reregulation of banking, insurance and securities issues. For all three areas there are some basic principles in common. These are as follows:

- The use of *harmonisation* and *mutual recognition* to ensure that only those areas which really need harmonising, such as the definition of capital, are harmonised. Where mutual recognition is allowed, in finance as in manufacturing, the presumption is that different national practices should be accepted.
- *Home country authorisation* and *host country regulation* of markets. Once the home country authorises a bank, the bank has a 'single passport' to operate in all other national markets without being required to meet further authorisation criteria. This is gradually being extended to other financial services. Host countries still have responsibilities for the regulation of financial markets and the maintenance of liquidity in national monetary systems. For example, although Deutsche Bank is authorised in Germany, its compliance with capital market rules in London is a matter for UK authorities.
- *Reciprocity* and *national treatment*. As regards banking, the EU allows firms from third countries to operate in EU markets, even making use of the single passport principle, so long as reciprocal access is given to their domestic markets. Reciprocity is qualified by national treatment, so that European banks in the US would only expect to provide services in that country consistent with its banking rules, rather than the more permissive European ones.

The most important achievements with regard to the provision of financial services and capital to industry are as follows:

1. *Banking*: The key measure is the Second Banking Directive (89/646/EEC), which is backed by two further directives which define and weight capital for the purposes of the banking business. These are the Own Funds Directive (89/2999/EEC) and the Solvency Ratio Directive (89/647/EEC). The Second Banking Directive covers a range of operations far beyond making loans and taking deposits. When taken along with other directives, the aim is manifestly to provide a framework within which financial conglomerates can function alongside more traditional firms.
2. *Insurance*: The Second Non-Life Insurance Directive (88/357/EEC) and the Third Non-Life Insurance Directive (92/49/EEC) both expand the goal of cross-border selling and use of subsidiaries across the EU by insurance companies. They generally open the range of business from large risks in the Second Directive to mass risks in the Third.
3. *Capital markets*: There are now directives concerning both the undertaking of securities business and the appropriate level of capital adequacy for firms engaged in such business. From the European manufacturing firm's perspective, a string of technical directives in the late 1980s are important. They cover such issues as the requirements to be published when securities are issued for sale to the public (89/298/EEC); the information to be published for listing on a stock exchange (87/345/EEC); mutual recognition of listing particulars for stock exchanges (90/211/EEC); and insider

trading (89/592/EEC). As the list indicates, the aim is to make it easier to buy and sell shares around Europe's capital markets as well as to raise capital across them. In this way firms can develop a capital structure that reflects the reality of where they manufacture and trade.

This short review of the key measures indicates the ways in which the financial services' directives build on the Capital Movements Directive to work at creating a EFA within which capital can be allocated more efficiently. It is important to note that national systems are not abolished or even totally harmonised. Rather, the aim is to create competitive openings so that market forces can remedy inefficiencies. The aim is to use the market to remedy imperfections and distortions that exist in the national allocation of capital. As argued above, with reference to the EIB and the EBRD (in Eastern Europe), there is an acceptance that the market has limitations, but also a wide recognition of the benefits to European industry of an efficient allocation of capital. After all, for most firms which purchase capital this means they will have to pay less for it than would otherwise be the case, and they will have a greater range of choice in the financial services they buy.

European financial integration in a global context

The drive to create a single European market-place in goods and services has undoubtedly been connected to the goal of making European industries more competitive in global markets (Cecchini, 1988). While the pace of the development of international trade may be subject to various factors, including the success or failure of international trade negotiations, the process has proved to be inexorable. The traditional model of trade between companies based in different countries has given way to the rise of multinational firms such as IBM, Glaxo, Kodak and St Gobain. In fact, the multinational firm has been in some ways superseded by the notion of a 'global market-place' in which firms disengage from a particular home state to become integrated by market requirements across continents (Ohmae, 1990).

This process of internationalisation has been most developed in the area of capital because of the fungible nature of the commodity (O'Brien, 1992). EU integration, in terms of the trade in financial services, extends beyond what has been achieved at the international regulatory level. Furthermore, whereas international capital markets deal with major players, such as sovereigns (i.e. governments), supranationals (e.g. the EIB) and major firms (i.e. large companies), the EU reforms extend down to medium-size firms and many of the financial services they require. Within the EFE even retail financial services will be subject to some restructuring and integration, as discussed above.

The existence of international capital markets has a number of causes, including domestic deregulation (led by the United States) and the development of new technologies which allow global trading in capital products (see, for example, Smith and Walter, 1990). Another major factor has been the Euromarkets, which were subject to minimal regulation when they grew up in London from the early 1960s. The success of these international markets, both as a means for surplus spending units (SSUs) to gain a better return on capital and for deficit spending units (DSUs) to be able to borrow at all, led to their rapid growth. This forced many governments to choose between further domestic deregulation or risk larger and larger amounts of domestic currency being traded outside any kind of national controls at all.

As such, these markets have helped to free up international capital flows and provide new options for larger national firms. For these companies, if national banking and capital markets cannot provide the capital they require, or seek to charge a premium which the credit standing of the firm does not merit, they can seek funding in the international markets. The markets concerned are vast and highly liquid; that is to say, the financial obligations established within them are easily sold and resold. To give some examples, the volume of new bonds issued in 1992 was effectively $350 billion (i.e. 350 000 million) (Bank of England, 1993b). The total of outstanding bond issues in the international markets was nearly $1700 billion (ibid.). The size and liquidity of these markets mean that issues can be priced very keenly and in the currencies that suit the issuer. Further, the use of products such as swaps mean that a borrowing in one currency, or perhaps only the coupon (the interest rate), can be swapped into another currency if required.

International Monetary Fund (IMF) data confirms the size and significance of these international capital markets with further evidence of international capital allocation (IMF, 1993). Taking the top 100 European fund managers (including those based in states such as Switzerland, Sweden and Liechtenstein) the following figures are found for 1991:

• Whereas $640 billion was invested in national (i.e. domestic) markets by fund managers, $358 billion was invested in foreign markets. In some cases (e.g. Holland and Italy) more was invested in foreign than domestic markets.
• Whereas funds managers invested $993 billion in domestic fixed income markets, they invested $348 billion in foreign ones (IMF, 1993).

Already then, international markets are massive and the potential for the breaking down of national preferences is by no means a spent force. In this light, the development of a single market for finance in Europe can be seen as an accelerated part of a global process. One of the main benefits of European financial market integration has been a move towards a restructuring of the corporate financial services industry, in order to make it more competitive at an international level. This section has provided some empirical evidence for this process and its importance has also been discussed elsewhere (see Gardener and Molyneux, 1990, especially chapter 12; Steinherr, 1992, especially Part One). Although size alone is not a solution to competitiveness, it can bring with it a large and strong balance sheet in terms of the amount of capital a bank or financial conglomerate has access to. In terms of participating in the provision of capital in international markets by debt or equity, let alone gaining the extra added value from being the principal involved, this really does make a difference.

The international financial markets are of real importance to larger firms and governments in the EU. Their existence has helped spur on European financial integration and helped create the momentum for giving European firms, financial and non-financial, a powerful European market that can function in many respects as a domestic market.

NATIONAL FINANCE WITHIN A SINGLE MARKET

National financial systems: the history

Just as the global environment has an impact in shaping the EFE, so the national environment remains an important factor. The analysis of the financial services sector given above showed how the creation of a single market was designed to open up national markets rather than replace them with a unitary EU level market managed from Brussels. National differences persist as do national product markets in some financial and non-financial markets.

The classic study of the relations between finance, industry and government was produced by Zysman (1983) on the basis of research in the 1970s. His researches led to a typology of 'financial systems and the adjustment process' (ibid., p. 94). The French system (somewhat like the Japanese) was argued to be credit based, with prices administered by the state. The key player was the state, in that it determined the price and allocation of credit to industry, as well as orchestrating industrial adjustment by forcing through mergers and investment in new industries. In contrast, the German system was based on the major banks, which supplied credit into a political-economic system in which finance (i.e. capital), labour, and industry each had a strong negotiating power in industrial adjustment. At times this resultant tripartite system seemed to involve finance as a representative of government and at other times government was perceived as an independent force, but one which played a relatively limited role in financing industrial change. In Zysman's words:

> The German system has two dominant characteristics. First, it is a credit based system of corporate finance ... the transformation of savings into investments and the allocation of financial resources are dominated by the major banks and achieved primarily by loans. Second, the government does not intervene in a detailed way to affect the allocation of credit ... As in France and Japan, the banks in Germany have close ties to industry; in Germany, however, resources are allocated in the markets by freely moving prices. (ibid., p. 260)

In the case of the UK, neither banks nor the state were argued to play a decisive role. In fact the UK was the more difficult of Zysman's cases to compartmentalise. Although the capital markets in the UK were (and are) very strong, their orientation was not towards domestic industry so much as international trade. The UK did not have the company-led adjustment policies so typical of the US capital market-based system. Without the state playing a key role, or the kind of role that banks had as part of a tripartite process in Germany, the UK system looked 'unclear' (ibid., p. 94) or 'ambiguous' (ibid., p. 302).

Zysman's arguments are now most useful as a counter-factual scenario, explaining a situation that might have continued had not the development of the EU and the internationalisation of capital, both discussed above, happened. In practice, all these and other national systems in the EU have had to change to accommodate the new international capital markets. In the process, differences between national financial systems have become less important, though they still exist.

National financial systems: similarities and differences

Although pronounced national differences continue to exist, any European firm in the 1990s can raise finance from a similar range of sources. At a generic level these are as follows:

1. *Retained earnings*: This basically means that after corporate taxation some of the remaining profit is kept back rather than distributed to shareholders as dividends. Such earnings have a number of advantages. For example, they carry no interest charge nor do they alter the balance of ownership within the firm. However, firms may need to invest in new capital even when they have no retained earnings and a firm that has a poor dividends payment record may find it increasingly difficult to get institutions to invest in it.

Given the problems of retained earnings most firms face a key choice of deciding between debt or equity:

2. *Debt*: This means borrowing the money from a financial intermediary, usually a bank. The borrowing can be very short term, as with an overdraft, or it can take the form of medium or longer term loans. The level of debt relative to the equity of a firm is called the gearing or leverage of the firm. High levels of borrowing, usually thereby making the firm highly geared, are acceptable if the borrowing generates the necessary revenues to pay off interest and the capital sum. Even if the debt is essentially simple, a highly geared firm has to make sure that the money it borrows can be invested with an appropriate return. In making this calculation, the firm has to make a judgement about the overall macroeconomic situ-

ation of the economy (national, European and, perhaps, international) in the years over which the investment will be paid back. Many firms have faced problems because much debt has a variable coupon; in other words, the interest rate can vary greatly dependent on the base rates set by the government or the central bank. This is known as the interest rate risk and it can sometimes be hedged against for a price, using derivative products. Debt can be borrowed internationally, but if it is not denominated in the borrowers own currency, then a foreign exchange risk may be incurred, which can also be hedged. In recent years a number of hybrid debt-equity products have become available allowing specified debt to be 'converted' into equity at some future date. All this goes to show that the decision to fund a firm using debt now takes the firm's finance team far beyond the traditional loan application to a bank!

3. *Equity*: The basic form of equity is the ordinary share. This involves the purchase, using capital, of a share in the ownership of the company. Each year, if profits are available, these can be distributed to ordinary shareholders as dividends, while the growth in value of the company should lead to the increase in value ('capital growth') of the ordinary share. The firm never pays back the capital, nor does it pay any interest on it. As such, the issuing of new ordinary shares injects new capital into the firm which it then has to use to promote growth. There are other forms of equity, such as preference shares, which usually have a fixed rate of return (say 7 per cent) that must be paid in full before any dividends can be issued to ordinary shares. The use of equity to raise capital is very common, but the practice is often complex. For an existing firm the issuing of new shares often involves a 'rights' issue, whereby existing shareholders can buy shares in proportion to the share of the company they already own. This prevents any change in the ownership of the firm unless existing shareholders choose not to exercise their rights. Equity capital can also be raised through sale by tender; placings with specific firms; and subscription offers. These methods can be underwritten by other financial institutions, so that if the equity is not sold the underwriter agrees to buy it and sell it on as best he can. As with debt, equity is thus a relatively simple notion which has endless variants and complexities in practice.

Most of the ways firms raise finance fall under these three headings, even if it is not always apparent. Commercial paper, for example, is a short-term promissory note issued by firms with a good credit rating. On examination, it turns out to be a kind of debt.

In most countries SMEs rely heavily on debt finance, delivered by banks. Often these banks are smaller or regional banks that have the advantage of local knowledge and are locked out of the international capital markets. In France, there are over thirty Banques Populaires, most with a specifically defined regional territory, and the Credit Mutuel, a group of cooperative banks dedicated to the support of small businesses (Economist, 1989a). In Spain there are no less than sixty-four commercial banks and twenty-two industrial banks, as well as the major national banking institutions. In addition, there are in the order of seventy *cajas* (savings banks), the largest of which have strong deposit bases and most of which lend on a strongly regional basis to support such things as infrastructure development (Economist, 1989b).

The existence of larger national banks providing commercial products (usually debt oriented) and investment banks providing equity related products is a mainstay of the financial system, though this is gradually blurring given the rise of the financial conglomerate (Steinherr, 1992). However, the durability of local finance, often working under geographical and functional restrictions which are sometimes self-imposed, is also a reality. Whereas Germany's 'big three' compete across Germany (and internationally), the major regional banks compete far less, and the 750 strong savings banks generally do not compete (because of geographical locations) with each other (Rudolph, 1993). Such firms survive because of factors such as superior local knowledge which enables a better quality of credit judgement, better management of operating costs, and traditional cultures of business practice within nation states. As many of them are cooperatives or have local ownership, this also helps them to focus on a specific mission and on a commitment to local economic interests beyond maximising the return on their own equity.

These strongly embedded traditions of local banking and financial intermediation contrast sharply with new means of providing finance for industry, for example by venture capital. This is used by both smaller and larger firms and involves the investment of capital in a firm which is unquoted on the stock exchange and usually at an early stage of development. The risks are extraordinarily high, but the potential rewards can be stunning if the right investments are made. The venture capital industry has been developed in the UK, but elsewhere in Europe its presence is very patchy, though it does exist to a degree in Holland, Belgium, France and Germany. A recent *Financial Times* survey – *Venture and Development Capital Survey* – shows that no leading venture funds are based in Spain or Greece and only one is to be found in Italy (Financial Times, 24/9/93). This particular form of financing industry is, however, relatively recent in origin and has fitted more easily and quickly into some countries than others, at a pace which is no doubt determined in part by the general level of economic growth.

A key point about financial systems in Europe is thus not that national systems remain different, but rather that despite different historical backgrounds national systems are gradually embodying similar features. The creation of the EFA accelerates this process because it removes the barriers to market entry and financial innovation which previously existed. In addition, as the Bank of England (1993a) survey cited above demonstrates, there are already numerous cross-border alliances and mergers which affect the range and nature of services on offer to firms seeking finance. It is too early to tell whether organisations such as the Credit Mutuel can survive within a more integrated financial environment or whether all German regional banks will merge into larger units. For many national financial institutions the fact that they are mutuals or cooperatives, or have other forms of strong local ownership, may enhance their chances of survival against the model of conglomerization that has been advocated by many and which is empirically evident in the operation of most major banks such as Paribas, Dresdner, or Barclays.

Their institutional survival should not, however, be confused with either the survival of a distinctive national product mix or the existence of an entirely national set of prices for the provision of finance to industry. The creation of a EFA, as well as the increasing relevance of globalisation, means that competitive forces are eroding such differences at a steady rate. If national differences remain, therefore, they will be at the institutional level of the delivery of finance and not in the price of capital or the range of products.

FINANCIAL REPORTING

This section focuses on the second component of the EFE, namely the European standards for financial reporting and the effect these standards have on the way companies use their financial assets. Rules about financial reporting are very important in that they affect the business decisions and strategic choices of firms. For example, if a business knows that any properties it purchases must be depreciated on its balance sheet, it will take a very different view of purchases from a firm which knows that properties can be revalued over time and used as a financial asset. The price a firm is willing to pay for a company in an acquisition will vary greatly depending on the extent to which factors such as 'good will' towards the purchased firm or brand value for its products can be included on the purchasing company's accounts. A financial product such as 'asset securitisation', the purpose of which is to get financial assets off the balance sheet and sold on via securitisation while still retaining a role (such as collecting interest payments) in relation to them, only makes sense under certain specific financial reporting rules. If accounting rules are ambiguous about such assets, or insist that they stay on the balance sheet in some form, then the entire financial transaction may not be worthwhile. This illustrates why financial reporting rules are very important to firms and why they merit extended consideration.

Although financial reporting has had a relatively higher profile in the EU in recent years, success in creating a genuinely European framework for it has been somewhat limited. So, as was shown above with the EFA, it is important to analyse the EFE at not just the European, but also at the international and the national levels. While national accounting standards have remained in existence, there has been a rapid development of international standard setting, coupled with a growing tendency to make use of US standards in order to facilitate access to the international capital markets. For these reasons it makes

sense to approach the subject, initially, through an examination of the international reporting environment.

International harmonisation

In the area of financial reporting there are national, European and international
bodies setting standards and regulating the behaviour of firms and their
accountants. Although this can create confusion and has obliged some companies, such as Ciba Geigy, to produce one set of accounts for its domestic regulators (the Swiss authorities) and another for its largely international
shareholders – this is an area where some harmonisation is continuing. In fact,
much of the driving force for harmonisation comes from the international level
and is articulated through the International Accounting Standards Committee
(IASC). This organisation has a membership of all the major professional bodies
in industrial countries and they collaborate in the IASC to develop international
standards. Over thirty of these standards now exist and they are subject to
periodic review (IASC, 1991). These International Accounting Standards (IASs)
cover basic issues such as consolidated financial statements and depreciation
accounting (IAS 3 and 4 respectively) and more complex issues such an
accounting for the effects of foreign exchange rate movements (IAS 21). The
IASC involves both users and preparers of financial reporting, and generally
enjoys the involvement of bodies such as the World Bank, the International
Organisation of Securities Commissions (IOSCO) and the European Commission.

The forces behind the adoption and implementation of international standards are mainly driven by the need of firms to make their financial affairs
transparent enough to gain access to global capital markets, and by national
authorities seeking to avoid having standards that conflict with the IASs. In
this latter case, the danger would be that national standards would carry less
weight in the global market-place and firms would be disadvantaged by having
to produce financial information according to different, and possibly conflicting, principles. For SMEs the issues are less important, but in so far as they
trade beyond a national jurisdiction, let alone seek capital beyond it, the last
thing they want to do is to pay the fees of accountants to produce a completely
new set of financial data. This is an area, therefore, where there is pressure to
harmonise both at the European level and the international level. Any alternative to harmonisation imposes costs on firms and restricts international trade
and the use of international capital markets. In consequence, the IASs carry
weight, not because they are ordained by governments or judges (they are
not), but because they are perceived to be the most efficient solution to the
problem of providing reliable financial data by companies and accounting
professions. The driving force in this area is the private sector more than the
public sector. Nevertheless, it is a tribute to the success of the IASC that
financial areas as diverse as Hong Kong and Eastern Europe are starting to

adopt these standards directly as the basis for national financial reporting. This may be because they lack any usable alternative, as in the case of the former communist countries, or because they wish to establish an internationally accepted standard which is independent of the UK, as in the case of Hong Kong. Nevertheless, it reflects well on the standing of the IASC.

One of the most important accountants in the world, Walter P. Schuetze, chief accountant of the Securities and Exchange Commission (SEC), recently commented on the possibility of mutual recognition in the field of accountancy standards. He said that it was

> the least efficient way possible ... it just does not seem possible for investors in all countries to be able to understand all the ins and outs and nuances of the accounting standards and the way or multiple ways those standards are applied in practice in various countries. Although many assert that the price of an issuer's securities is set by investors in the issuer's home country, it seems to me, intuitively, that an issuer's securities will not be priced efficiently around the world if investors around the world do not fully understand the issuer's financial statements. (Schuetze, 1992)

He went on to argue that as the IASC standards improved and were shown to be reliable, relevant, practical and as simple as possible, this may well 'force national standards to converge along the lines of international standards. And that convergence would be a good thing' (ibid.). While some academics may argue the case for different standards-setting bodies in order to promote competition between regulators, most business leaders, facing an economy that is at least European and often global, regard such debates as unhelpful. Wherever possible, manufacturing firms and most service firms would prefer a single accounting system. They are concerned to appear as the 'same' company around the world rather than be reported through different, and sometimes non-comparable, financial procedures. As Michael Lawrence, Chairman of the One Hundred Group of UK finance directors, put it,

> At the moment, a multinational company registered in the UK and reporting in London, New York and Tokyo has to cope with a bewildering diversity of accounting standards. People investing in those companies, or thinking of investing in them, can find it virtually impossible to understand what is going on in the company and why ... If the aim of financial statements is to help companies gain access to (international capital) markets, then the different reporting regulations ... inevitably act as a barrier to listing and capital raising (Lawrence, 1993).

The process of harmonisation in financial reporting would be hard enough if the subject matter 'stood still' long enough to be harmonised! Unfortunately it does not, and just as established positions need to be re-examined, new and important issues emerge. In response to these the IASC issues 'exposure drafts', such as E40 on the reporting of financial instruments. Exposure drafts become the basis of IASs. In the case of E40, issues such as securitisation of assets, compound instruments made up of component parts, offsetting and hedging are all considered. All these problems have been created by the very processes of financial deregulation and innovation in capital markets, referred to in the earlier sections of this chapter.

Powerful business interests, with a capacity to take a clear functional view of tasks that need to be achieved, have greatly contributed to the development of an effective international standards setting machinery. This process has one other great advantage that the EU level lacks – there is an absence of national political lobbies seeking to defend traditional national ways of doing or not doing aspects of financial intermediation. This absence has proved a valuable asset!

Financial reporting in European states and in the Single Market

Issues such as those referred to in the E40 draft, cited above, are also picked up in national settings. In the UK, for example, a financial reporting exposure draft (FRED 3) exists, entitled 'Accounting for Capital Instruments'. Generally, these national procedures seek to avoid conflict with international standards. In the UK, accepted standards, generally promulgated by the Accounting Standards Committee (ASC), are called Statements of Standard Accounting Practice (SSAPs) and are designed to give a 'true and fair view' of a company's financial position. Recently, SSAPs have been replaced with Financial Reporting Statement (FRSs) which fulfil the same function. While the UK and Ireland use much the same accounting rules, there are variations in other EU states. Many of the basic concepts are still present, but, for example, French accounts are drawn up according to a specific plan (Plan Compatable) rather than merely conforming to accounting rules. Another example is the issue of depreciation, which in the UK and US is largely decided by individual companies and, as such, is accounts driven, but in France is decided by reference to the Code General des Impots and is, therefore, decided more by tax considerations (Nobes, 1990).

National differences in the EU spring from national cultures and the status of the accounting profession, as much as they do from current business practices (these differences have been documented in *Accounting Standards Setting in the EU Member States*, Commission, 1993a). Remembering, however, that even the IASC does not try to harmonise everything, the main thrust of the EU's work, through DG XV (Financial Institutions and Company Law), has been to try to achieve some comparability between financial reporting, particularly with reference to that between financial statements. To this end, the Fourth Directive on Company Accounts (79/660/EEC) lays down EU standards on the annual accounts of a wide range of firms, mainly public limited companies. It was agreed in 1979 and was followed by the Seventh Directive on Consolidated Accounting (83/349/EEC) which was agreed in 1983 (Commission, 1993a). This latter Directive is important in that it permits companies to consolidate their subsidiaries across the EU into one balance sheet, thus giving a more complete representation of their financial position. It must be added that both of these directives have exception clauses and their coverage is far from complete.

Other directives on technical issues have been agreed, but the area has not shown great advancement in recent years. Proposals such as the Fifth Directive and the so called 'Vredeling' Directive have proved so controversial in raising issues concerning worker participation that the area as a whole has made relatively little progress.

Even when agreement has been reached, as on the inclusion of the notion of 'true and fair view' in the Fourth Directive, there remain problems. As recent research has indicated, 'countries are tending to interpret "true and fair view" in the context of national culture, national accounting traditions and national [accounting principles]' (Alexander, 1993, p. 59). While the *image fidèle*, of the French system is supposed to be equivalent to a true and fair view, as is the German *Massgelichkeitsprinzip*, neither would give a true and fair view in the British sense. From this line of argument it seems reasonable to agree with Alexander: 'If European accounting harmonization is going to progress sufficiently to be able to make its proper contribution to the Single Market then such differences must be fully exposed and discussed' (Alexander, 1993, p. 72).

However, a more awkward issue emerges in this context: 'Should the major target of European accounting be commonality, or knowledge and understanding of differences?' (ibid., p. 75). The answer appears to be the latter, not the former. Writing to an American audience, the head of the Fédération des Experts Comptables Européens (which represents thirty European accounting organisations in twenty countries), reminded his audience to 'keep in mind there is no such thing as a "European Accountant". A tremendous range and diversity exist in European countries' (Hegarty, 1993, p. 94). In many ways there is less emphasis on harmonisation at the European level than at the international level. Hegarty, for one, dismisses it as 'unrealistic' and 'unworkable', and goes on to argue that

> no further legislative initiatives are expected for the foreseeable future. Nor is there any prospect of European accounting standards. Instead the emphasis will be on greater consultation between the EU Commission in Brussels, national standard setters, European representative organization of various prepare and user groups and the accounting profession. (ibid., p. 94)

While this sombre assessment portrays the reality of European policy-making, caught between the national and international standard setters for financial reporting, it is unduly negative in terms of the prospects for EU action. The functional spillover from other areas of economic activity means that firms will press for more comparable ways of indicating company performance in order to facilitate such things as mergers and acquisitions, and gaining access to the new complex financial instruments now available in some of Europe's capital markets.

Although EU successes in this area have been limited, it is true that the 'quality of financial reporting in the EU has considerably improved with the implementation of the accounting directives' (Van Hulle, 1993, p. 390). This judgement, by perhaps the leading expert in this field, is reinforced by his point: 'People tend to forget that most member states of the EU did not have any detailed accounting rules prior to the adoption of the Fourth Directive . . . Accounting has become something serious in all member states of the EU' (ibid., p. 391).

There remains a powerful case for more effective progress in the company law and financial reporting areas. This case rests on the disharmonisation (Van Hulle's term) that results as national standard setters, such as the British, bring forward new financial reporting requirements to deal with developments such as the creation of new capital market products. These problems are compounded by failures of implementation at the national level, failures which are by no means confined to the less developed EU states. Germany, for example, is subject (at the time of writing) to an infringement procedure introduced by the Commission because more than 90 per cent of German limited liability companies refuse to publish accounts as required by the EU directives (Van Hulle, 1993). The Europeanisation and globalisation of business require more progress in financial reporting. Without such progress the failure in this area will constitute a dysfunctional spillover, inhibiting the growth of business, the raising of new capital, and the development of the SEM.

This last point can be extended to the international level, where arrangements such as those which are embodied in the North American Free Trade Area (NAFTA) and the General Agreement on Tariffs and Trade (GATT) mean that Europe's market is, as Hegarty admits, 'increasingly regional and less national'. Many US organisations, such as the SEC, do not accept national European standards, whereas US Generally Agreed Accounting Principles (GAAP) standards are accepted in most European capital markets. Mercedes Benz, for example, broke ranks with the rest of the German industrial sector in 1993 by giving an undertaking to produce US style financial information in order to get its shares fully listed on the New York Stock Exchange and thereby extend its credibility as a global company (Van Hulle, 1993). There is a powerful case for European harmonisation of financial reporting consistent with IAS, and it will be interesting to see how far this case is translated into new directives during the 1990s, at the expense of traditional, national standard setting. If there is not a European response commensurate with the tasks, then both EU and European national standards will face a declining role in business affairs, even within the EU, as IASs and US GAAP rules come to be more and more influential.

TAXING BUSINESSES

Taxation, the third component of the EFE, affects the behaviour of firms in many ways. Firms do not simply accept a national tax system, overlaid with EU rules, and continue with their business. Instead they react to a changing situation and seek to adapt their operation to the tax environment which they face. Although corporation taxation, that is, the taxing of company profits, is the most important tax firms face in making decisions on such matters as company location and investment, other taxes also have effects on the behaviour of firms and these are explained below.

It is important to remember that as well as tax payments, taxes can have a deleterious impact on the operation of firms because of the administrative costs of dealing with them. For SMEs the complexities of some taxes are a disincentive to economic expansion. Furthermore, firms face a variety of obligatory charges on their use of the factors of production – land, labour and capital – and these are taxes, even when they masquerade under other names such as social security charges.

Not surprisingly, the idea of EU-wide taxes has long been controversial, touching as it does on national sovereignty and fiscal policy, as well as on the comparative position of firms in different national sectors. In fairness though, it ought to be mentioned that not all EU states even operated a Value Added Tax system (which is a key element of EU taxation policy) before joining, and that consideration of tax harmonisation for corporate profits – which is now very much on the agenda – would not have been politically acceptable for some member states a few years ago. Progress needs to be measured against the historical differences of these nation states as well as against the functional requirements of a single market.

Although the national and European taxation environments are clear to see, the idea that there is a global financial environment for taxation may seem less obvious. After all, there is no global government to pay taxes to. However, it does make sense to think of an international tax environment, particularly in the context of the globalisation of production. Many European firms, led most notably by Barclays Bank, have long objected to the unitary taxation system adopted by the state of California in the USA. Put simply, such a system, while it generates additional income for that state, imposes effective double taxation on the profits of international firms operating there, while Californian resident firms do not face the same discrimination in Europe. The so called 'unitary tax law' of California has been the subject of substantive trade negotiations and court cases in the USA. The Federal Government in Washington has not been able to move as quickly or decisively as it might have wished because of states' rights in the USA, perhaps indicating that the EU is further towards a federal system, in economic terms at least, then may be commonly thought. This is a specific example of a general problem, highlighting a point made elsewhere in this chapter, of the need to harmonise the framework of regulations governing the financial operation of firms. This does not imply that the financial regulations must be the same for firms, far less that they should face the same fiscal costs around the world. Rather, that taxation and other financial rules should not lay contradictory or discriminatory burdens on firms. As the Californian case indicates, achieving these goals is still some way off.

Taxing business in the Single Market: Value-Added Tax

Creating a EFE with regard to taxation has proved difficult and the task has hardly begun in the field of corporate taxation. As regards VAT and excise duties, however, more progress has been made, though as late as September 1992 a proposed Directive (Com(87)324) for convergence in excise and VAT rates was withdrawn by the Commission for want of agreement between states. The new regime for VAT, which came into existence as of 1 January 1993, will last until the beginning of 1997 when a new and 'definitive' regime will be introduced. The new rules were set out in a Directive (91/680/EEC), which was further reinforced by another Directive on the approximation of VAT rates (92/77/EEC) and a Regulation (EEC/218/92) on administrative cooperation in the field of indirect taxation.

The main achievement is that all customs formalities and cross-border checks have been abandoned. Under the old system, exports carried a VAT rate of zero per cent but were charged at the appropriate rate (17.5 per cent, for example, in the UK) on entry to the country importing the goods. The goods were then treated as standard domestic products and sold as such, with a deduction of all VAT paid on imports in the final domestic VAT return. In the new system, exports are still rated at zero per cent but VAT is charged at the appropriate rate for the country which imports the goods. However, this declaration of VAT and its deduction is solely in the final VAT return. In other words, the mechanism for VAT has been greatly simplified and an obstacle (a fiscal barrier) to trade has been removed (Commission, 1992, 1993b).

Rates and applications of VAT vary considerably across the EU, with Italy, Greece and Spain being amongst the higher rated countries, Luxembourg being the most notable of the lower rated countries, and the UK having the largest number of items which are exempt from VAT. Convergence measures are, however, narrowing these differences. Where VAT is charged on goods and services, it has been agreed that the standard rate shall be at least 15 per cent and the expectation is that it shall not normally be above 19 per cent. Most EU countries have a rate within this band and there will be a gradual abolition of other rates. This convergence will be aided in part by market arbitrage as customers shop across borders to pay lower tax rates. However, as VAT rates converge within a few percentage points, the transaction costs of doing this will outweigh the benefits and the practice will stop. Of course, unless the same process is followed on products carrying excise tax, cross-border shopping will continue.

As to the position after 1997, the situation is still fluid but it is likely that the Commission will push for broadly comparable VAT rates across the EU. Its goal is to have all VAT transactions treated as if the EU were a single state, so that the idea of exports being zero-rated will end. One of the consequences of this is that more VAT receipts will end up in some states than others, reflecting the final destination of the exports, and this may require a central EU clearing house to reallocate tax revenues if this outcome is felt to be unacceptable. Either way, in a period when indirect taxes such as VAT are becoming more important for EU states as a source of revenue, the proposal is contentious. It could lead, eventually, to a greatly enhanced role for the EU in tax raising at the expense of member states.

One of the practical consequences of this development which is widely apparent in the SEM is that when a VAT registered firm sells to another in a different state of the EU it issues an invoice with zero per cent VAT, but keeps a record of both companies' VAT numbers. This information is passed on to the national tax authorities which collaborate to avoid fraud. There are various special cases, such as cross-border direct sales, and special rules for firms such as insurance companies and banks which are normally VAT exempt in all states.

Overall, considerable progress has been made in Europeanising VAT, and a new system has been created. National political opposition to a genuinely integrated VAT system has yet to be overcome, however, and it remains to be seen if it will be so in the years ahead.

Taxing business in the Single Market: company taxation

Progress in the field of company taxation has been slow and shows few signs of a major change in gear. Late in 1992 the Council approved some general guidelines on company taxation, but these were very broad and non-binding (*Official Journal of the European Communities*, 1993). The area of company taxation is one of considerable complexity and it is by no means clear exactly how a harmonised system would operate. As the following examination indicates, the policy issues are so difficult that the process of policy development is as much hampered by its complexity, as by the wish of nation states to remain fully in control of company taxation.

From an economist's perspective, the case for harmonisation is not based solely on the existence of technical barriers, such as transfer pricing (the selling of goods and services within the same group of companies), or the enhanced tax liabilities that can be encountered from cross-border mergers. Undoubtedly these problems exist and marginally distort the Single Market. Beyond them, there is the broader resource allocation issue of capital neutrality both as regards capital exports and capital imports (Devereux and Pearson, 1989). The issue becomes important, for example, when a more efficient firm is displaced by a less efficient firm because the latter is less heavily taxed. The lack of tax neutrality in these circumstances leads to a suboptimal allocation of resources.

While the general case for harmonisation can be made, the policy has remained very difficult to progress, with the sheer technical difficulty of changes proving almost insurmountable. Even basic questions, such as the rate of taxation and the basis on which it should be levied, are still open issues. The current position within the EU is examined below, as are the Ruding proposals for more radical change (Gammie, 1992; Jeffcote, 1993). Given the present situation, attention is also given to the way in which different national corporation tax systems vary.

Although proposals for corporate tax harmonisation reach as far back as the 1962 Neumark Report, progress has been slow. Much of the progress that has been made focuses on cross-border transfers of goods, profits and shares in companies. The Mergers Directive (90/434/EEC), attempts to make cross-border mergers tax neutral in effect, thus facilitating company restructuring and the creation of larger EU firms. The companies involved must meet a wide number of criteria, including being in different member states and both being resident in EU states for tax purposes. Another important measure is the Directive on Dividends from Subsidiary to Parent (90/435/EEC), the main aim of which is to abolish 'withholding tax' being charged on dividends from a subsidiary to a parent company by the state where the subsidiary is based. The state where the parent company is based may still charge corporate tax on the distributed profits, but it must give appropriate exemptions or tax credits for those profits emanating from the subsidiary (Jeffcote, 1993).

An EU convention on transfer pricing to deal with double taxation has also been adopted (90/463/EEC), but it has not yet been fully ratified by member states. This is important because it comes up for renegotiation in the mid–1990s and, until it is ratified by the EU member states, it does not come into legal force. Further directives may well come into effect in areas such as cross-border loss relief, loss carry forward harmonisation, and the question of royalties and interest (Jeffcote, 1993).

More radical proposals for change, which it must be stressed have not yet been accepted by member states, have come from the Ruding Committee, which reported in May 1992 (Ruding, 1992). These proposals, which have been placed in a three stage process on a par with monetary union, deal with a number of issues, of which the most discussed is the proposal to keep company tax within a 30–40 per cent range in all EU states, to be levied on a more standardised basis than at present (Gammie, 1992). Most EU states fall within or near this band, though the UK has a lower rate for SMEs earning profits below a threshold, and the Irish Republic has much lower rates of tax on manufacturing firms (10 per cent).

In the absence of a strong EU company taxation system, national differences remain, both as to the rates and the method of taxation. Allowances for firms to set against their tax bill also vary considerably. Using 1989 data, Devereux and Pearson were able to show that the Irish had a vastly lower than average corporation tax, while the highest tax rate, of 56 per cent, was in Germany and was only levied on undistributed profits. A group of states levied corporation taxes at around 35 per cent (e.g. Spain, The Netherlands, and the UK), while several taxed in the lower 40 per cent region (Devereux and Pearson, 1989). Although methods of taxation vary, the 'imputation method' has become more and more widely used within the EU. Under this approach there is one rate of corporation tax on all profits, but dividends distributed to shareholders (as opposed to retained earnings) carry a tax credit which reduces their liability to personal tax (usually income tax). This means that a shareholder's income from dividends is subject to less double taxation. As the shareholders may be individual or institutional, such a system makes it more likely that both would be willing to invest in equity and help broaden the financing options for industry beyond borrowing from banks.

Although development of EU harmonisation in this area will be slow, the existence and continuing development of the SEM will put continuing pressure on policy-makers to develop a solution to the technical problems in this part of the EFE.

Taxing business in the Single Market: other issues

Corporation tax is the major direct tax which business bears in the EU, while VAT is the major indirect tax. Although the latter involves businesses in con-siderable administrative costs, the former is more likely to affect the location and investment decisions of firms. Firms in the EU face a variety of other taxes, however, which affect the financial environment in which they operate. Many of these taxes are not levied directly on the firm, but on the workforce, and some, such as compulsory national insurance schemes, are not even called taxes. From a company's perspective, a high tax economy, including high insurance and social security contributions, is a cost imposed on their business. This cost can be offset by a more productive labour force, but this in turn requires an investment in capital goods and training which the market for the product may not be able to bear.

The clearest example of the importance of these issues can be seen in Ger-many, where tax and social security payments by firms and individuals amoun-ted to 43.7 per cent of GDP in 1992, as opposed to 30.7 per cent in the USA (*Financial Times*, Germany Survey, 25 October 1993). This generally undermines the incentives of firms to invest in Germany and is one factor, amongst others, in encouraging German firms to manufacture abroad rather than export from domestic plants. Both BMW and Mercedes Benz have recently committed capital for new manufacturing sites in the southern states of the USA, for example, rather than export from domestic plants. At the individual level, recent figures from the German Economics Ministry underline the problems German industry faces: total labour costs are DM 42 per hour, of which DM 20 are various taxes. This compares with DM 28 and 13, respectively, in France and DM 9 and 4 respectively in Portugal (ibid.). This does not necessarily mean that production in Germany will always be more expensive – it may be offset by greater German labour productivity – but it does show a greater tax burden on German businesses. For industrial companies involved in major capital expenditure, possibly using a new 'green field site' to produce a commodity type product where margins are low and control of costs crucial, these figures could have considerable significance.

Most income taxes and social security taxes are national, but there is some evidence of growing European influence in this sphere, most notably via the implications of the social protocol of the Treaty of European Union (see Chapter 4). Extended European level involvement in policy areas such as social benefits and minimum wages has implications for the levels of taxation facing all EU firms, and there is evidence that firms are starting to react to this particular part of the EFE by shedding direct employment and outsourcing as many functions as possible (i.e. buying in goods and services rather than producing them within the firm). In so far as the costs of employment rise because of social and income taxes, firms will always seek to calculate how the production function can be improved by substituting capital for labour, or by importing from elsewhere in an increasingly global economy.

Seen in this light, it can be understood just how important tax issues really are. They affect investment decisions, intra-company sales, and mediate relationships with the international economy. In addition, they have a direct impact on the functional organisation of firms and the level and kind of employment they provide. Taxation issues are thus crucial to the business environment of all firms in Europe.

CONCLUDING REMARKS

The EU has created a financial environment for firms operating within it. Some of the EFE's components are far more developed than others: more, for example, has been achieved in freeing the movement of capital and providing competitively priced financial services across the EU, than in providing an adequate framework for financial reporting. However, progress has been made, to some degree, in all areas. Van Hulle's remark, that at least all member states have had some kind of accounting standards since the Fourth Directive, could be generalised to other parts of the EFE (Van Hulle, 1993, p. 391). This chapter has sought to specify the extent of that progress and to indicate the areas, such as company taxation and controls on capital movements, where more progress is needed.

In doing this, however, it has become clear that the EFE will only ever be one of three such environments. It is possible that, as the SEM becomes more like the integrated market envisaged by leading Commission economists, the EFE will be a unitary market in some regards (Jacquemin and Wright, 1993).

That is to say, the cost and availability of capital, as well as the rules governing taxation and financial reporting, will be much the same in different member states. However, this chapter has provided strong evidence that such a development will require a long time scale to be implemented, and that there are many reasons for believing that it may never come to full fruition. The power of national, and indeed subnational governments may have declined in these areas, but there is no evidence to suggest a permanent process of atrophy has set in. States will continue to exercise sway in many areas, such as taxation, and will continue to own financial institutions in order to influence national and local economic development. The EFE will continue to function as a set of rules overlaying and linking national financial environments rather than replacing them.

If the national financial environment looks set to continue, the international one looks set to expand in significance as the globalisation of business, especially financial business, continues. From a European perspective, the goal must be to have a EFE which enhances the efficiency and thereby the competitiveness of European firms within both the EU and the global business markets. This requires a continued emphasis on the reregulation of financial markets and financial institutions so as to assist in the creation of competitive opportunities.

Guide to Further Reading

The best place to start is with the *Financial Times* newspaper (*FT*), which covers the full gamut of issues in a readable and informed way. *The Banker*, and *Euromoney* are worth following on a monthly basis. Various on-line databases are now available, including *Datastream* which provides vast amounts of data and is relatively user friendly.

As regards journals, both *Economic Policy*, and *The Journal of Common Market Studies* (*JCMS*) carry relevant material at times. The *Bank of England Quarterly Bulletin* provides regular and clear analyses of financial affairs in Europe. Other journals are usually more specialised: the *European Accounting Review* is a good example of such a journal, as is the *European Journal of Management*.

Turning to books, the collection edited by A. Steinherr (1992) covers a variety of pertinent issues, including the strategic choices of financial firms and the problems of providing finance in Eastern Europe. Gardener and Molyneux (1990) are very thorough and particularly strong on financial institutions. The edited collections by Dermine (1993) and Mullineux (1992) both contain some very useful material, although the perspectives articles are written from, as well as their quality, is variable. Dermine's book is more focused on different national systems than Mullineux's.

Two single-authored books that focus on the financial environment of contemporary Europe are those of Henderson (1993) and Balling (1993). Henderson's text is easy to read and tends to take a public policy perspective, focusing on matters such as the EMU debate, public sector funding, and broader questions of funding for industry. Balling's deals more directly with financial instruments and has particular strengths in the application of these instruments in the context of corporate finance. He also indicates the relation of these practical issues to theoretical debates in areas such as the Capital Asset Pricing Model.

Kaufman (1992) provides an almost encyclopaedic study of different national banking systems, including the US and Japan. The edited collection by Cerny (1993) on finance and world politics includes a chapter on Europe and generally explores the impact of the deregulation and reregulation of finance for the international politico-economic order.

CHAPTER 6

The marketing environment

John A. Murray and John Fahy

INTRODUCTION

Europe has long been a huge economic force, accounting for more than 40 per cent of world trade. However, its own market remained a complex web of internal non-tariff barriers until the Single European Market (SEM) project took shape in the mid-1980s. The effects of the SEM will take time to make their full impact, but it is clear that for many industries the new structure is having radical implications. Industries that were built on nationally regulated frameworks, such as financial services, or those that lived on contracts from their own governments, such as telecommunication, are experiencing enormous change. The national markets for public procurement contracts have, or soon will have, become open competitive markets on a European scale. Companies with strategies based on serving local markets protected by physical and regulatory barriers to trade now have to deal with direct international competition. Start up companies and those with growth objectives can aim for an EU market of almost 350 million people to support marketing strategies based on low-cost and 'world class' product quality. European consumers increasingly view the same media, listen to the same music, respond to similar fashion trends and are ever more aware of each others' consumption behaviour. Europe is in transition – as perhaps it has always been – but especially now with the added pace and urgency of the SEM programme and with the changes in political and social values that lie behind it. In so far as business success relies on well-judged adaptation to a changing environment, the 1990s is a decade in which environmental responsiveness will be vital. In so far as marketing is the managerial function with special responsibility for reading and interpreting the environment, it is also a critical decade for marketing practitioners.

Kotler (1991) suggests that the marketing environment consists of all those external actors and forces that affect a company's ability to develop and manage

183

successful transactions and relationships with its target customers. Defined in this manner, the scope of the 'environment' is very wide indeed, encompassing economic, physical, political, legal, technological, demographic and socio-cultural factors, as well as the more immediate competitor, stakeholder, and business system participants who are related to the individual enterprise. Other chapters in this book deal with many of the broad environmental forces and influences, so the focus here will be, first, on some of the demographic and consumer features of the European marketing environment, and then on the more 'immediate' forces involved in shaping competitive market structures and the business systems of Europe.

THE EUROPEAN MARKET: SOME DEMOGRAPHIC AND CONSUMER FEATURES

Defined in its single market scope, the European Union is one of the three largest markets for goods and services on a global scale, with a population of approximately 345 million (Eurostat estimate for 1991), a Gross Domestic Product (GDP) of US$4.8 billion (1989), and a per capital GDP of US$14 700. These figures compare with approximately 248 million, US$5.23 billion, and US$21 000 for the USA, and with 123 million, US$2.8 billion, and US$23 000 for Japan. In simple demographic and economic terms the single market is thus one of enormous size and importance to firms worldwide. If the seven member states of EFTA – which together with the EU member states constitute the European Economic Area (EEA) free trade zone – are included, then 380 million people are encompassed in a step that may well define the next stage of expansion of the EU itself. Beyond this group of countries the question arises as to whether the EEA and eventually the EU, will, in due course, expand to include East and Central European countries.

Demographic trends in Europe signal an important medium-term growth in the older age groups. European teenagers and pre-teenagers are predicted to decline in numbers by approximately 9 per cent during the 1990s, from their current 25 per cent of the population. By contrast, those of 60 and more years of age, who already account for 20 per cent of the EU population, are set to increase further (Eurostat, 1992). By the year 2000 it is estimated that some 34 per cent of Europe's population will be over 60 years of age, compared with 29 per cent in the USA and 36 per cent in Japan (World Bank, 1987–8). The 'greying of Europe' will bring special market demands on competing firms as an increasingly large, demanding and longer lived group of consumers makes itself heard in the market-place. This trend is already causing shifts in large sectors of industry and service, from pharmaceuticals to tourism. Pharmaceutical companies have to focus increasingly in their marketing, planning, R&D, and product policy, on responding to the growing demand for drugs and treatment related to the ailments of old age and to the needs of institutions that take care of the elderly. In tourism, the rise of a very large segment of demand based on the travel needs of those in retirement and with pension-based disposable income to devote to leisure activities dictates change. New marketing responses, ranging from the reconfiguration of tourism 'products' to the physical planning of tourism plant and facilities (accommodation, transport and personal service), are widespread.

The size of households is falling throughout the EU, with the exception of Portugal which has been stable in recent years (Lambkin, 1993), resulting in an average household size in 1986 of 2.7, compared to 2.8 in 1981 (Eurostat, 1991). In addition, women's participation in the labour force has been steadily increasing – to 39 per cent in 1990 (ibid., 1992), with a high of 46 per cent in Denmark and a low of 32 per cent in Spain. The implications of these trends are the subject of debate, but it is generally felt that as household size diminishes and as more women take up paid employment, major impacts are felt in various consumer markets. For example, it is often argued that in the market for food, declining household size, combined with the increased number of working parents and the rise of what consumer researchers term 'latch-key kids', has fuelled the rise of prepared frozen and chilled meals in small serving sizes for preparation with microwave technology. Changes to accommodate these trends have already led to radical alterations in product policy, manufacturing methods, and packaging design in consumer foods companies. The market for cookers has been similarly changed by the needs of small households, whose members often eat alone and value convenience highly. The explosion in demand for microwave cookers is not unrelated. Similarly, transportation and logistics demands have changed because of the shift in the nature of food products and especially the rise in demand for fresh chilled foods, with the result that the infrastructure to service and support supermarket retailing has had to follow. Fewer children per household is also noted as leading to more expenditure per head on children, in areas as diverse as toys and clothing, with consequent changes in the importance and character of demand in these segments.

European consumers spend the single largest percentage (29 per cent) of their disposable income on food and non-alcoholic drinks, followed by housing and household fuels, and transport and communication (Euromonitor, 1992). So Europeans still spend their incomes on the 'basics' – nourishment, shelter and movement. It is notable that leisure and health now account for more than 7 per cent and 5 per cent respectively of household expenditure, statistics that are reflected in the growth of sectors and companies supplying these markets.

Demographic and consumer trends vary across Europe, but in general terms it is an ageing market with high disposable income wielded by increasingly smaller households in which female members are more and more likely to work outside the home. Like consumers everywhere, Europe's population still spends most of its income on food and shelter while paying increasing attention to leisure, health and education.

COMPETITIVE MARKET STRUCTURE

One of the central challenges to those managing marketing in European companies is to develop an understanding of how the political, legal and economic restructuring of the EU is affecting the competitive forces that dictate success and failure in local, regional and pan-European markets. The driving forces in the restructuring of the market are broadly twofold. On the one hand, the political and regulatory agenda of the European institutions and their implementation through negotiation and legislation is driving change through the environment to the firm. On the other hand, the strategic initiatives of European companies, seeking to anticipate the new structures and to position themselves in advance of the new realities with early pan-European marketing policies, is altering the nature of inter-firm competition in fundamental ways. The political and regulatory momentum gained by attempts to meet the 1992 target date was important in radically altering the pace of change in the EC. It would now appear to be a distant memory to hark back to the time when it took fourteen years of negotiation to agree a jam standard (*Wall Street Journal*, 1989). Over 800 standards were agreed between 1984 and 1990, more than three times as many as in the previous twenty years (Thompson, 1990). Issues with a critical influence on market structure and the competitive environment, such as legislation on trademarks and patents, international mergers and acquisitions, and the harmonisation of VAT rates, remain controversial, and the full impact of structural change will not be visible for quite a number of years yet. In the area of initiative-taking by firms, a long list of companies pursuing European-wide marketing strategies already exists, ranging from Nestlé in food markets, to Electrolux in household durables, to Asea Brown Boveri (ABB) in industrial and capital goods. For example, Nestlé's sales doubled between 1981 and 1993 through a series of acquisitions across Europe designed to secure its market position and to capture brands with multi-country appeal. Similarly, Electrolux set out to acquire and coordinate electrical white goods brands and distribution channels from Italy to Scandinavia, while ABB has created a European giant by combining and rationalising the operations of two traditional Swedish and Swiss companies.

Commentators from many perspectives argue that the development of the new market structure in Europe is producing an overall intensification of competition. Commentaries covering marketing (Bertrand, 1989; Quelch, Buzzell and Salama, 1990), management (Higgins and Santalainen, 1989), economics (Bennett and Hakkio, 1989; Calingaert, 1989) and finance (Hexter, 1989; Haufbauer, 1990; Simpson and Korbel, 1990) all typically stress the development of a more competitive market environment. Clearly the relationship between industry and market structure, firm conduct, and expected performance is an important one to explore in the context of the significant changes Europe is now witnessing. There is no doubt that the SEM is restructuring European industries and, in so far as one accepts the proposition that structure, conduct and performance are linked, then significant implications for market-ing and competitive strategy are inevitable.

In this context, Porter's (1980) framework for industry analysis might be expected to suggest some of the most likely changes in market-place competi-tion. Porter suggested that the combined effect of five industry forces deter-mines the nature of competition in an industry and the expected profitability of the competitors. The forces consist of (1) inter-firm rivalry, (2) the threat of entry to a market, (3) the threat of substitution from alternative products, services, technologies or materials, (4) the bargaining power of buyers, and (5) the power of suppliers. Fahy (1992) has suggested elsewhere that this fivefold framework may add some greater conceptual force to the assessment of emerg-ing market structures in Europe. The framework will therefore be used now to look at the likely impact of the restructured European environment on marketing practice.

Firm rivalry

Intermittent overcapacity, decreasing switching costs, increasing exit barriers and increasing numbers of rival firms are all factors that are expected to intensify rivalry among competitors in many European markets. In industries such as steel, detergents, pharmaceuticals, and banking, overcapacity is seen as a well-established reality (Friberg, 1989). The switching costs facing buyers in most industries inevitably decrease with the opening of borders and the harmonisation of technical standards. This liberalisation leads to greater price and other competitive pressures, especially on nationally oriented companies. On the other hand, a harmonised market allows the achievement of greater economies in production and distribution in those firms that pursue more pan-European strategies, reducing both fixed and storage costs (Aron, 1990). For example, companies such as Jacobs Suchard of Swiss chocolate fame and SKF bearings in the industrial products market have been consolidating production of individual products in specific European-scale plants to gain focus and scale in manufacturing. This has involved shutting down the overcapacity that was characteristic of a nationally structured European market and exploiting pan-Europeanism through quality, service and price advantages in marketing strategies.

Exit barriers are high in many industries and are unlikely to be lowered, especially where government shareholding and national pride is involved, as in the case of airlines. It seems unlikely that the Single Market can support all European national airlines and even with their reduction in number through strategic alliances and mergers, protracted competitive uncertainty seems likely to result from both overcapacity and political barriers to exit.

Several commentators have suggested that rivalry will increase and profit-ability decrease due to increases in the number of rivals in most European markets (Bertrand, 1989; Van der Hoop, 1989). It has also been suggested that the sheer size and global importance of the Single Market will attract American and Pacific Rim competitors as well as further competitors from within Europe. As an indicator of this possibility it may be noted that Japanese manufacturing presence in Europe increased from 276 to 392 plants between 1987 and 1988 alone (Berger, 1990). In 1990 Japanese investment of US$13.3 billion in the EC accounted for almost one quarter of Japan's total direct foreign investment, with its major concentrations being in electronics, machinery, chemicals and general machinery markets (JETRO, 1992). A 1992 survey of ninety executives in twenty-five leading Japanese companies reported that: (1) 58 per cent saw Europe post 1992 as an opportunity and only 2 per cent saw it as a threat; (2) the focus for their expansion in the 1990s would be 32 per cent in the USA (versus 60 per cent in the previous 5–10 years), 27 per cent in Western Europe (versus 20 per cent), 10 per cent in Eastern Europe (versus 2 per cent) and 16 per cent in Asia outside Japan (versus 11 per cent) (Abravanel and Ernst, 1992).

Set against these trends which signal increased numbers of competitors, it must be noted that Europe is being swept by consolidation, mergers, acquisitions and strategic alliances among those supplying its markets. In the first nine months of 1990 alone, 1190 European concerns changed hands (Berney, 1990). Conflicting forces are therefore at work in determining the state of rivalry among firms competing for the markets of Europe, but they might be expected, on balance, and when combined with slow economic growth, to lead to the intensification of rivalry in most markets. The pressure on marketers to compete simultaneously on the basis of lower price and higher quality is making a necessity of fundamental cost restructuring and innovation for quality in manufacturing, logistics, distribution and marketing on a European scale.

The threat of entry

High barriers to entry are generally assumed to lessen the intensity of competition and to support high profitability for incumbent companies. In European marketing, barriers often reflect past investment in local or international brand assets and the creation or exploitation of local or national niches free from the full force of international competition. The removal of entry barriers to markets within the SEM has been the central objective of the harmonisation process and changes the 'rules of the game' for all nationally oriented companies. Perhaps because of its traditionally fragmented nature, the European market has not produced many global brands. Indeed, among the ten best known brands worldwide, Nestlé is the only European brand, compared with six American brands and three Japanese. In Ireland, a recent survey of the top grocery brands (by sales value) indicated that among the top twenty, seven were global, six had a European scope, two a British and Irish base, and five a primarily local Irish base (Lambkin, 1993). The SEM restructuring process is expected to encourage the emergence of more pan-European brands. This would reflect the opportunity to exploit economies of scale in both marketing and manufacturing and the manoeuvring of European competitors to build barriers to entry based on brand assets as protection against marketers from North America and Japan. In the area of consumer products this likelihood is confirmed by the growth of very large-scale retailers with significant buying power and their success in transferring customer loyalty to retail brands and away from manufacturer brands. Thus retailers such as Marks & Spencer and C&A have already initiated European expansion strategies which gain leverage from their brand identities but which weaken that of traditional manufacturers. However, their sourcing strategies for 'own brand' products increasingly stress supply partnerships with European rather than non-European companies. This reflects a new era of intense relationship marketing in business-to-business markets, based on long-term partnership concepts, service as the key marketing variable, and real-time electronic exchange of marketing data to underwrite fast and flexible supplier response.

In the services sector, financial services provide an illustration of just how slowly market restructuring can proceed and how long it takes for the threat of entry across internal market boundaries to be translated into practice. Despite the fact that financial services account for an estimated 7 per cent of EU GDP, there has been less progress in the dismantling of national barriers than in tackling barriers to trade in goods (DTI, 1992). However, progress towards a free market in financial services is generally expected to result in significant concentration as a result of pan-European competition and also in new forms of market specialisation.

The implications for the market in financial services are expected to flow from three areas of impact. First, any institution licensed to sell in any one EU country is being given the right to sell in all EU countries. Second, those financial services companies incorporated in any one member country can establish or acquire branches or subsidiaries throughout the market. Third, all remaining capital and foreign exchange controls are to be abolished. The implementation of regulatory provisions on these three fronts varies from country to country, so the full emergence of a free market in financial services still seems some time away. None the less, the trend is clear – companies and consumers will enjoy more and more freedom to 'shop around' on a regional basis for their financial services. One commentary on the process notes that by the year 2000 industry sources expect 'greater competition within each country as well as more concentration in the region as a whole. Likely "winners" in the 1990s are expected to be the leading banks in each country, with deep penetration of their home markets and large resources of capital and people' (Harvard Business School, 1991).

The threat of substitution

As a force influencing structure and performance, the threat of substitute products is generally expected to reduce profitability. Substitution operates not just within narrowly defined product categories or immediate substitutes, but also between near substitutes. Thus, in the market for energy, the individual fuel sources – gas, oil, electricity and solid fuels – represent a persistent threat of substitution to each other and create price boundaries beyond which each energy form may become a substitute for another. The development of European grids for both natural gas and electricity has already redefined the market dynamics of these sectors and the relative market shares of both. It is interesting that the logistical infrastructure to enable this now extends throughout Europe, even including Ireland with its unique location off the west coast of the Continent.

The harmonisation of fiscal barriers can have a far reaching impact through altering the probability of substitution. For example, excise-related harmonisation may dramatically reduce liquor prices in Ireland, Denmark and the UK while greatly increasing them in Italy and Luxembourg. In the UK, price decreases for wine should be greater than for beer, suggesting the likelihood of substitution between these two classes of alcoholic beverages in a market that has already seen a consumer taste shift in favour of wines (Quelch, Buzzell and Salama, 1990).

Bargaining power of buyers

In general, it may be argued that the bargaining power of buyers is likely to increase as a result of structural shifts in European markets, although the impact will vary greatly across industries (Fahy, 1992). This is predicted on the grounds that there will be, in general, greater concentration of buying power, and greater availability of substitutes both from within and beyond the EU. In the retail and wholesale sectors for example, buying groups are emerging that transcend traditional national boundaries and that promise to create formidable market power. The recent alliance in grocery retailing between the Argyll Group (UK), the Ahold Group (Holland) and Casio (France) is an example of the creation and deployment of pan-European purchasing power, based on convergence in consumer tastes and demand, and the harmonisation of trade. The traditional national structure of European markets allowed pricing policy to vary by country without undue danger of 'parallel importing' or arbitrage across national boundaries. However, with the implementation of harmonisation and the concentration of retail and industrial purchasing power, pricing policies are rapidly becoming standardised as a matter of necessity across Europe. This puts an end to many traditional price discrimination policies that were used to increase overall profitability or to cross-subsidise various national marketing strategies.

Bargaining power of suppliers

The pressure for consolidation among producers in Europe and the general intensity of rivalry already noted suggests that the widespread restructuring of industry to create lower cost structures will continue unabated. This process of cost restructuring typically involves reconsideration of supply relationships and, in general, a movement away from multiple suppliers towards single supplier relationships or a very few supply linkages. For example, in the course of its drive to regain competitiveness, Philips has ceased to deal with 10 000 traditional suppliers (Fahy, 1992). The same process of supplier rationalisation is visible in sectors as disparate as automobile components and clothing. This would seem to suggest that the forces working towards industry consolidation and concentration spell out a future of lower power for sub-supply sectors. However, the balance of power will also reflect the uniqueness of suppliers' products or services and the dependence of buyers on their differentiated inputs. In so far as a shift to single rather than multiple supplier relationships is occurring, this may reflect an underlying change in the nature of industrial and business-to-business markets as much as it reflects the forces at work in the emergence of a single market. Single sourcing arrangements, or supply partnerships as they are often called, also confer power on the effective sub-supplier as dependency becomes mutual between buyer and supplier.

EUROPEAN BUSINESS SYSTEMS AND THEIR MARKETS

An alternative view of structural forces at work in European markets is suggested by taking a business systems view (Murray and O'Driscoll, 1993). A business system analysis traces the chain of value adding activities that is undertaken in order to bring a product or service from raw material stage to the provision of final customer service and support after its sale. In recent years, such analysis has had to include the activities involved in the recovery and recycling of products and their residues after use. Observation of marketing strategies in Europe in the 1990s suggests that many companies are exploiting or anticipating the advantages of a unified market by moving to integrate and systematise their business systems on a pan-European scale. In order to build the critical market advantages required for success and sustainability, companies must increasingly seek to compete on a combination of product quality, low delivered cost, and speed to market (ibid.). This market imperative drives business systems towards the consolidation of 'upstream' companies through tightly linked single supplier relationships and the careful location of each element of the value chain across Europe, in a manner that reflects cost, factor availability, and logistical forces in different country locations. Within the ambit of marketing, the redesign of distribution and logistics arrangements is widespread and often radical. For example, Ford of Europe now manages its parts distribution to dealerships across Europe in a centralised manner so as to minimise locally held and duplicate stocks while still guaranteeing rapid fulfilment of parts orders for the repairs of customers' cars. Such reconfiguration of business systems' cost structures and responsiveness is based on being able to operate in an integrated fashion through the whole system across Europe – from suppliers, via manufacturing, to marketing. It is also based on investment in information technology infrastructure that allows a multicountry management of response to demand and of inventory positions.

At the consumer end of business systems one of the most heated debates in marketing analysis and practice rages over the issue of whether consumer tastes and behaviours are converging on a pan-European basis. Increases in international communication, urbanisation, disposable income, education, English language ability, similar product ownership patterns, and a continuing surge in travel, are all presented as reasons for a convergence in consumer behaviour in Europe. Companies such as IKEA or Benetton are often advanced as exemplars of companies which choose marketing strategies to exploit this process of convergence. IKEA, a Swedish furniture company, addresses a segment or niche consisting of relatively young consumers across Europe with its common marketing strategy of reasonably priced, self-assembly products, retailed in combination showroom-warehouses across the Continent. To the young urban couples with mid-range but rising incomes that they target through their marketing, IKEA is as attractive in Italy or Hungary as it is in Sweden. The advantage of targeting such pan-European segments lies in the ability to exploit the consequential economies of scale in everything from investment in design to brand building. In integrated business systems of European scale, the key to success lies in control of the complete system – but not necessarily in ownership. IKEA, for example, makes no furniture but rather relies on over 17 000 sub-suppliers, despite being the largest furniture company in Europe. Its success and profitability to date reflects its control of the important elements of the business system – especially design and retailing – underwritten by a deep investment in information technology to provide the instantaneous information flows it takes to coordinate the full system. Benetton's strategy reflects similar commitments. It manufactures almost none of the garments that bear its label, just as it owns almost none of the shops that retail them. However, it does own its design, information technology, and distribution infrastructure, while controlling the rest of its business system tightly without bearing the costs of ownership.

While these companies have exploited trends towards consumer convergence, there are also examples of markets in which convergence has not occurred and which illustrate the alternative viewpoint in the consumer convergence debate. In the area of domestic electrical appliances, Baden-Fuller and Stopford (1991) found that attempts by manufacturers to implement standardised strategies have failed. Their research indicates that this market has been characterised by increasing divergence since the early 1970s, with growing demand for variety *within* countries compounded by growing differences in demand *between* countries. Electrolux attempted to pursue a pan-European strategy with its many acquisitions but, even today, it produces 120 basic designs and 1500 variants. After failing in its efforts to standardise its products and marketing strategy it now plans to standardise when it may and to 'localise' when it must, in response to the persistence of variety in consumer demand, based on deep-seated differences in national usage habits and taste (Echikson, 1993).

As a consequence of social and political concern about the physical environment, business systems are now being redesigned across Europe to recover waste and used products and to recycle them where possible or to return them to nature in a harmless manner. EU Directives have been important levers on change in this area as they typically reflect the increased concern of citizens about pollution and health. For marketing strategy it has meant that 'environmental friendliness' has become one of the common criteria for product acceptability in both industrial and consumer markets. To guarantee the 'greenness' of products, marketers have had to adapt product design to incorporate 'recyclability' and to eliminate the use of certain materials, such as CFCs in aerosols. As a result, the EC's production of CFCs as a percentage of world production had fallen from 40 per cent in 1980 to 33 per cent in 1987 (Eurostat, 1992). But differences in regulatory requirements have caused considerable disparities in competitive ability and economic rewards across markets. In general, Germany was the first to establish demanding environmental standards and its companies were necessarily the first to adapt – but often to their own short-term disadvantage in competition with suppliers from less 'advanced' European nations. In the medium to long term this competitive disadvantage may be reversed as both EU and national environmental legislation spreads, as its enforcement becomes more uniform, and as the early mover advantages that have been gained in making, marketing, recovering and recycling environmentally friendly products pay off. The advantage to the 'early movers' is most likely to arise from: (1) positive consumer perceptions and attitudes which become attached to companies and their brands; (2) the accumulated experience of dealing with new materials, technologies and processes; and (3) the ownership of proprietary design, recovery and recycling technologies and processes.

An interesting example of how far reaching this environmental force has been in its impact is the change that has taken place in the European paint industry. Solvents have been the traditional 'carriers' for paints. However, they present a pollution, health and safety threat in use. Between 1970 and 1992 the proportion of decorative paint that was water based rather than solvent based consequentially grew, from about 30 per cent to 70 per cent, and is expected to grow to 85 per cent by the year 2000. In industrial applications, where water borne paint is less appropriate, a major change to powder paints has been experienced and continues. Car and appliance manufacturers, on the other hand, are the subject of marketing campaigns by manufacturers of steel who would like to supply them with prepainted steel coil which the manufacturers would then stamp or fabricate without having to worry about painting or dealing with waste and effluent and worker health problems (IMD, 1993).

MARKETING STRATEGIES IN A EUROPEAN CONTEXT

It has been suggested that all strategies for competitive advantage in markets may be reduced to the generic categories of uniqueness, cost, and speed, with the added dimension of whether such strategies should be deployed on an industry-wide basis or on a segment or niche basis (Murray and O'Driscoll, 1993). Porter (1980) suggested two bases for competing – uniqueness and cost – and claimed that these could be combined only in exceptional circumstances. The experience and research of the 1980s suggests that the strategic winners were in fact those who managed to combine the advantages of both product uniqueness and low cost, and have since gone on to add further advantages through various mechanisms that compress the time taken to respond to market demands (Gilbert and Strebel, 1988; Loomis, 1989).

The strategic decision concerning choice of scope – whether to market to an entire industry's markets or to focus on one segment – has been lent added drama by the changes in European integration. Many traditional, nationally oriented, European companies effectively implemented strategies of regional market segmentation that were reinforced and protected by barriers to trade between the countries of the EU. This situation made focused strategies based on premium pricing, which in turn reflected the small scale and investment characteristics of local small enterprise, commonplace across the Continent. With the unification of the internal market, competitors have increasingly moved to strategies of consolidating national niche markets into pan-European segments that, in aggregate, change the economics of design, production, distribution and marketing in a radical manner. Those who have moved to take advantage of such opportunities can acquire radical improvements in cost advantage which they can then exploit through investment in quality improvements and in marketing. The consequences for competitors who chose to remain nationally focused with a premium pricing strategy are usually disastrous. Marketing strategies that are based on low cost, product quality, and sharp focus across national markets, have become a distinctive feature of the 1990s. Guido (1992) presents evidence for the emergence of cross-national segments among young people, trend setters, and business people, each with common attitudes, behaviours and preferences. Vandermerwe and L'Huillier (1989) forecast the emergence of six clusters of 'Euro-consumers' based on geographic proximity as well as cultural, demographic and economic factors. They suggest that even small companies can compete effectively in the 'new Europe' by accurately targeting the needs of narrow multi-country segments.

The pressure to compete on a combination of cost, quality, and speed of response has also led to some thematic changes. The pressure for cost competitiveness to support keen pricing policies has dictated the continuing wave of restructuring in European industry and, more recently, the widespread investment in the redesign or 're-engineering' of whole business systems, including basic marketing activities such as order fulfilment processes. The 'fashion' for business re-engineering has been born of this parentage. The simultaneous pressure for improvement in product quality and environmental friendliness has emphasised the importance of integrating strategy and implementation practice in such previously diverse areas as R&D, design, manufacturing, marketing, waste management, and recovery and recycling. While responsiveness to these pressures has yielded significant advantage in certain markets for some competitors, the same forces have encouraged industry concentration where the attendant cost of change has been substantial. In the paint industry, for example, it is estimated that the investment in resin technology alone to support new environmentally friendly products may typically cost US$2.5–3.0 million per major research project. Given the uncertainty about success and the number of such R&D projects that are required, it is easy to appreciate the extent of financial resources needed to support strategies of product innovation. Only large companies with deep financial resources can sustain such investment levels, leading to significant consolidation in industry membership (IMD, 1993)

The demand for speed of response is best seen in the intense pressure to reduce new product lead times and to move 'just in time' arrangements in many physical distribution systems. This, in turn, has necessitated a new level of investment in information technology to track activities and inventories throughout organisations and logistical systems.

THE PAN-EUROPEAN DEBATE

The hypothesis that European consumers are set on a road of social convergence has already been mentioned. The protagonists of this view argue for a future of 'standardised' demand across Europe, that may then be addressed by pan-European companies marketing pan-European brands with scale and depth of resources that cannot be matched by smaller competitors. The argument is a variant on the debate about the globalisation of markets sparked by Levitt's controversial 1983 article (Levitt, 1983). Kashani (1992) summarises the 'globalisation' hypothesis as arguing that markets increasingly reflect: (1) the disappearance of national market boundaries; (2) declining numbers of competitors and increasing size of survivors; (3) competition between essentially the same set of 'world-class' companies in each national market; (4) interdependence between local marketing strategies as what is done in one market increasingly affects what happens in another; and (5) growing similarity among segments of customers worldwide as divergence in lifestyle, tastes and behaviour narrows.

There is evidence to support the existence of the trends that underlie this scenario for the future. Firms' strategies are shaped by the intense pressure to reduce costs and to fund increasingly large investments in R&D and new technology. These forces prompt companies to search for scale by consolidating markets. From the market side there are clear developments in media and communication – for example, *The European* newspaper or *Sky* television – and in the acceptance of 'world brands' in a manner that suggests convergence in taste and consumption patterns. One might expect all these forces to be even more powerful on a European scale than on a grand global scale. However, the reality of European social, market, and industrial structures seems to be such that the hypothesis of convergence receives only partial confirmation.

One reason for this is the persistence of divergences in consumer preferences. So, to take food consumption as an example, per capita consumption of bread ranges from 131 kg in Italy to 30 kg in Denmark; frozen food consumption ranges from a high of 38 kg in Denmark to a low of 6 kg in Greece; while yogurt consumption ranges from a high of 20 kg in The Netherlands to a low of 3 kg in Ireland. In beverage markets the EU market looks equally divergent, with Ireland (3.1kg per capita) consuming five times the EU average for tea; Denmark (10.8 kg) consuming twice the coffee average; the UK (125 litres) consuming twice the average of carbonated drinks; and Greece (15 litres) consuming three times the average in spirits (Euromonitor, 1992). Distribution also demonstrates the difficulties involved in establishing pan-Europeanism, with marketers seeking to implement standardised strategies facing the problem of quite dramatically different retailing structures. Retail multiple chain stores account for 51 per cent of retail trade in the UK, but only 10 per cent in Italy and Luxembourg. In Spain there are 23 retail outlets per thousand of population compared with 4.5 in the former East Germany (ibid.). At the corporate level, twenty-two of Europe's top seventy-five companies have home country sales of greater than 50 per cent, which hardly speaks for rampant pan-Europeanism (Abravanel and Ernst, 1992).

Several features of the SEM are promoting the further development of pan-European strategies. The harmonisation of product standards, testing and certification procedures, patent regulations, labelling, and processing requirements are all advancing standardisation. Common guidelines on television broadcasting and changes in advertising regulations are making the production of standard advertising material easier. The simplification of transit documents and procedures and the elimination of customs formalities are encouraging the development of pan-European distribution networks. Despite the presence of these changes, however, empirical research reveals only limited successes with pan-European marketing strategies to date. For example, Whitelock (1987) shows that tastes and company strategies vary across eight European countries in the market for bed linen. Reichel (1989) suggests that while products will be increasingly suited to all European markets in a legal and regulatory sense, deep-seated differences in culture, language and consumer preferences will continue to necessitate country by country adaptation. Reisenbeck and Freeling (1991) found evidence that while the product, brand, positioning and advertising were likely to be standardised, packaging, pricing, sales promotion and public relations were usually tailored to each market. A study of 'expert opinion' by Daser and Hylton (1991) forecasts greater pan-European coordination of brand names, product image, advertising themes, distribution and marketing information systems, but continued diversity by local region in pricing, service, and product design and development.

The danger with the debate about pan-European marketing is that it is badly framed, leading participants to argue for a polarised scenario of future markets: either pan-European or local. Bartlett and Goshal (1989) propose a framework arising from their empirical work with companies that suggests neither viewpoint is right or wrong. They note that in international markets companies seek cost advantage through standardisation of strategies across national boundaries and that they also seek advantages arising from customer responsiveness through the 'localisation' of strategy. Resolving the apparently conflicting demands of these two desires may not be as complex as it at first appears. Taking a business system viewpoint, it is apparent that different activities or stages in any value chain – whether for an industry or a company – may respond differently to the possibilities for market advantage based on standardisation or local responsiveness. For example, the scale and depth required in R&D in technology-intensive industries almost inevitably argues for centralisation and standardisation on a European scale. Investing in R&D facilities on a country by country basis is almost always an impossibility. In sharp contrast, activities at the other end of business systems, such as sales promotion and selling, must almost always be tailored to local circumstances – reflecting differences in language, culture, legal regulation, or distribution structures. Thus, if one isolates marketing in the business system, it is clear that its constituent elements are differentially affected – product policy is most likely to become pan-European; pricing policies are rapidly converging in response to market unification; distribution strategies are still necessarily locally configured because of the radically different national distribution structures across Europe; and sales, service and promotional strategies are most likely of all to be quite localised, even where a standardised product is being brought to market. Pan-European marketing strategies are, therefore, emerging that reflect a combination of both localisation and standardisation. And that seems entirely appropriate as an adaptation to a Europe that embodies the two themes of broad convergence and resolute and proud adherence to national differences in many areas of behaviour and taste.

Guide to Further Reading

The literature and source material that has been referred to in this chapter is diverse in origin and typically partial in its treatment of the broad theme it addresses – there are far more specialist contributions than there are wide-ranging synoptic ones. In suggesting further reading it therefore seems most helpful to direct the reader towards two areas: the conceptual and the documentary.

In seeking to come to terms with concepts which may, and have been, applied to ordering and interpreting marketing phenomena Kotler's standard text (1991) provides a good overview of the managerial school of thought on marketing. Quelch *et al.* (1990) provide a view on the European marketing environment which is consistent with the more general Kotler framework. In pursuing thoughts on, and in structuring analysis of, competitive dynamics Porter (1980) is valuable. To explore issues that relate to the issue of 'pan-European' strategies and firm structures Bartlett and Goshal (1989) should be read.

On the empirical and documentary front, there are numerous statistical and similar sources. However, for those principally interested in marketing issues, a combination of two sources in their most recent editions provides the best overview and starting point. These are: *Europe in Figures*, which is published by the Statistical Office of the EU, EUROSTAT; and two Euromonitor publications – *The European Compendium of Marketing Information* and *European Marketing Data and Statistics*.

CHAPTER 7

The technological and infrastructural environment

David Jacobson[1]

The business environment in which European firms operate is shaped by the technology and the infrastructure that are available to them. These two dimensions will be examined in this chapter. Following a brief introduction, the chapter is divided into four main sections, three on technology and one on infrastructure.

Both technology and infrastructure can influence firms in two interrelated ways: internally and externally. In relation to technology, innovations can take place within a firm as a result of the efforts, skills and abilities of people working in that firm. On the other hand, the level of sophistication of a firm's suppliers of inputs, the demands of the buyers of a firm's outputs, and the technology of a firm's competitors, are all part of the external technological environment of the firm. Also part of the external technological environment are the universities and other educational institutions, the general level of skills, and the cultures and traditions that have contributed to that general level of skills. Through other firms with which it interacts, and through national institutions and traditions, the external technological environment impinges on the internal technological capabilities of the firm.

In relation to infrastructure, and focusing for the sake of illustration on communications, internally a firm may have a highly sophisticated telecommunications system, linking all branches of the firm in different parts of the country. Externally, the firm's infrastructural environment includes all aspects of the communication networks in that country. Relevant aspects include the sophistication and reliability of the networks, their degree of diffusion among users throughout the country, and interconnectivity to other countries. The type of system that can be installed within a firm depends on the general level of development of telecommunications in the economy as whole. In relation to infrastructure, as to technology, the external impinges on the internal.

The focus in this chapter will be on technology and infrastructure as significant parts of the environment of the firm. A key question in relation to both the technological and infrastructural environments is the relative significance of the European as against the national aspects of those environments. The main aim of the chapter, in conjunction with a description of the main features of these environments, is to assess this relative significance.

THE TECHNOLOGICAL ENVIRONMENT IN EUROPE: INTRODUCTORY CONCEPTS AND DATA

A new technology can be defined as new knowledge applicable in the production of goods and services. The innovative capacity of firms is their ability to apply, adopt and/or adapt a new body of (technical) knowledge, transforming new ideas into practice. Innovation refers to the upgrading or improvement of a process or a product. The procedure of developing new processes and products has traditionally been described in three stages: the invention (a purely creative and intellectual act), the innovation (the transformation of the new idea into a practical use), and the diffusion (which implies standardisation and, eventually, obsolescence). Recently, research has begun to focus on innovation and technological change not as discontinuous jumps but as cumulative and ubiquitous. 'In such a perspective the distinction made in innovation theory, between invention, innovation, and diffusion, as three separate stages necessarily becomes blurred' (Lundvall, 1992a, p. 8).

The diffusion of an innovation can be interindustry or spatial diffusion. Within a single nation, a new product or process, generated in a given industry, can spread across the industrial structure of that nation. Improvements in machine tools or in computers, for example, while the results of innovation in those industries, will lead not only to process improvements but also to product upgrading within the user industries. Innovation and diffusion of this type can occur almost simultaneously, as, for example, where increased precision in production of a product arising from a particular innovation necessitates the introduction of the same or similar innovation in the firms supplying subcomponents.

Spatially, and specifically internationally, diffusion is enhanced by transfers through foreign direct investment (FDI), joint ventures (JVs), licensing, and other strategic alliances. Diffusion can be both interindustry and, simultaneously, international, as for example when it is a by-product of 'normal' market operations, such as the purchasing of capital equipment or of intermediate inputs into a production process. Imitation, scientific exchanges, specialist publications, and the interfirm mobility of employees at various levels, all also enhance the diffusion process.

The risk faced by the innovating firm is fast imitation before the costs of innovation have been retrieved, sometimes referred to as the 'free rider problem'. Patents are a device aimed at protecting the innovator against quick diffusion; they also constitute an indicator of innovative performance.

Measuring innovation in Europe

Research and development (R&D) spending is usually considered to be a precondition for successful patent performance. Table 7.1 shows R&D expenditure as a percentage of GNP in the major European countries, Japan and the USA.

TABLE 7.1   R&D expenditure as a percentage of GNP

	France	West Germany	UK	Japan	USA
1964	1.8	1.6	2.3	1.5	2.9
1975	1.8	2.2	2.1	2.0	2.2
1986	2.3	2.7	2.4	2.8	2.7
1989	2.3	2.9	2.2	2.7	2.8

SOURCE   Nelson (1993), various tables.

During the 1980s, Japan, West Germany and the USA had significantly higher R&D expenditures as a percentage of GNP than France and the UK. Moreover, West Germany and Japan, in terms of this indicator, came from behind France and the UK in the 1960s to equal or exceed the USA by the end of the 1980s. Since its reunification, Germany has declined somewhat, due to the relatively lower level of R&D expenditure in East Germany. However, it should be noted that the use of R&D as a percentage of GNP to measure innovativeness has limitations. In what follows, in the context of comparing Europe with Japan and the USA, and the major European countries with one another, some other ways in which R&D and innovativeness can be measured will be considered.

Expenditure by governments accounts for significantly more of R&D in some countries than in others. Table 7.2 shows a general decline between 1985 and 1991, but in France government still accounts for almost half of total R&D expenditures, as indeed does the Federal Government in the US. In both Germany and the UK, the figure is closer to one third. The Japanese govern-

TABLE 7.2   Government funding as a percentage of GERD,* 1985–91

Year	France	Germany	UK	Japan	US
1985	52.9	36.7	42.7	21.0	48.3
1991	48.8	36.5	34.2	18.2	46.8

NOTE

* Gross Domestic Expenditure on R&D, based on constant 1985 $.

SOURCE   OECD (1993).

ment's contribution to R&D expenditure is lower than that in other industrial-ised countries, although in other respects, the role of the government in Japan is greater than elsewhere.

The pattern is somewhat different in relation to defence R&D, and, to quote Nelson (1993, p. 508), defence R&D 'accounts for the majority of the differences among the countries in government funding on industrial R&D, and the pres-ence of large military programs thus explains why government industrial R&D spending in the United States, and the United Kingdom, and France is so much greater than in Japan and Germany'. For most of the countries in Nelson's study, 'military R&D accounts for the largest portion of government funding of industrial R&D' (ibid. p. 513); Japan and Germany are exceptions. This is reflected in Table 7.3, showing percentage of government R&D expenditure accounted for by defence. The US is by far the highest, followed by the UK and France. Germany and Japan, as a continuing legacy from their post-World War II demilitarisation, are the lowest. The figure for the European Union (EU) as a whole, at around 25 per cent, is between Germany and France.

TABLE 7.3   Defence as a percentage of government expenditure on R&D, 1991

France	Germany	UK	Japan	US*
37.4	11.0	44.3	5.7	59.7

NOTE
* Federal Government only, excluding capital expenditure.

SOURCE   OECD (1993).

Tables 7.1, 7.2 and 7.3 together raise two key questions. First, does the high proportion of R&D accounted for by government, particularly in France and the US (Table 7.2), reflect strengths or weaknesses in the national innovation systems of these countries?[2] Second, do the high proportions of government R&D expenditure accounted for by defence in France and the UK, and particu-larly in the US (Table 7.3), enhance or reduce the innovativeness of these economies? In short, to what extent do Tables 7.2 and 7.3 change the picture presented in Table 7.1? These questions will be returned to later in the chapter.

In the 1950s and 1960s, the USA and Britain had the highest R&D expenditure to GNP ratios and yet, at the same time, showed the lowest rates of productivity growth. As Lundvall (1992a, p. 6) points out, the measure 'reflects only an input effort and does not say anything about what comes out of the effort'. Using R&D expenditures as a proxy of innovation intensity also implies the existence of the following linear pattern:

R&D ▶ new idea ▶ new product ▶ market definition ▶ product launch.

This is associated with a smooth flow of operations from the research labora-tory, to the design, and then to the market analysis departments. However, this linear pattern does not hold true in all cases. In many instances innovations are born in the production department (factory floor) itself; many others are suggested by end users (customers), or by suppliers. Some innovative firms do not have research departments and, thus, apparently no R&D expenditure at all. To quote Lundvall again, 'R&D expenditure is not the only kind of relevant input to the process of innovation – learning in connection with routine activities may be more important than R&D' (ibid., p. 6). Even in industries in which there is a research function, such as the pharmaceutical industry, there have been changes in traditionally understood patterns of development from invention to product launch. The market is an increasingly important first element in the very identification of the need for research. Moreover, there are many ways of differentiating pharmaceutical products, including different types of delivery systems (e.g. liquids, tablets, patches), different strengths, packaging, distribution outlets, and, more fundamentally, research to slightly alter molecular structure – which, in many cases, is influenced by national regulations. This means that the linear pattern outlined above is an oversimplification. The reality is often far more complex, with most of the stages able to influence developments in most other stages.

The fact that different elements of the technology change process, though located within a single company, may be located in different countries, also reduces the accuracy of R&D data. The UK, for example, is an R&D base for many firms whose headquarters are elsewhere. As a result, the expected relationship between R&D expenditure and innovation may not be realised within the UK because the results of the research there may be used to develop products and processes which are introduced in the countries where these firms' headquarters are located.

It is clear, then, that as an alternative to R&D expenditures, other indications of innovativeness must sometimes be used.[3] Basic research, done in universities, national research laboratories, and to a significant extent in a limited number of large firms, is at least the foundation for innovation. It 'provides the knowledge and skills on which national systems of business R&D can build' (Patel and Pavitt, 1991, p. 42). Table 7.4 relates research inputs (as measured by government funding) to outputs (as measured by scientific publications).

TABLE 7.4 Per capita inputs and outputs of basic research: West Europe, Japan and USA

Measure	West Europe	Japan	USA
Government funding (inputs)			
1987	100	52	104
1980	100	55	97
Publications (outputs)			
1986	100	51	118
1981	100	46	125

SOURCE Patel and Pavitt (1991), table 3.2.

According to Patel and Pavitt, the table is 'based on the most thorough attempts made so far to compare per capita inputs and outputs of basic research' in these countries (ibid.). The figures for Japan and the US are an index with Western Europe (France, UK, Germany and the Netherlands) set equal to 100. The publication indices are based on the CHI/NSF Science Literature Indicators Database. The table suggests that the US is the most productive of the three and that Japan became relatively more productive during the 1980s. Though Patel and Pavitt do not say so, one reason for the apparent improvement in Japan may be the English language bias of the literature base, publications by Japanese scientists in English language journals having become more common over time.

How do the major European countries compare to each other? Patel and Pavitt combine a number of different indicators in order to identify aspects of the inputs into and results of R&D. Some of their data substantiates the findings of Tables 7.1 to 7.3: Germany spends most, and has the highest proportion of R&D accounted for by non-government sources; France has the lowest proportion accounted for by non-government sources. What Patel and Pavitt add is that there are very sharp differences in the basic indicators of industrial technology among the three main European countries. Germany's industry-funded R&D is nearly twice that of the UK and more than twice that of France. In relation to the granting of patents in the USA, there is an even larger gap between Germany and the other two. The largest gap of all is that between Germany and the UK in craft and technician level qualifications; and, with respect to this last measure, the UK is significantly below France as well.[4] The only measure in relation to which the UK appears to be ahead of France and Germany is the output of scientific publications, and here, as mentioned before, there is an English language bias – though it may not account for all the difference.

The reason why US patents granted to France, Germany and the UK is used, rather than patents granted within each of these countries, is because data on the latter are distorted by different national systems of registration of patents. In Japan, for example, 'patents are granted separately even when inventions behind them were closely related technologically' (Odagiri and Goto, 1993, p. 104). For the same reason, in Figure 7.1, only external patent applications per capita are used as a measure of research output. These are applications by residents of each country for registration of patents abroad. What Figure 7.1 shows is that, from more recent data, Germany has higher external patent applications than its European partners but also that it has higher external patent applications than either Japan or the USA. (The figure also shows that Japan has had a more substantial growth in Gross Domestic Expenditure on R&D per capita than either the European countries or the USA.)

In the EU, the problem of different patent rules is gradually disappearing since a future European patent system is being implemented. The principle was agreed in Luxembourg in 1975 and was completed in 1989; it represents a serious attempt at transnational harmonisation of patent systems. However,

FIGURE 7.1   Indicators of R&D inputs and outputs:
GERD and external patent applications per capita

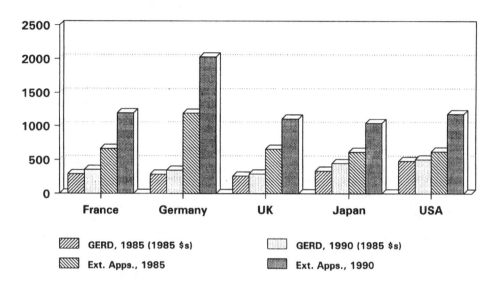

SOURCE   OECD (1993).

the use of patents as an indication of the output of R&D, or of innovativeness, will continue to suffer from the problem that many patents issued are not actually used in products or processes within firms. A tendency to apply for patents may be a characteristic of a particular (national or sectoral) group of firms, without that group of firms necessarily being more innovative than less patent oriented groups of firms.

Another way to indicate the inputs and outputs of R&D is to compare the change in Gross Domestic Expenditure on Research and Development (GERD) per capita over a period with the change in the Technology Balance of Payments (TBP) over the same period. The TBP 'registers the commercial transactions related to international technology and know-how transfers. It consists of money paid or received for the use of patents, licences, know-how, marks, models, designs, technical services and for industrial R&D carried out abroad, etc.' (OECD, 1993, p. 333). There are differences in coverage from country to country, and there may also be problems arising from profit switching transfer pricing, where firms adjust prices so as to shift profits to low tax areas. This measure is therefore also not perfect and should be used in conjunction with others to give broad indications. Figure 7.2 shows, first, how GERD per capita has changed between 1985 and 1990. (Greater than one is an increase and less

FIGURE 7.2   Indicators of R&D inputs and outputs:
GERD per capita and technology balance of payments, 1990/1985

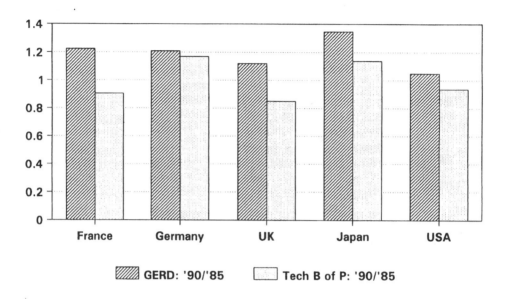

SOURCE   OECD (1993).

than one is a decrease.) It has increased in all the countries, but particularly in Japan. Second, it provides, through the TBP, an indication of change in the output of R&D. (Here the ratio of receipts to payments for 1990 is divided by the ratio of receipts to payments for 1985. An index greater than one suggests an improvement in the TBP, and less than one a deterioration in the TBP.) Only Germany and Japan have improved.

It is clear, even from the partially comparable data that is available, that in terms of innovation intensity there are significant differences among the three industrialised world regions, and among the countries of Europe itself. The focus has thus far been on the three major countries within the EU and this has shown that there are significant differences among them. Nevertheless, in the wider European context, Germany, the UK and France are among the most innovative. Data similar to that presented in the tables above would show that, in most respects, Portugal, Greece and Ireland are the least innovative. On the basis of many of the measures introduced above, Italy and Denmark are also well below Germany, the UK and France, but as will be shown in the next section, Italy and Denmark are, in other respects, more innovative than their major neighbours.

NATIONAL INNOVATION SYSTEMS

Following on the work of economists such as Freeman (1988), Nelson (1993) and Lundvall (1992b), innovation and the general level of technology in a country are believed to be systematically related to a whole series of institutional and cultural factors. Rather than focusing exclusively on narrow, quantifiable variables like expenditure on R&D, patents, etc., these writers have developed the idea of 'national systems of innovation'.

Here the concepts of national systems of innovation (NSI) will be used to refer to the set of institutions, within an economy, 'whose interactions determine the innovative performance of national firms', where innovation is understood to refer to 'the processes by which firms master and get into practice product designs and manufacturing processes that are new to them, whether or not they are new to the universe, or even to the nation' (Nelson, 1992, p. 349). Lundvall (1992a, p. 12) emphasises the learning consequences of these interactions, and this enables him to differentiate between narrow and broad definitions of NSI. The narrow definition is the one underlying most of the first section of this chapter, including, as it does, only those organisations and institutions directly involved in 'searching and exploring – such as R&D departments, technological institutes and universities'. The broad definition, which is close to that of Nelson, 'includes all parts and aspects of the economic structure and the institutional set-up affecting learning as well as searching and exploring'.

Given that historical, social, cultural and other factors – many aspects of which are nation-specific – influence the development of institutions, it follows that any country's NSI will be unique. In an attempt to operationalise this notion, Niosi *et al.* (1992) suggest that NSIs can be differentiated on the basis of a number of criteria. Somewhat adjusted, these are as follows:

- *Size of the country*: A large country (like the USA) is characterised by a more diversified system than small ones (like Austria or Finland) which have tended to focus on particular sectors.
- *Role of the country in the world*: In the UK, France and the USA, past colonialism/imperialism explains the development of R&D in military-based technology.
- *Existence and nature of natural resources*: The nuclear programme in France was developed because of the lack of fossil fuels; the success of the petrochemical industry in the USA is linked to the abundance of petrol in that country.
- *Socio-cultural factors*: Culture or 'habits of thought' are specific to societies, interacting with institutions to process information. Know-how or learned routines are as important as knowledge and can be communicated to the population as a whole. This places the training and education systems at the centre of the innovation process.

- *Political factors*: These have a substantial impact on the institutional frame-work of a nation (role of the state, banking system, education system) and, through policy, on its economic features as well.

These ideas will inform the examination of some of the NSIs in Europe, to which attention is now turned. France and the UK are examined in some detail, followed by a brief review of Germany and Italy. Consideration is then given to whether a European system of innovation can be said to exist. The aim of what follows is to identify the significant aspects of the technological environments within which firms operate, and to consider the relative importance of the national and European scopes of these environments.

National system of innovation in France

As was seen above, France has a lower R&D/GNP ratio than Germany, and a higher government R&D/total R&D ratio than either Germany or the UK; its defence R&D is as significant as that of the UK, and well above that of Germany. From these findings, a number of more detailed questions suggest themselves. Why is the state so important in R&D in France? Does this have positive or negative implications for the output of R&D? Does France's military R&D produce commercial results exploitable by French companies? Other questions are suggested by the criteria for assessing NSIs. How is France's R&D distributed? How successful is the French education system? Is there a culture of innovation within firms, and to what extent is it diffused among firms?

The extensive role of the state in the French economy in general, and in science and technology in particular, has roots as far back as the Colbertism of the seventeenth century. However, apart from its involvement in the education system, the state's association with the actual organizations and mechanisms involved in the production and distribution of R&D has evolved only since World War II.[5]

At the centre of the NSI (narrowly defined) is the National Centre for Scientific Research (CNRS), which dates in its present form from 1945. It has had a pervasive effect on the organisation of basic and long-term research in science, and on the availability of scientific and technical personnel. In particular, the CNRS directly administers laboratories and research facilities in areas not covered by universities, and, in addition, it funds university research and makes its own personnel and equipment available to universities for specific projects. More broadly, the CNRS provides services to the scientific community, including documentation, training and 'assistance on patentable inventions' (Chesnais, 1993, p. 203).

That an institution such as the CNRS was necessary, was a consequence of the traditional weaknesses in R&D in the third level education system. This system contains two separate types of institution, the professional schools (*Grandes Ecoles*), established by Napoleon, and the universities. The *Grandes*

Ecoles gave priority to technical education, and French engineers were among
the best in the world in the nineteenth century. French scientists, too, were
very advanced and the *Ecole Normale Supérieure* became a leading scientific
institution. In terms of science graduates, however, it was too small, providing
'much too narrow a base on which to build a sound scientific edifice' (ibid., p. 198;
emphasis in original). The university system remained secondary to the *Grandes
Ecoles*, and had a tradition of small, personal laboratories that went with the
professorial chair and reflected the interests of individual professors. This
situation was not corrected until the formation of the CNRS.

Despite this weakness of science in the higher education system, there is
little evidence before World War II of attempts within industry to undertake
scientific research. This contrasts sharply with the situation in the USA, where,
during the late nineteenth and early twentieth centuries, a large number of
corporate research laboratories were established.[6] Where France did excel
during the first half of the twentieth century was in areas in which the engineering skills, built up over the previous hundred years, could impinge on product
and process development. French inventors and entrepreneurs were most active
in 'sectors where technological development took the form of pragmatic, step-
by-step innovations as in automobiles and aeronautics' (ibid., p. 199).[7]

In addition to the CNRS, the French government established a number of
other research institutions, both civil and military after World War II. Among
these were the Energy Commission (CEA), which included R&D into and
production of nuclear energy, a National Centre for the Study of Telecommunications (CNET), and a National Office of Aeronautical Studies and Research
(ONERA). These, and a number of other research institutions in such areas as
tropical agriculture, health sciences, and military research, were mostly under
the relevant government ministries. In the international scientific context, the
most significant step was the establishment of the Saclay R&D laboratories by
the CEA. In a country where no large firm, even at this late stage, had yet set
up a major industrial R&D laboratory based on the US and German model,
'Saclay was France's first real step into twentieth-century fundamental and
applied science' (ibid., p. 202).

Driven in part by a desire for technological independence from the United
States, the state began to select particular firms and particular industries.
'National champions' – some publicly and some privately owned – were selected for support by the state, both directly and through state-owned financial
institutions. From the 1960s onwards, this evolved into a planned restructuring
of French industry in general, and a sharpening of French technological competitiveness in particular. In the late 1960s and early 1970s, four *grands programmes* were developed, covering the nuclear, aerospace, space technology,
and electronics industries – each of which, it should be noted, have significant
military aspects.

Industrial policy in the period since the early 1980s has witnessed significant
changes, but the principle features of the technological environment in France
have not varied greatly.

> With respect to the overall structure and working of the French innovation system, the 1970s and 1980s have essentially brought about only *shifts in emphasis* in the area of overall R&D resource allocation and the location of entrepreneurial capacity, along with a clearer spelling out of features that were already contained within the system. (ibid., p. 204)

There are a number of weak elements to this system, which arise from the fundamental nature of the control and organisation of French industry. First, there is the extremely important role of the state.[8] From the end of World War II to the end of the 1960s, both through the establishment of institutions and the implementation of policies, the state contributed an essential coordination role to the success of the French economy. However, this role also enhanced features of the system which would later emerge as weaknesses (de Bandt, 1987). Nelson's (1992) conclusion from studies of systems of innovation in fifteen countries is that few have 'active coherent industrial policies', and government policies supporting industrial innovation are 'generally fragmented'. This concurs with de Bandt's assessment of the role of the state in the relative lack of success of French industrial innovation since the early 1970s: 'While the transfers from the state to enterprises remain very important, no attempt is now being made to define and implement a consistent industrial policy' (de Bandt, 1987, p. 49). The nationalisations by the Socialist government in 1981–2 were aimed at integrating 'some of the big firms into a consistent plan-rational approach for the redeployment and further development of the French industrial system' but they were followed by an industrial policy of 'hesitations and obfuscation' (ibid., p. 48). Since the early 1980s, France – along with virtually all other governments in Europe – has reduced the degree of direct intervention and progressively privatised its nationalised industries.

Given its importance in military-related technologies, the state's role has become associated with a need for secrecy.[9] This is the second weakness, because technological information that might have contributed to commercial innovations remained within organisations developing and implementing those technologies for military purposes. Moreover, the significance of the military in directing the subsystems of innovation in France is increasing. The Délégation Générale à l'Armement (DGA) plays a key role, in most cases along with other government agencies, in innovation subsystems of nuclear power, telecommunications, defence electronics, aerospace and aeronautics. The increasing influence of the military 'even in telecommunications and nonmilitary space [is] a result of the current post-Gulf war reorientation of military-strategic priorities to space observation and telecommunications systems' (Chesnais, 1993, p. 214).

As with government involvement in general, military control of R&D is not *ipso facto* negative. There might be different contributions to commercial competitiveness of military R&D, depending on whether this R&D aims at 'opening up a broad new generic technology', or whether it goes into 'highly specialized systems development'. The former is associated with greater 'spin-off', the latter with less. French and British military R&D have 'from the beginning focused largely on the latter', and 'most of the companies [from those countries] receiving R&D contracts have shown little capability to crack into non-military markets' (Nelson, 1992).

An exception to this generalisation about limited spin-off of military R&D in France is the case of aerospace. Aerospace and drugs and medicines (see p. 212) are the only two industry groups in the high-technology sector that have positive trade balances. Strong institutions, established relatively early, form the background to the success of the aerospace industry in France. The first such institution was ONERA in the immediate post-war period, followed by the establishment of a Committee for Space Research in 1959 (see p. 209), and a National Centre for Space Studies (CNES) in 1961. A key difference in aerospace was that the CNES, unlike other state institutions, involved 'public and private firms in the program from the outset by contracting out a large part of the R&D to the business sector' (Chesnais, 1993, p. 203). The main firms were Matra, Aérospatiale and Thomson-CSF. A second difference is in the scale of this industry which is such that, from the beginning, international partners were sought. This led to the central role that France has played in Arianespace, the European competitor to the US satellite launchers.[10]

The third broad weakness of the French NSI is its organisation into vertical subsystems. Both industrial and technological policies have been implemented through programmes aimed at particular industries, and on the basis of the 'national champion' ethos, at particular large firms. While the overall economic 'plan' approach in the early post-war period also relied on large firms, this was appropriate and successful in the context of the French economy in that period. However, both the 'programme' and large-firm aspects of state intervention in the later period resulted in an overly vertically organised set of subsystems in the 1970s and 1980s, when increasing flexibility, rapid change and globalisation required a different type of state intervention. The vertical organisation of industries reduced the rate of diffusion of innovation between industries.

The state is not exclusively responsible for problems in the French system of innovation. Among other aspects of French industry that impede the diffusion of innovations are: the absence of an integrated industrial infrastructure at decentralised geographical levels; the poor relations between big and small firms, particularly in the case of subcontracting; the unfavourable power relations between industry and distribution; and the weak research-business relations (de Bandt, 1987, p. 54). To these may be added characteristics of French firms and industry that reduce innovation in general: the 'more hierarchical and bureaucratic attribute of French enterprises (compared with German firms) prove particularly ill-suited to the needs of advanced technological change' (OECD, 1988, p. 79); and the influence of stock markets which (as in the UK, but unlike Germany and Japan) impose short time horizons and deter changes or investments that might reduce current profitability, but enhance future competitiveness.

The focus has thus far been on R&D undertaken or controlled by government and the military. The pharmaceutical industry is the main high-technology industry which is, at least in part, outside the state's system of innovation.[11] While in some ways this industry builds on France's traditional strengths in the chemical sciences, in other ways it differs from the typical French pattern. Like other research-based industries in France, it is dominated by large firms, the main ones being Rhône-Poulenc (which merged with the American firm Rorer in 1989) and Sanofi. They have strong in-house R&D capacity, and in this are unusual (though not unique) in France. R&D expenditure as a percentage of sales (around 19 per cent) for both these firms is well above the average for the top twenty-five pharmaceutical companies in Europe (16.8 per cent) (Sharp, 1991a, table 13.5). This R&D is largely self-funded by the industry and this also differentiates pharmaceuticals from most of the other innovation subsystems, including electronics, armaments and aerospace. It does obtain transfers of technology from its joint ventures with the public sector's Institut Pasteur – Pasteur-Mérieux-Sérums et Vaccins in the case of Rhône-Poulenc, and Diagnostics-Pasteur in the case of Sanofi – but in the allocation of state R&D funding, 'one finds an *overwhelming bias in favor of the nuclear, aeronautics, space, telecommunications, and electronics sectors* to the detriment of the chemical, biological, and life science based sectors ... as well as to that of the machine tool and robotics industries and other small firm dominated industries'[12] (Chesnais, 1993, fn. 18; pp. 207–8).

In terms of competitiveness, the pharmaceutical industry in France has a positive trade balance, but there appear to be long-term problems – which the merger with Rorer may diminish for Rhône-Poulenc. First, while French companies tend to have very high numbers of compounds under development, the proportion that are successful in world markets when launched are smaller than in Germany or the UK. According to Sharp (1991a, p. 218), French companies 'have introduced many new drugs but mainly for local market needs; they were not sufficiently innovative to reach world markets'. As compared to the UK's twelve and Germany's ten, French companies did not have one in the world's top fifty best-selling drugs in 1990 (ibid., table 13.3A). A second problem facing the French pharmaceutical industry is that France has not experienced the same 'swarming' of new, innovative firms in biotechnology as the US. France shares this weakness with the other major European countries, but biotechnology research in new firms has been even less prevalent in France than elsewhere in Europe.

It would appear that the French NSI is dominated by state institutions and particularly the military. The pharmaceutical industry is to some extent outside this. Even more independent, though largely unresearched, is the innovative activity of small firms. A key to this is the development and transmission of skills. The French system of vocational education is, as would be expected, public, and although work experience contracts have been used since the late 1970s to combine workplace and school-based learning, this has tended to reproduce the large-firm, narrowly defined skills, Taylorist mentality that impedes innovation.

National system of innovation in the UK

The UK national system of innovation is, in some respects, even weaker than that of France. French industry-funded R&D was below that of the UK at the beginning of the 1980s, and it declined relative to that of the UK into the 1990s (OECD, 1993). But, while overall R&D expenditure as a percentage of GNP (Table 7.1) grew substantially in France from the 1960s to the 1990s, in the UK it was at best constant. Also, in terms of external patent applications, while the UK was ahead of France in 1985 (though both were, and remain, behind Germany), by the 1990s the UK had been overtaken by France (Figure 7.1). More significantly, in terms of the number of people obtaining mechanical and engineering qualifications at the craft and technician level, the UK, well below either France or Germany in the 1970s, also grew more slowly than either over the period up to the late 1980s (Patel and Pavitt, 1991, table 3.8) and, between 1985 and 1990, the UK's Technology Balance of Payments deteriorated to a greater extent even than that of France (Figure 7.2).

How does an examination of the British NSI contribute to our understanding of the strengths and weaknesses of R&D inputs and outputs in the UK? Does it facilitate a better understanding of technological aspects of the business environment in the UK? Does the less interventionist role of the state mean a greater rate of diffusion? Is there more commercialisation of the results of military R&D in the UK? As with France, the discussion begins with the historical background, followed by a description of relevant aspects of the educational system and key R&D institutions, and concludes with some indication of the innovativeness of the UK economy.

The UK, as was shown in Chapter 1, has not had the *étatist* tradition of France. While the reasons for this are complex, they are related to Britain's position as the first industrialised nation, and its early and long standing commitment to free trade. The economic role of the state in Britain between the mid-eighteenth and last quarter of the nineteenth centuries was confined to the regulation of a small number of markets, including financial and property markets, and to the advancement and protection, by military means where necessary, of foreign trade. While intervention increased over the next hundred years, it was never as coherent or determined as in France or Japan. Whether despite or because of this,[13] for much of the 200 years up to the end of the nineteenth century, the national system of innovation in Britain 'had no match, generating revolutionary changes in the techniques of energy and material transformation (the coal, iron, and steam nexus), in the organization of production (the factory system), and in transportation (railways and the steam ship)' (Walker, 1993, pp. 187–8).

Britain has not declined since then, but it has lost its leadership position.[14]

There are different theories as to why this change occurred, though few attribute a significant role to the British state. Among the main explanations are the inappropriateness of culture and institutions to the conditions of the twentieth century, despite their success in the previous two centuries; a change in attitude from industrial enterprise to a rentier mentality; and the inevitable catch-up of competitor nations as industrialisation spread.[15] While there is an element of truth in each of these explanations, the first fits best with the NSI framework's focus on culture and 'habits of thought'. Chandler (1984) provides a material basis to the argument by suggesting that 'Britain was the only nation to industrialize before the coming of modern transportation and communication. So its industrialists had become attuned to a slower, smaller-scale process of industrial production and distribution.'

Some writers have emphasised the weakness of education and training in Britain as reasons for its loss of leadership.[16] One weakness is that, although having a long and excellent tradition, particularly in science, Oxford and Cambridge universities are part of an elitist system, access to which is obtained through wealth as well as ability. The Oxbridge student output may be small in comparison to the total, but nevertheless it still provides a disproportionately large part of the country's economic and political elite. The system is, moreover, more service than production oriented. 'The French phenomenon of bright young Polytechniciens developing careers that span both government service and industrial management has no parallel in Britain'.[17] A second weakness is that while at the highest level (doctorate) the UK education of scientists and engineers is comparable in terms both of quality and quantity with other European countries, at the middle level (bachelor, technician and craft) it is relatively weak. Engineering in particular is weak at the technician and craft levels. This reflects the low standing of the engineering profession in British society.

Why engineering underwent such a decline, having been a part of Britain's earlier success story, may be attributable to the onset of the rentier mentality.[18] Thus it is not just the weaknesses in the education and training systems themselves that account for the low level of engineering skills. It is also the lack of recognition of the need for a more highly skilled labour force on the part of employers. This is illustrated in the contrast between an estimated investment in training by industry of only 0.15 per cent of revenue in Britain and 2 per cent in Germany. Intervention by the state could have imposed selective qualification prerequisites, but the state has traditionally had a *laissez-faire* attitude to the economy. This does not mean that there are no significant state institutions in the NSI or that government policy has never impinged on innovation. Policy and institutions in the UK are almost inseparable, with the latter more or less determined by the former.[19]

As in France, policy has been inconsistent. In the 1960s, the state was more interventionist than at any other time. Industrial policy (industrial restructuring, corporation tax, capital grants), particularly under the Labour government between 1964 and 1970, aimed to reorganise industry through consolidation in particular sectors – notably steel, cars, machine tools and computers – to form national champions. At the same time, science and technology (S&T) policy (S&T education, public sector laboratories, patent laws) acting through the education system, direct support of R&D, and other measures, attempted to regain technological leadership for Britain. Generally, however, there was a lack of coordination, with industrial policy under the Department of Trade and Industry and S&T policy under the Department of Education and Science. In the late 1960s and during the 1970s attempts were made to simplify matters through, for example, the creation of a Ministry of Technology and a National Enterprise Board (NEB), but with only limited success.

Under Conservative governments since 1979 direct intervention has been largely ruled out, and a policy of creating the right environment, or climate, for encouraging innovation has been adopted. The NEB was initially instructed to act commercially but its most public function became the bailing out of failing companies such as Rolls-Royce. Partly in consequence of this, in 1981 it merged with another state corporation to become the British Technology Group (BTG), providing venture capital through equity mainly in small firms. By the mid–1980s, BTG had an investment portfolio of about £230 million in 430 companies. Other schemes introduced in the 1980s with the aim of advancing venture capital to facilitate the introduction or development of new technologies included the Loan Guarantee Scheme and the Business Expansion Scheme. One problem with all these schemes is that many of the firms which have obtained capital through them are not actually innovative in terms of products, processes or structures.

Among the important institutions in the British system of innovation under the Conservatives have been, at various times, the Advisory Council for Applied Research and Development (ACARD), the Advisory Committee on Science and Technology – both advising the Cabinet Office – and, as before, the Department of Trade and Industry. Significant programmes, like the Alvey Programme for information technology, were launched, and defence R&D expenditure remained high – a higher proportion of government R&D than in France and much higher than in Germany. But despite these elements of continuity in innovation policy, during the second half of the 1980s and into the 1990s there has been a substantial reduction in the state's role in the innovation system. Moreover, as Table 7.2 shows, the decline in the government's contribution to R&D in the UK has been much greater than that in any other major country. A number of initiatives, including many begun by the Conservative government itself during the early 1980s, have been terminated, including the Alvey project.

How important has defence R&D been to the British NSI and how much spin-off has there been? The answer to this question is very similar to that for France. Most defence R&D goes on development rather than basic or applied research and there is a sharp distinction between civil and military activities. Defence R&D may occupy an even greater proportion of Britain's technological resources than in France, and almost certainly defence procurement absorbs a higher proportion of high technology *engineering* resources. There 'is broad agreement that defense spending has sapped, rather than strengthened, Britain's industrial economy' (Walker, 1993, p. 177). Until recently, amongst the significant differences between the UK and France in relation to defence technology was that while the UK was willing to remain dependent on the US in certain key areas – such as nuclear missiles – France went for independence across the board, and solved the scale problem by relying to a greater extent than the UK on exports. This is now changing as 'a French-style policy of export maximisation has been adopted that discourages product complexity' (ibid.).

Among similarities between the UK and France is that the only high-technology industries with positive trade balances are aerospace and pharmaceuticals, and that aerospace is therefore an exception to the generalisation that there is little spin-off of military R&D.[20] Britain's heavy post-war commitment to defence procurement has contributed directly to the strength of this industry. The main firms benefiting from this have been British Aerospace, Rolls-Royce and Lucas Aerospace. As in France, the pharmaceutical industry is the only high-technology industry that has performed well in international terms. Companies like ICI, Glaxo and Beecham have been aggressive investors in R&D, establishing close links with university researchers in related fields. In comparison to France, British companies have far fewer new drugs under development, but the drugs they do develop have greater success in world markets. One reason for this is the British companies' strict policies of dropping products which, from the early screening process, seem unlikely to be successful.

A key difference in the pharmaceutical industries, and of the two national economies in general, is in the significance of multinational companies (MNCs). Subsidiaries of MNCs are far more important to the UK economy than they are either to France or Germany. There has been a long tradition, beginning in the late nineteenth and early twentieth centuries and increasing sharply after World War II, of American direct investment. With companies like Ford and General Motors – and more recently the Japanese car companies – owning manufacturing subsidiaries in the UK, it is not surprising that foreign companies account for 45 per cent of gross value added in motor vehicles. But even in chemicals and pharmaceuticals, dominated by giant UK companies like ICI and Glaxo, foreign companies account for 32 per cent of value added (ibid., table 5.5).

There are differences of opinion amongst commentators as to the implications for national economies of a significant presence of MNCs, particularly in high-technology areas. Vernon's (1966) product cycle model suggested that the more sophisticated parts of a MNC's production process, including R&D, would be located in the country of the firm's headquarters. Porter elaborates on this, arguing that production of sophisticated components, and core R&D, are activities 'first and foremost, for either the multinational's home base, or nations with attributes (such as demand conditions) that make locating in them important to innovation. In addition, foreign subsidiaries do not necessarily breed managers with an orientation toward exports and international competition' (Porter, 1990, p. 679). Vernon himself, among others,[21] now disagrees with this view: 'explanations of the behaviour of TNCs which draw on the national origins of the enterprise as a major explanatory variable are rapidly losing their value, to be replaced by an increased emphasis on the characteristics of the product markets in which the enterprises participate' (Vernon, 1992). Dunning, whose work on MNCs has been seminal, takes a position somewhere between those of Porter and Vernon. He argues that an increasing proportion of economic activity is potentially footloose in its location, though the extent to which enterprises 'are able and willing to switch locations varies according to industry, firm and country-specific differences' (Dunning, 1992).

In a detailed case study of foreign owned firms in the UK machine tool industry, Young and Dunlop (1992) point out that 'most UK production of machining centres . . . is under licence from Japanese makers'. Young and Hood (1992), referring to the same study, conclude that UK competitiveness in this industry will depend on the extent of Japanese FDI and sourcing strategies – which in turn may depend on EU local content rules. What emerges is a picture of an industry in which the presence of foreign, and particularly Japanese, firms may have reduced – or been a result of a decline in – the competitiveness of the indigenous machine tool industry in the UK. As the industry has advanced technologically, so has it become, in the UK, more dependent on foreign owned firms.[22] Thus, whether as a causal or resultant factor, the high proportion of foreign owned firms in this high-technology industry in the UK is an expression of the relative weakness of the innovativeness of the indigenous industry. At least in this industry, location of ownership is important.

Walker (1993, pp. 167–8) generalises this finding by emphasising the importance of distinguishing between those competitive manufacturing industries in the UK in which the strengths are indigenous – chemicals and pharmaceuticals, aerospace, and food, drink and tobacco – and those in which they derive from foreign multinationals – motor vehicles and electronics. He goes further than Young and Hood by stating that Britain's entire industrial development in the 1990s (not just in the machine tool industry) will depend on the behaviour of foreign multinationals, and in particular on the decisions of Japanese companies.

As with foreign direct investment, so with foreign investment specifically in R&D in the UK, there is no consensus as to its effect on UK indigenous technological capabilities. Either way, it is a significant characteristic of the British system of innovation that the proportion of UK patents registered in the US accounted for by foreign owned firms in the UK is far above the European average, and that the proportion of large British firms' patents registered in the US accounted for by those firms' foreign subsidiaries is also above that average (Patel and Pavitt, 1991, table 3.6). These characteristics firmly underline the relatively international nature of the British NSI. Yet, at least in the high-technology sectors, Britain has very few 'giant' manufacturing companies. At the other end of the scale, while there is a profusion of dynamic small firms in the service sector, in manufacturing 'Britain is relatively poorly endowed with small firms' (Walker, 1993, p. 167).[23]

There are weaknesses in Britain's indigenous NSI. One must conclude that the possibility of regenerating British technological leadership is slight. Among the key weaknesses are those in the areas of technical education and training, and, more broadly, general attitudes to technical skills. As to what the impact of European integration will therefore be, positive results will be derived more from effective institutional developments than from the further extension of market mechanisms.

National systems of innovation in other European countries

Both France and the UK have strengths and weaknesses in their NSIs. In this section these will become clearer through comparisons with aspects of the NSIs of other European countries, in particular Germany and Italy.

Germany and the importance of the financial system

The control and financing of firms and, in particular, of investment in R&D and innovation, varies from country to country. Moreover, different systems of control and financing – or governance – may be associated with different rates and types of innovation. According to Ozaki:

> Management of the capitalistic firm is constrained by the propensity of the institutional investors or major individual capitalists to intervene in management decisions (they may, for example, opt for higher dividends and object to a proposed increase in R and D expenditures). The same management also faces another interventionist force, the union, which, concerned with job security of its members, may oppose management's attempt to introduce a new automation technology. (Ozaki, 1991, p. 58)

Ozaki's argument is that Japan has had innovative success because of a hybrid form of enterprise, the 'humanistic firm', in which these problems are obviated by the fact that management and unions both act in the long-term interests of the firm. While this may be part of the explanation, others (e.g. Christensen, 1992) emphasise the close relationships of Japanese firms to banks.

Germany's innovative success, it can be argued, has also been based, among other factors, on aspects of industrial relations and banking. In Germany, too, there has been a 'system of industrial relations that has limited trade union conflict within industries' and a 'banking system that enables the banks to support the restructuring of industries' (Keck, 1993).[24]

Christensen's (1992) analysis suggests that the role of finance is particularly important in Germany[25] with a tradition of strong banking influence in the process of industrialisation going back to the middle of the nineteenth century.

This influence on large firms has declined somewhat in recent years – firms like Siemens, for example, are now largely internally financed – but the banks (and, to some extent, government grants) remain important in the financing of small and medium enterprises. Moreover, the German financial system continues to have an indirect influence on large firms. In contrast to the financial systems in the UK and the US, for example, the institutional features of the German system make takeovers difficult. This lower frequency of takeovers means less disruption in the establishment of reputations and the building of relations – inter- and intra-firm – that arises from frequent changes in ownership.

A distinction can be drawn between credit-based and capital-market-based financial systems. In the first, firms' financing is based mainly on bank credit, and in the second, firms raise funds mainly through the stock market. It is inappropriate to identify the German (or Japanese) system as exclusively credit based, and the UK (or US) system as exclusively equity based. However, to the extent that the UK is more capital market based than Germany, the problem of 'diverse shareholders who take little interest in the development of the firm, except for the short term prices of their shares' (Christensen, 1992, p. 161), is more a British one than a German one. And to that extent, investment in R& D with returns expected over a long time horizon are more likely in Germany than the UK.

The picture is, however, rather more complicated than this suggests, because each of the two systems, credit based and capital market based, has advantages – the former in the financing of R&D within existing firms, and the latter in the one-off selection of projects, such as new firms based on single innovations. Furthermore, financial systems may emerge from, as well as influence, industrial development. The expertise that financial institutions have in relation to the business of their clients, and the relationships between credit institutions and the firms they finance, also influences the efficacy of credit-based systems. What is clear, at least, is that there is an interrelationship between the development of a country's financial system, and its industrial and technological change. Despite a great deal of internationalisation of financial markets and institutions, national financial systems – with all the historical, cultural, legal, linguistic and economic factors that go into differentiating them – continue to be of primary importance.[26]

German success relative to other European countries is thus based, in part, on its financial system. The technical education system is also usually mentioned as a basis of that success. Ironically, the German perspective on the German NSI emphasises its weaknesses relative to Japan rather than its strengths *vis-à-vis* its European partners: 'Japan has caught up with Germany or overtaken it on nearly all counts that make up for a strong national technological capability: business financed R&D as percentage of gross domestic product, patents held in the United States, scientists and engineers in nonacademic jobs per 10,000 labor force' (Keck, 1993, p. 146). With respect to some indicators of technological capability, Germany has outperformed even Japan, as can be seen from Table 7.1, Figure 7.1 and Figure 7.2. The Japanese system is also not without faults, and Odagiri and Goto (1993), for example, fear that the sharp diminution in the share of universities in basic research in Japan may not augur well for the future of the Japanese NSI. Germany's continuing success over a much longer period than Japan, notwithstanding the increasing challenges it faces in the context of its reunification, increasing European integration, and the intensification of technological competition from South-East Asia, leave room for confidence about the future of its NSI.

Italy and industrial districts

Thus far, attention here has been on national and to some extent sectoral factors in systems of innovation. There are also, however, in most EU countries, important subnational, regional systems of innovation. In Italy, for example, in addition to a NSI which is comparable (though inferior) to those of the UK, France and Germany, there is also a second, much more successful, system of innovation – a small firms network.

> These two systems are quite different in terms of capabilities, organisation, and performance. The small firms network is composed of a large population of small and medium size firms (in some cases located in industrial districts), which interact intensively at the local level . . . Firms in the network are engaged in rapid adoption of technology generated externally and in the adaptation and continuous improvement of this technology. (Malerba, 1993, p. 230)

Within the small firms network, Malerba identifies three types of firms: (1) those in industrial districts; (2) the equipment suppliers (some of which are also in industrial districts); and (3) non-industrial district firms in traditional sectors. These will now each be considered.

1. Industrial districts are defined as production systems characterised by a myriad of firms specialised in various stages of the production of a homogeneous product, often using flexible production technology and connected by extensive local interfirm linkages. While competing at some levels, at others the activities of these independent firms are strongly coordinated; information, including innovations, diffuses rapidly among them. They contribute to the production of the same good within the same geographical area (e.g. toys in Canneto sull'Oglio in Lombardy, ceramic tiles in Sassuolo). These geographically defined districts are said to form a 'social and economic whole' and have been at least in part responsible for the rejuvenation of the dormant economy of the 'Third Italy' (Best, 1990). The Emilia-Romagna region has been a particular focus of attention because of its ceramic tile, textiles and clothing, metalworking and machine making industrial districts, among others. As can be seen from the traditional nature of these products, the innovative nature of the

industrial districts is concentrated in their processes. There are other industrial agglomerations (or regional innovation systems) in which product innovations are more prevalent.

2. Metalworking and machine-making firms are examples of the large number of innovative, internationally competitive, small- and medium-sized equipment manufacturers which are common in a number of different regions in the Third Italy. Among these firms, those in the machine tool industry have been particularly successful. This is illustrated by the growth in the Italian share of machine tool production – which, in contrast to UK machine tool production, is accounted for almost exclusively by indigenous firms. In 1986 the Italian share of world machine tool production was 5.6 per cent; by 1990 it had grown to 8.5 per cent (*American Machinist*, various issues). The success of these firms derives partly from the high levels of skill among technicians and engineers – which transfers rapidly horizontally where the firms are part of an industrial district – and partly from the needs of sophisticated users in close vertical relationships with the suppliers. Major Italian firms like Fiat and Olivetti, and the flexibly specialised, small-firm districts (such as the textile machinery district in Biella), interact closely with machinery designers and manufacturers. This provides 'an innovative stimulus and a continuous feedback on the use of the machinery' (Malerba, 1993, p. 239).

3. Benetton has been cited as an example of an innovative firm in the traditional sector. But many of these firms are not particularly innovative. Those, like Benetton, that are, represent a new organisational model for the Third Italy regions in which they have emerged in recent years – including Emilia-Romagna and Toscana – especially in sectors such as clothing and textiles. This is the large vertically integrated firm, which has been more typical of other regions. Using advanced information and communication technologies to provide remote production control, linking sales with production management, this type of firm has also established 'tight relationships with fashion creation and international marketing' (Camagni, 1991, p. 156). Such firms use the most sophisticated telecommunications and/or production technologies to emulate some of the flexibility of the industrial districts.

Industrial districts are a very important part of the recent innovative success of small firms in Italy. Other examples of localised agglomerations of innovative firms in Europe that have been discussed, either as extant or potential, include those in Spain (Benton, 1992), Germany (Schmitz, 1992), and Denmark (Hansen, 1991; Kristensen, 1992). While successful innovative districts are internationally competitive, the local focus of the innovation process offsets the emergence of an integrated European system of innovation. In the next section aspects of this latter system will be considered.

A EUROPEAN SYSTEM OF INNOVATION?

Impediments to flows of information about innovations have been shown in this chapter to exist both within and between countries. The dual systems of innovation in Italy, and subnational regional systems of innovation elsewhere in Europe, reduce the flow of information about innovations within these countries. Military R&D and other institutional factors also impede diffusion to varying extents in each EU country. Between EU members such impediments exist to an even greater extent, despite the completion of the Single European Market (SEM). The role of the military in the innovation system can, as has been shown, limit spillover into commercial applications, but it has also limited international diffusion:

> Despite belonging to the same military alliance, countries lent a high degree of protection to their defence industries, thereby placing limits on the international division of labour, multinational investment and the diffusion of technology. Within countries, a high degree of tolerance was shown to monopolistic supply structures. (Walker, 1991, p. 367)

Nationally focused assistance for defence industries has continued despite the efforts within NATO of the Independent European Programme Group (IEPG), and largely failed exercises like the European Fighter Aircraft project. The military aspects of the NSI have thus enhanced national, and diminished international, aspects of systems of innovation in Europe. However, given the end of the Cold War and the collapse of the Soviet bloc, this particular obstacle to diffusion is declining. Also, according to Harbor (1990, p. 145), the European Commission 'cannot afford to cede national autonomy in defence industrial matters, for to do so would be to create a massive loophole through which governments and companies could circumvent EC legislation on the single market on the grounds of national security'. While such autonomy is not, in most respects, in the Commission's power to cede (and such loopholes are therefore likely to continue to exist), there are at the same time a number of other factors that are contributing to the generation of elements of a European system of innovation. Such factors include the development of institutions and programmes in the EU, and the improvements in information and communication technologies. In the context of defence matters, an important development is the increasing coordination of defence policy via the Western European Union and – since the Treaty on European Union entered into force – via the EU itself.

European integration and technology: the impact of European Union policy

The relationship between technology and integration can be examined in two separate ways: first, in terms of attempts within the EU to 'Europeanise' (or denationalise) efforts to influence firms to create, produce and introduce new technologies; second, and in the opposite direction, in terms of how new technologies have brought firms to focus on Europe (or even the world) as a terrain, both for production and distribution. The two directions of causality – from EU institutions to firms to technology, and from technology to firms to EU institutions – reinforce one another, but, for the sake of presentation, this section will examine the former and the next section will examine the latter.

During the 1970s and early 1980s, it began to be perceived that a technology gap existed, with Europe lagging behind the US (and Japan), particularly in the area of microelectronics.[27] There were a number of unsuccessful attempts, including Unidata, to generate research cooperation within Europe. There was also success, like the European Space Agency and the Ariane rocket, but, as suggested above, though these did include technological collaboration among firms and governments of different European countries, they were more or less dominated by France. Concorde, an Anglo-French technological success of the 1960s, was a commercial failure. More recently, Airbus has also been a technological success, and may become a commercial success. But if it does, it will do so on the basis of a great deal of support by a number of European governments, as well as by the EU.

Against the background of this mixed record, in the early 1980s EC Commissioner Davignon initiated discussions with the managing directors of the twelve leading electronics firms in Europe. Davignon's aim was to reduce the fragmentation arising from the support for national champions provided by individual member states. Out of these discussions emerged a collaborative R&D programme, the European Strategic Programme for Research in Information Technology (ESPRIT). Starting as a small pilot programme, ESPRIT grew into a significant institutional context for cooperation between the major European firms, involving Community expenditure of 750 million ECUs in 1984–8, and 1.6 billion ECUs in 1988–92. More important than either the expenditure or the projects generated was ESPRIT's symbolic value: first, ESPRIT was the first EC programme providing funds on the ('demand-led') basis of competitive bidding by groups of firms and researchers; second, subsequent programmes, such as RACE (Research in Advanced Communications for Europe) and BRITE (Basic Research in Industrial Technologies of Europe), were modelled on ESPRIT; third, it provided a context for cooperation and encouraged converging technological expectations; and fourth, it helped generate support among large firms – accepting that for success they had to be competitive beyond their national markets – for the completion of the SEM.[28]

The 1986 Single European Act formalised and intensified much of this collaborative R&D effort. In the words of Riccardo Petrella, head of the EC's FAST programme (Forecasting and Assessment in Science and Technology), 'For the first time since the creation of the EC, member countries have decided to adopt a common European policy for research and technological development' (Petrella, 1991, p. 10). In particular, under the Framework Programme, beginning in 1984 all EC R&D and Science and Technology (S&T) programmes were brought together, with a 1987–91 budget of 5.6 billion ECU. The Third Framework Programme had a similar budget for the years 1990–4, its main features responding to a 1989 review of the First Programme by, among other things, giving more attention to the creation or support of 'European centres of excellence'. The Fourth Framework Programme (1994–8) was allocated a budget by the December 1993 Brussels European Council of 'not less than 12 billion Ecu'. The guidelines of the Fourth Programme include, in addition to a number of specific technology-related focuses, greater coordination of the research being undertaken in the context of the national programmes of member countries. (See also Chapter 1 on the Fourth Framework Programme.)

Another programme under which funding is obtained for R&D collaboration among West European firms and institutions is the European Research Coordinating Agency (EUREKA). EUREKA, which includes countries outside the EU, does not fund research, but merely acts as a match-maker. The funding comes from the national governments and participating firms and institutions. There is some overlap between the EU programmes and EUREKA, but the former concentrate on precompetitive R&D and the latter on the competitive end of R&D.

Sharp (1991b) has commented in a largely positive and optimistic manner on the impact of integration on the technology and competitiveness of European industry.[29] Others, however, are more cautious. Petrella (1991, p. 13), for example, sees dangers in the fact that 'the process of globalisation of competition and technological strategies seems as yet to be happening faster than European economic integration'. There are, indeed, a number of grounds for moderating optimism about the impact of EU programmes and institutions. First, as Petrella (ibid, p. 15) has pointed out, most interfirm collaborative agreements have been between European firms on the one hand, and US or Japanese on the other.[30] Second, there are vastly greater levels of public expenditure on R&D within individual countries than there are in the Framework Programme and EUREKA combined. Third, there is little in the present EU technology policy that will offset the imbalance between the technological capacity of the European core and that of the periphery.[31] Fourth, EU member countries and regions continue to compete through various incentives for the mobile investment projects of US and Japanese firms. Finally, there is the unsolved problem of actual and potential national support for nationally based MNCs that continue to be seen as national champions.

Technology and European integration: the technological drive to internationalisation

The development of certain technologies has greatly facilitated the emergence of firms whose terrain of activity transcends national boundaries. The most important 'enabling technologies' are transportation and communications. In relation to transportation, jet aircraft have significantly reduced the time taken to move people and goods from one part of the world to another. In communications, the application of information technology, and the convergence between computer and communication technologies into information and communication technologies (ICT), have facilitated the transmission, virtually instantaneously, of spoken and written words and data, and of images. While these technologies by themselves have not made inevitable the emergence of MNCs, the growth in scale and number of these firms would certainly not have been possible without such technologies. Related to the ways in which enabling technologies have given rise to MNCs, particularly during the second half of this century, are the developments in production processes which have required large volumes of output – and hence large firms and large markets – for competitiveness, and the continued accumulation of technologies by firms in their attempts to remain competitive.

Among the practical results of these forces acting on the advanced technology firms in the member countries of the EU has been the support that many of these firms have offered for the removal of trading and other barriers. To some extent this support, as shown above, is attributable to the efforts of the Commission, and to the ESPRIT programme, which 'created an important constituency in big business, pressing for the completion of the internal market and the abolition of all remaining internal barriers to trade, such as divergent standards and regulations' (Sharp, 1990, p. 59). At least some of this constituency, irrespective of ESPRIT, would have been pressing for these ends because of technological and competitive imperatives. Indeed, some authors go so far as to suggest that firms' needs resulted in such programmes as ESPRIT: 'Market pressure and rising R&D cost were among the main factors [in the 1980s] underlining the willingness of both managers and politicians to engage in (international) inter-firm collaboration. Shared-cost R&D programmes like ESPRIT and EUREKA are a very clear expression of this phenomenon' (Roscam Abbing and Schakenraad, 1991, p. 27).

International, interfirm collaboration in Europe does not unequivocally enhance European integration, however. Thus alliances of various kinds were much more common, at least until the mid-1980s, between European firms on the one hand and non-European (and particularly US) firms on the other. On the basis of a study of the ICT industry in the second half of the 1980s, there were, according to Petrella (1991, table 2 and p. 17), some signs of change towards intra-European agreements, but it was not at all clear whether this would continue.

Hamill (1992, p. 137), apparently confirming this trend, writes of recent years having 'witnessed a wave of mergers, acquisitions and strategic alliances (MAAs) in Europe'. This includes a growth in intra-EU cross-border MAAs, but some of the most significant MAAs he identifies are, as in the early 1980s, between non-European firms (US and Japanese) and EU firms. He concludes that the rationalisation arising from intra-EU MAAs may have an adverse effect on employment and on concentration, and that there may be a loss of EU sovereignty arising from non-EU acquisitions of EU firms. The 'main beneficiaries of the Single European Market may not be European companies, consumers or workers, but rather non-EC firms which have consolidated their market positions in the EC through MAAs' (ibid., p. 158). This rather negative view is consonant with that of Kay (1990), who finds, among other things, that high-technology firms are particularly likely to collaborate with firms 'outside their natural market sphere'. On the basis of this and other similar findings, Kay concludes that, in the aftermath of the Single European Market, it could, ironically, 'be easier and cheaper to stimulate joint ventures between EC and non-EC firms than between EC firms' (ibid., p. 269). This may make an EU science and technology policy of encouraging intra-EU collaboration more difficult and expensive, notwithstanding the aims and objectives of the Fourth Framework Programme.

This doubt about the extent to which increasing European integration and technological development can interrelate with European firms to create a European system of innovation is strengthened by the organisation and behaviour of most of the large, research-based companies. While many MNCs with headquarters in EU member countries have supported increasing integration, there has not emerged a significant number of integrated European firms. The national base of advanced technology firms remains important. As Petrella (1991, p. 91) states, 'the country of origin remains the preponderant site of location of R&D units in Europe, USA and Japan'.

What the apparently contradictory evidence suggests is that while individual European firms may support and gain from EU S&T policies in particular, and from European integration in general, pressures arising from technological change, though they may contribute to MAAs, are – by themselves – unlikely to generate industrial integration in Europe. As a context within which R&D and innovation take place, the European system of innovation, for most research and for most firms, is far less significant than national – and in some cases subnational – systems of innovation.

A EUROPEAN INFRASTRUCTURE?

The key issue to be addressed in this part of the chapter is the relationship between infrastructure and European integration and its implications for the business environment. While infrastructure includes a range of mainly public utility services such as electricity and other energy distribution networks, water and sanitary services, transport and telecommunications, attention here will focus on the latter two. As in the discussion of technology, an underlying issue is the extent to which the infrastructural environment is, or is becoming, European.

Transport

Following the political and military struggles in Europe during the nineteenth and early twentieth centuries, it is not surprising that 'the layout of the railways and roads in the Community reflects national economic and in some cases strategic needs dating back a century or more' (Cole and Cole, 1993, p. 172). In some cases these needs included international access. Rail and road links between the Continental European countries have existed, though to a minor extent, since or soon after road and rail transport were first used. It has even been argued that because the railways in the nineteenth century were more efficient if they did not have to stop at frontiers, 'their own internal logic forced the countries of Europe to give up some of their own decision-making power in order to obtain things the railways required, such as a common gauge, timetable alignments, or through traffic agreements' (Pollard, 1981, p. 13). From this, and other examples of the development of technologies, Pollard shows that a degree of integration was imposed on the countries of Europe. However, the transport networks have been, and still are, far more orientated towards the movement of goods and people between the cities within European countries than between countries.

In relation to *freight* traffic in the EU, which has volumes of around 1000 billion tons per km, 30 per cent is between member countries (Commission, 1991, p. 72). This varies sharply depending on the means by which the freight is transported. Of the freight that is transported by water (sea, river, canal), over 70 per cent is between countries. By road, which is the most important mode of freight transport, only 12 per cent of the traffic is between countries. Rail accounts for less than 15 per cent of total freight, but 25 per cent of freight moved by rail is between countries. To summarise this information in a different form, about a third of all international freight transport within the EU is by sea, about 15 per cent by rail, and the rest mainly by road.

Another sharp difference within freight transport is with respect to the core and peripheral countries and regions in Europe. In fact, among the core countries – France, Germany, the Benelux countries and the UK – international traffic exceeds internal. The peripheral countries – Denmark, Ireland, Portugal and Greece – together account for less than 5 per cent of total EU, intercountry freight. The difference between inter-core-country traffic and intercountry traffic to or from a peripheral area is not surprising – whether in relation to freight or passenger traffic. It is a consequence, in part, of the smaller populations in outlying areas, though population is not the only determinant of transport use: the type of industry in a city, and whether it is a business centre or national capital – a core within a periphery – also influences the amount of traffic to that city.

Overall, the growth of freight traffic over the last ten years has been substantial. It has been dominated by the use of road for freight, such use more than doubling over the period. Intercountry freight has increased more rapidly than internal freight, and this is a trend that is expected to continue.

The picture in relation to *passenger* transport in the EU is similar, with an even greater concentration on road use. Over the last four decades, the passenger/kilometres of traffic carried by rail in the EU increased by less than half, while that on the roads increased several times. Of about 100 million cross-border journeys annually within the EU (and Austria and Switzerland), 55 per cent are by road (mostly in private cars), 30 per cent by air and 8 per cent by rail.

In the context of an awareness of the problems both of the national focus of transport systems, and the disadvantages of peripheral regions, the EEC Treaty expressed the intention of establishing 'a common transport policy to enable the free movement of people and goods over national boundaries'. Attempts to create the common transport policy have focused on three main approaches: harmonisation – for example in the setting of a maximum permitted weight for freight vehicles of 40 tonnes; deregulation – which has been only partially effective in relation to airlines, but has steadily liberalised the road freight market; and infrastructure investment – with the aim of providing EU monies for specific projects in order to increase cohesiveness within the Union. A key weakness in relation to infrastructure investment and the EU transport policy in general is that, despite the existence of integrated European transport plans, funds are allocated on the basis of competitive bidding between countries. It may be more logical for the infrastructural investment funds to be allocated directly to individual projects.

Plans for European road and rail networks

Plans for the internationalisation of the European road and rail infrastructure emanate almost exclusively from the EU, rather than from member countries. As stated by the Commission in 1991, there are a number of projects which are 'well advanced in the preparatory process at the Commission and some of them, especially in the field of inland transport, already form the subject of decisions by the appropriate Community bodies. Their common aim is to identify and overcome inadequacies in existing trans-European networks' (Commission, 1991, p. 84). In relation to road networks, among the projects which will receive EU financial support are a number of road links across the Pyrenees, and a road link to Ireland connecting Crewe and Holyhead in the UK.

A high-speed train network has also been the subject of EU attention:

Two major axes have been considered as priorities for Community financial intervention:

- in the North: Paris-London-Brussels-Amsterdam-Cologne, with connections to other Member States
- in the South: Seville-Madrid-Barcelona-Lyon-Turin-Milan-Venice, and then to Tarvisio and Trieste, and Oporto-Lisbon-Madrid. (Commission, 1991, p. 85)

A rather optimistic picture of the future of the international transport network in Europe emerges from an examination of EU sources.[32] Even at this early stage in the twenty-year high-speed rail network plan that was initiated in 1989, ominous national disparities have been noted: French high-speed trains cannot run on German tracks because the power supply is different; German trains are too heavy for French tracks; the high-speed Eurostar trains, successfully tested in France and Belgium, and intended for use in the Channel Tunnel, cannot run smoothly on British tracks. In other areas, such as sea and air transport, there is even less cooperation at the European level than in relation to road and rail. Cole and Cole (1993, p. 181) conclude that if 'the desultory progress on the transport infrastructure in the last 20 years is a guide, some drastic changes in priorities and funding are needed'.

There has been some Europeanisation of the transport network, particularly in relation to the core countries, and more is expected in the future. However, as with the technological environment of firms in Europe, the predominant focus of the transport environment remains the national economies of the member states. This has obvious implications for both the conduct and the costs of business.

Telecommunications

As in relation to transport, so for communications, Pollard (1981, p. 50) has argued that developments in the nineteenth century necessitated cooperation and even integration between countries. The international distribution of mail required agreement within the Universal Postal Union. An international convention (in 1863) was required in order to agree rules for the regulation of submarine cables. Marconi's patent for radio telegraphy led to other systems coming into use in other countries, which 'threatened the usefulness of the invention ... but at the Berlin conference the leading powers agreed to a Radiotelegraphic Union with an obligation to use all systems' (ibid.). There are modern equivalents of most of the above, and, in addition, new methods of communication require new agreements on standards. For example, a clearing system for international telephone charges required agreement among countries, under the auspices of the International Telephone and Telegraph Consultative Committee (CCITT) in Geneva.

However, 'the regulatory and administrative structures that have bounded the world of the ICTs [information and communication technologies] are being torn down and rebuilt in a different fashion' (Locksley, 1990b, p. 2). The changing ICTs, deregulation and privatisation, and increasing integration in Europe are all interacting to alter the face of the telecommunications infrastructure as a key aspect of the environment of business in Europe. The fundamental question for our purposes is whether this infrastructure is becoming more or less European.

The telecommunications infrastructure consists of the institutions and networks for voice telephony, text services, mobile communications, data and image communication, videotext and ISDN (Integrated Services Digital Network).[33] The institutions controlling and developing these networks are the mainly state-owned Public Telecommunications Operators (PTOs). In particular in relation to voice transmission, which accounts for 80 per cent of the total, the PTOs remain dominant. This part of the market is growing at around 5 per cent per annum, which is not as rapidly as other parts, some of which have reached rates of growth of 20 per cent per annum. In response to deregulation, new firms have entered the telecom service sector, but mainly in value added and other niche areas.

The manufacturing of telecommunications equipment is directly related to the infrastructure, but the equipment manufacturers and suppliers are, generally, MNCs. Until recently, national regulations ensured that the manufacturers from which the PTOs obtained their equipment were the 'national champions' where such existed, or multinationals that had local plants where there were no indigenous equipment manufacturers. The impetus towards the completion of the SEM has imposed on EU member countries the need to liberalise the procurement market, opening tendering for telecom equipment – among other things – to international competition. Together with the 'mutual recognition' rule for standards, which aims to ensure interconnectivity of equipment of different European equipment suppliers, liberalisation of procurement provides a regulatory framework for the most technologically advanced telecoms infrastructure uniformly throughout the EU.

The telecoms systems of the member countries of the EU are not starting, in the post–1992 period, from level pegging. In recognition of the continued existence of separate and divergent telecommunications networks in the EU, the Commission sees four options for progress:

1. Freezing the liberalisation process and maintaining the situation as it was at the end of 1992.
2. Regulating extensively on tariffs and investments, in order to remove the surcharge on intra-EU tariffs.
3. Liberalising all voice telephone services internationally (within and outside the EU) and domestically.
4. Opening competition on voice telephone services between member states.

Of these, the Commission favours the fourth option, because it would stimulate competition between existing telephone operators within the EU, and would encourage cooperative agreements between operators and other companies (Commission, 1992).

National and regional disparities in regard to telecommunications services are considerable. Peripheral regions, in the south of Europe in particular, suffer from the poor quality of even very basic telecommunication services. In 1989, Portugal had fewer than 20 lines per 100 inhabitants, compared with 56 for Denmark and 46 for France (Commission, 1991, pp. 93–4). Even more serious is the disparity in relation to future developments. The installation of the new universal ISDN networks will make possible the transmission of both voice and data on the same medium at greatly increased speeds. However, at least initially, these installations:

> will tend to follow established patterns. They will therefore be concentrated in the most developed and highly populated areas, so preventing many small and medium-sized companies in more remote regions, which do not have access to private networks or are deterred from using them by the cost, from being able to take advantage of them. (Commission, 1991, p. 93)

In a number of ways the EU is attempting to remove these disparities. First, telecommunications services are explicitly recognised as a priority for assistance through the Structural Funds. Second, STAR (Special Telecommunications Actions for Regions) provides some funds for investment in infrastructure. Third, TELEMATIQUE aims at strengthening the implementation of telematic services in less favoured regions. Fourth, PRISMA provides assistance for the use of advanced information technology services by small and medium enterprises. In addition, a number of other programmes and initiatives aimed at stimulating a pan-European telecommunications network have been set up within the EU framework. These include agreement on a European digital cellular radio standard, called GSM (Groupe Speciale Mobile) after the special group – the European PTOs and the European Commission – that established the standard. GSM is, according to Roobeek and Broeders (1993), a breakthrough for the mobile telephone market, enabling subscribers to use the same mobile telephone system right across Europe, and equipment suppliers to market the same mobile telephones to all the populations of the EU.

Increasing integration in the EU has had a significant impact on the telecommunications infrastructure. From the basis that the Commission has a political agenda to achieve political integration in Europe by increasing its own power, one writer goes so far as to argue that the 'Commission is purposefully eroding national sovereignty and using the ICTs as an instrument in its game plan' (Holmes, 1990). Whether this is true or not, there are – as with the new technology environment in general – a wide array of institutional and business interests seeking to increase integration of the telecommunications environment in Europe.

However, national differences, and the will to maintain them, remain. Telecommunications is a sector in which interventionism and national barriers to competition are particularly prevalent. Indeed, Cole and Cole (1993, p. 151) apparently contradict Roobeek and Broeders by asserting that 'the existence of at least three different and incompatible mobile communications systems within the EC means that it remains impossible for a British-system carphone to be used in France or for a mobile phone system originating in Denmark to be of any use in Italy'. Cole and Cole are referring to the situation as it is at present; Roobeek and Broeders' allusion to a breakthrough in this area of telecommunications is a reference to a new GSM standard which will make Europeanisation possible. The telecommunications environment of the firms using mobile phones remains national, but the regulatory environment of the firms manufacturing the equipment has become increasingly European. When these latter firms respond to the new standard, then the telecommunications environment of the user firms will also become European. At that point it is quite likely that the European standard will be identical to that in other parts of the world, and both environments will, in effect, have become global.

Given that telecommunications are increasingly global, and, given the possibility and increasing application of satellite communications, the remnant of national intervention in some aspects of this infrastructure is likely to be relatively insignificant. A distinctive European pattern is likely to prevail in only some elements of telecommunications services. Ironically in those parts of telecommunications where national intervention is likely to be least significant, the infrastructural environment of firms in Europe is likely to become more global than European.

CONCLUSION

In both the technological and infrastructural environments of business in Europe, the European dimension is significant. Firms in all sectors have been made increasingly aware of this dimension, partly through competitive pressures and partly through the changing regulatory environment imposed by the EU. However, what has been shown in this chapter is that the European dimension is of varying significance across sectors. This variation runs all the way from a relative predominance of subnational regional systems of innovation in the case of the technological environment for some small European firms, to the global domain of telecommunications in the infrastructural environment of the larger European firms.

Notes

1. The author wishes to thank Bernadette Andreosso for contributions to, and Jim Stewart for comments on, an earlier draft of this chapter.
2. Precisely what is meant by 'national system of innovation' will be discussed in the next section of the chapter.

3. One way of measuring output, or performance with respect to innovation, is to examine international trade in high-tech products. This is done in Chapter 2 of this book, and shows a generally high and worsening deficit in the EU's trade in high-tech products between 1982 and 1991. See also Figure 7.2.
4. Barnett (1986, pp. 204–5) points out a similar disparity just before World War II, when there were 39 000 students between the ages of 13 and 21 in full-time vocational education in England and Wales, and 164 000 in Germany.
5. This paragraph and much of the rest of this section are drawn from Chesnais, 1993.
6. In Germany, too, to a greater extent than the UK, there was growth in industrial research during the first half of the century (Mowery, 1990).
7. The engineering tradition was at the level of trained engineers; in general in France, even after World War II the 'level of industrialisation was quite low and the industrial relations – cultural, behavioural, institutional – were rather poor' (de Bandt 1987, p. 46).
8. For more on the role of the state in Europe in general and in France in particular, see Chapter 1.
9. De Bandt (1987, p. 50) writes of the absence of transparency in the decision-making process because it is 'internalised within the state apparatus'.
10. French shares in the Arianespace industrial consortium, held by CNES and the four main contractors, are still 48 per cent, having been reduced from 60 per cent. It should be noted that the French leadership in Europe, in relation to space research, was not least a result of the Gaullist search for a leadership role for France in Europe in general.
11. It is part of the chemicals, pharmaceutical and agrochemicals complex, which, Chesnais (1993, p. 220) suggests, is a partly separate innovation subsystem. It should be noted that while the state has had significant shares in the major French pharmaceutical companies, particularly since 1982, these firms have behaved by and large commercially.
12. It may well be that in the absence of state funding, and even in the absence of self-funded R&D, these firms are nevertheless innovative. There is, indeed, some evidence that the innovative activity of small firms is 'much greater . . . than that reflected in the formal R&D data' (Chesnais, 1993, p. 222).
13. It could be neither despite nor because of the role of the state from the mid-eighteenth century; the success of the British economy in the eighteenth and nineteenth centuries could be a result of – among other things – the role of the state during the mercantilist period up to the second half of the eighteenth century.
14. Losing its leadership means, as McCloskey (1990) points out, a relative decline, though some writers fail to emphasise the fact that it is relative. See for example, Porter (1990): 'Britain declined because of growing disadvantages in each part of the "diamond" '. The diamond is Porter's explanatory framework, consisting of firm strategy, structure and rivalry, related and supporting industries, factor conditions, and demand conditions.
15. See Walker (1993, pp. 158–9) for a brief elaboration of these three theories. Porter (1990, p. 506) in some ways combines each of them when he states that the most significant causes were 'weaknesses in human resources, low motivations, the lack of rivalry, and eroding demand conditions'. The main factor according to Chandler (1984) was the continuation of control by the owning families of the main corporations, long after control by salaried managers had become the norm in Germany and the US.

16. See, for example, Barnett (1986, chapter 11). The discussion on the British education and training systems that follows draws mainly on Walker (1993). See also Porter (1990, pp. 497–8).
17. This quote from Walker (1993) shows that he sees this characteristic of the French system as a strength. Chesnais (1993, p. 214) sees the same characteristic as a weakness of the French system.
18. Walker (1993), referencing Hobsbawm (1987), writes: 'resources became overextended as the Empire grew, middle class culture turned against industrial enterprise, and a rentier mentality took hold'. See also Lazonick (1990a, p. 90): 'The heads of the most successful firms, typically of middle-class origin, sought to have their sons educated at the elite public schools, and Oxford and Cambridge – institutions that remained firmly under the control of an aristocracy of landowners and financiers who had little use for industry and technology.'
19. The discussion that follows draws on Rothwell (1987), Porter (1990, pp. 504–6) and Walker (1993).
20. There is, however, an interesting contrast within this similarity. Chesnais (1993) identifies French success in aerospace as having derived, in part, from the need for international collaboration. The result, he writes, is that, in this area 'the French subsystem of innovation has *provided the overall structure and represented the backbone of Europe's involvement in space.*' On the other hand, Walker (1993), using similar evidence of need for international collaboration, concludes that it has led to a diminution in the 'autonomy of the British innovation system'.
21. See, for example, Robert Reich's argument (1992, p. 137) that 'the important question – from the standpoint of national wealth – is not which nation's citizens own what, but which nation's citizens learn how to do what'.
22. Jacobson and Andréosso argued in 1988 that the conclusion of agreements between British and Japanese firms in the UK machine tool industry, in order to give the British firms access to newer technologies, amounted, in some respects, 'to the "peripheralisation" of Europe. The high-skill, advanced-technology parts of the production process will end up being located outside Europe – in the US and Japan' (Jacobson and Andréosso, 1988). See also Andréosso and Jacobson (1991). For a detailed discussion of the relationships between multinational corporations and national systems of innovation see Chesnais (1992).
23. The argument that manufacturing is the source of innovation in industry and services is presented in Coriat and Petit (1991, pp. 30–2).
24. Keck considers the industrial relations and banking systems to be 'other factors', outside the 'national system for technical innovation'. According to Nelson's definition of NSI quoted above, they would fall within the 'national system of innovation'. Industrial relations in particular deserves more attention than is possible in this chapter. See Chapter 4 of this book; see also Lazonick (1990b).
25. There are, as is clear from the early part of this chapter, other important characteristics of Germany's NSI. Particularly significant is technical education. This is discussed by Keck (1993) in some detail.
26. In addition to Christensen (1992), on the relationship between financial systems and innovation see also Zysman (1990) and Dosi (1990). On the financial environment in general see Chapter 5 of this book.
27. This discussion draws heavily upon Sharp (1990, pp. 57–60). See also Sharp (1991b, pp. 60–7).
28. In addition to the manufacturers, research institutions and small and medium firms

have also gained from ESPRIT: 'The SMEs in particular are very positive about ESPRIT and the Commission now claim that 70 per cent of the ESPRIT budget goes to SMEs, a considerable turn-around from its early days' (Sharp, 1991b, p. 67).

29. This optimism is tempered only by doubts about the outcome of the dialectic between 'the pressures towards liberalisation and deregulation on the one hand and towards collaboration and concentration on the other' (Sharp, 1991b, p. 75).
30. More recent data may show a change in the late 1980s and early 1990s – see below; see also Chapter 2 of this book.
31. 'The gap ... between technology-rich and technology-poor countries in Europe is not likely to diminish as a result of *à la carte* programmes [like] EUREKA or technology specific programmes [like] ESPRIT' (Roscam Abbing and Schakenraad, 1991, p. 27).
32. There is, admittedly, also some warning of the potentially negative effects on peripheral regions. A Commission-funded study of the effects of the Channel Tunnel, for example, found that Ireland could become more peripheral (Commission, 1991, p. 82).
33. This section draws on Roobeek and Broeders (1993, especially p. 275).

Guide to Further Reading

The technological environment in Europe

The book edited by Nelson (1993), though its focus is not particularly European, provides in different chapters descriptions of the main features of the national systems of innovation of the main European countries. For comparative purposes there are also chapters on the American and Japanese, and a number of other smaller countries', NSIs. On the development of the institutional approaches to the technological environment of firms, the book edited by Lundvall (1992b) is important. For a specifically European focus, Freeman, Sharp and Walker (eds) (1991) is an excellent compilation. The regular publications of organisations like MERIT (Maastricht Economic Research Institute on Innovation and Technology) and SPRU (Science Policy Research Unit, at Sussex University) provide up to date information and analysis of developments in this area. Journals such as *Industrial and Corporate Change* and *Research Policy* are also useful for the more recent writings. Finally, the most important source for data is the OECD's publication *Basic Science and Technology Statistics*, though the section on R&D in the EU's *Europe in Figures* is also useful.

Infrastructure

For information on European infrastructure the main readings are those published by the EU. Both one-off reports and regular bulletins provide details of the Commission's attitudes to, and EU funding of, infrastructural improvements. The geography literature, such as the book by Cole and Cole (1993), provides general information and objective analysis of the situation and the potential for change. For more detail on specific infrastructures, specialist literature needs to be consulted; on telecommunications, for example, Locksley (1990a) is useful.

References

Chapter 1: The Political Environment

Cawson, A. *et al.* (1990) *Hostile Brothers: Competition and Closure in the European Electronics Industry* (Oxford: Clarendon Press).

Commission of the EC (1990a) *Industrial Policy in an Open and Competitive Environment: Guidelines for a Community Approach,* COM (90) 556 Final (Brussels). This Communication was subsequently incorporated in *Bulletin of the European Communities: European Industrial Policy for the 1990s,* Supplement 3/91 (Luxembourg).

Commission of the EC (1990b) *Enterprise Policy: A New Dimension for Small and Medium-sized Enterprises,* COM (90) 328 Final (Brussels).

Commission of the EC (1991) *The European Electronics and Information Technology Industry: State of Play, Issues at Stake, and Proposals for Action,* SEC (91) 565 (Brussels). This Commission Communication was subsequently published in *Bulletin of the European Communities,* Supplement 3/91. For the Council Resolution on the industry see Council of Ministers of the EC, *Press Release* 9298/91 (Presse 208) 18 November 1991 (Brussels).

Commission of the EC (1992a) *The European Aircraft Industry: First Assessment and Possible Community Actions,* COM (92) 164 Final (Brussels). For the Council Conclusions on the industry see Council of Ministers of the EC, *Press Release* 7275/92 (Presse 117) 17 June 1992 (Brussels).

Commission of the EC (1992b) *The Motor Vehicle Industry: Situation, Issues at Stake and Proposals for Action,* COM (92) 166 Final (Brussels). For the Council Resolution on the industry see Council of Ministers of the EC, *Press Release* 7275/92 (Presse 117) 17 June 1992 (Brussels).

Commission of the EC (1992c) *The European Telecommunications Equipment Industry: The State of Play, Issues at Stake and Proposals for Action,* SEC (92) 1049 Final (Brussels). For the Council Resolution on the industry see Council of Ministers of the EC, *Press Release* 10085/92 (Presse 213) 19 November 1992 (Brussels).

Council of Ministers of the EC (1993a) *Press Release* 7278/93 (Presse 102) 14 June 1993 (Brussels).

Council of Ministers of the EU (1993b) *Press Release* 9624/93 (Presse 180) 11 November 1993 (Brussels).

Duchene, F. and Shepherd, G. (eds) (1987) *Managing Industrial Change in Western Europe* (London: Frances Pinter).

Dunleavy, P. *et al.* (1993) *Developments in British Politics 4* (London: Macmillan).

Fennell, R. (1988) *The Common Agricultural Policy of the Community*, 2nd edn (London: Granada).

Grant, W. with Sargent, J. (1987) *Business and Politics in Britain* (London: Macmillan).

Grant, W. *et al.* (1988) *International Industry, National Governments and the European Community: A Comparative Study of the Chemical Industry in Britain and West Germany* (Oxford: Clarendon Press).

Grant, W., Martinelli, A. and Paterson, W. (1989) 'Large Firms as Political Actors: A Comparative Analysis of the Chemical Industry in Britain, Italy and West Germany', *West European Politics*, vol. 12, no. 2, pp. 72–90.

Greenwood, J. (1991) 'Organised Interests and the Internal Market', paper presented to the 1991 Annual Conference of the Political Studies Association (unpublished).

Greenwood, J., Grote, J. R. and Ronit, K. (1992) *Organised Interests and the European Community* (London: Sage).

Hall, P. A. *et al.* (1992) *Developments in French Politics* (London: Macmillan).

Harrop, J. (1992) *The Political Economy of Integration in the European Community* (Aldershot: Edward Elgar).

Hart, P. *et al.* (1993) *Shipping Policy in the European Community* (Aldershot: Avebury).

Hine, R. C. (1989) *The Political Economy of European Trade: An Introduction to the Trade Policies of the EEC* (Brighton: Wheatsheaf).

Horn, E. J. (1987) 'West Germany: A Market-led Process', in Duchene and Shepherd, *Managing Industrial Change in Western Europe*.

Maresceau, M. (ed.) (1993) *The European Community's Commercial Policy After 1992* (Dordrecht: Martinus Nijhoff).

Martinelli, A. (1991) *International Markets and Global Firms: A Comparative Study of Organised Business in the Chemical Industry* (London: Sage).

Mazey, S. and Richardson, J. (1993) *Lobbying in the European Community* (Oxford: Oxford University Press).

Moyer, H. W. and Josling, T. E. (1990) *Agricultural Policy Reform: Politics and Process in the EC and USA* (Hemel Hempstead: Harvester Wheatsheaf).

Nicoll, W. and Salmon, T. (1993) *Understanding the New European Community* (Hemel Hempstead: Harvester Wheatsheaf).

Nugent, N. (1994) *The Government and Politics of the European Union* (London: Macmillan).

Peterson, J. (1992) 'Technology Policy in Europe: Explaining the Framework Programme and Eureka in Theory and Practice', *Journal of Common Market Studies*, vol. XXIX, no. 3, March, pp. 269–90.

Peterson, J. (1993) 'Towards a Common European Industrial Policy? The Case of High Definition Television', *Government and Opposition*, vol. 28, no. 4, Autumn, pp. 496–511.

Sandholtz, W. (1992) 'ESPRIT and the Politics of International Collective Action', *Journal of Common Market Studies*, vol. XXI, no. 1, March, pp. 1–19.

Sharp, M. and Pavitt, K. (1993) 'Technology Policy in the 1990s: Old Trends and New Realities', *Journal of Common Market Studies*, vol. 31, no. 2, June, pp. 129–51.

Single European Act (1986) (Brussels: Council of the European Communities).

Smith, G. *et al.* (1992) *Developments in German Politics* (London: Macmillan).

Treaties establishing the European Communities (1978) (Luxembourg: Office of Official Publications of the European Communities).

Treaty on European Union, together with the complete text of the Treaty establishing the European Community (1992), in *Official Journal of the European Communities*, C244, 31 August.

Tsoukalis, L. (1993) *The New European Economy: The Politics and Economics of Integration* (Oxford: Oxford University Press).

Van Schenden, M. P. C. M. and Jackson, R. J. (1987) *The Politicisation of Business in Western Europe* (London: Croom Helm).

Wilks, S. and Wright, M. (1987) *Comparative Government-Industry Relations* (Oxford: Clarendon Press).

Wilson, G. K. (1990) *Business and Politics: A Comparative Introduction* (London: Macmillan).

Wright, M. (1988) 'Policy Community, Policy Network and Comparative Industrial Policies', *Political Studies*, vol. XXXVI, pp. 593–612.

Chapter 2: The Economic Environment

Albert, M. and Ball, R. J. (1983) *Towards European Economic Recovery in the 1980s*, European Parliament Working Document (Luxembourg: European Parliament).

Amin, A. and Dietrich, M. (1991) *Towards a New Europe? Structural Change in the European Economy* (Aldershot: Edward Elgar).

Baldwin, R. (1989) 'The Growth Effects of 1992', *Economic Policy*, vol. 9, October, pp. 247–81.

Bean, C. (1992) 'Economic and Monetary Union in Europe', *Journal of Economic Perspectives*, vol. 6, no, 4, pp. 31–52.

Blanchard, O. J. and Muet, P. A. (1993) 'Competitiveness Through Disinflation: An Assessment of the French Macroeconomic Strategy', *Economic Policy*, vol. 15, pp. 12–56.

Bliss, C. (1987) 'The New Trade Theory and Economic Policy', *Oxford Review of Economic Policy*, vol. 3, no. 1, pp. 20–36.

Britton, A. and Mayes, D. (1992) *Achieving Monetary Union in Europe* (London: Sage).

Buigues, P., Ilzkovitz, F. and Lebrun, J. F. (1990) 'The Impact of Internal Market by Industrial Sector: The Challenge for the Member States', *European Economy/Social Europe, Special Edition*, pp. 19–113.

Buiter, W., Corsetti, G. and Roubini, M. (1993) 'Excessive Deficits: Sense and Nonsense in the Treaty of Maastricht', *Economic Policy*, vol. 15, pp. 58–100.

Cantwell, J. (ed.) (1992) *Multinational Investment in Modern Europe* (Aldershot: Edward Elgar).

Caves, R. (1991) 'Corporate Mergers in International Economic Integration', in A. Giovanni and C. Mayer (eds), *European Financial Integration* (Cambridge: Cambridge University Press), pp. 136–71.

Cobham, D. (1991) 'European Monetary Integration: A Survey of Recent Literature', *Journal of Common Market Studies*, vol. 29, no. 4, pp. 363–83.

Commission of the EC (1989) 'Horizontal Mergers and Competition Policy in the European Community', *European Economy*, no. 40.

Commission of the EC (1990) 'One Market, One Money: An Evaluation of the Potential Benefits and Costs of Forming an Economic and Monetary Union', *European Economy*, no. 44, October, p. 1.

Commission of the EC (1993) 'The European Community as a world trade partner', *European Economy*, no. 52.

Cutler, T., Haslam, C., Williams, J. and Williams, K. (1989) *1992 – The Struggle for Europe: A Critical Evaluation of the European Community* (London: Berg).

De Grauwe, P. (1992) *The Economics of Monetary Integration* (Oxford: Oxford University Press).

Dunning, J. and Robson, P. (1988) *Multinationals and the European Community* (Oxford: Basil Blackwell).

Dyker, D. (ed.) (1992) *The European Economy* (London: Longman).

Eichengreen, B. (1993) 'European Monetary Union', *Journal of Economic Literature*, vol. 31, September, pp. 1321–57.

Eichengreen, B. and Wyplosz, C. (1993) 'Taming Speculation', *European Economic Perspectives*, no. 1, October, pp. 8–11.

Emerson, M. *et al.* (1988) 'The Economics of 1992', *European Economy*, no. 35, March (Brussels: European Commissions).

Ergas, H. (1984) 'Corporate Strategies in Transition', in A. Jacquemin (ed.), *European Industry: Public and Corporate Strategy* (Oxford: Clarendon Press).

Flamm, H. (1992) 'Product Markets and 1992: Full Integration, Large Gains?', *Journal of Economic Perspectives*, vol. 6, no. 4, pp. 7–30.

Geroski, P and Jacquemin A. (1985) 'Industrial Change, Barriers to Mobility, and European Industrial Policy', *Economic Policy*, vol. 1, November, pp. 169–218.

Geroski, P. (1988) 'Competition and Innovation', *European Commission, Economic Papers*, no. 71.

Geroski, P. (1989a) 'The Choice Between Diversity and Scale', in E. Davis (ed.), *1992: Myths and Realities* (London: Centre for Business Strategy, London Business School).

Geroski, P. (1989b) 'European Industrial Policy and Industrial Policy in Europe', *Oxford Review of Economic Policy*, vol. 5, no. 2, pp. 20–36.

Giavazzi, F. and Giovannini, A. (1986) 'The EMS and the Dollar', *Economic Policy*, vol. 2, April, pp. 456–85.

Grahl, J. and Teague, P. (1990) *1992 – The Big Market: The Future of the European Community* (London: Lawrence & Wishart).

Gros, D. and Thygesen, M. (1988) *The EMS: Achievements, Current Issues and Directions for the Future* (Brussels: Centre for European Policy Studies).

Gros, D. and Thygesen, M. (1992) *European Monetary Integration: From the European Monetary System to European Monetary Union* (London: Longman).

Grossman, G. M. (ed.) (1992) *Imperfect Competition and International Trade* (Cambridge: Mass.: MIT Press).

Hamill, J. (1992) 'Cross-border Mergers, Acquisitions and Alliances in Europe', in S. Young and J. Hamill (eds), *Europe and the Multinationals: Issue and Responses for the 1990s* (Aldershot: Edward Elgar).

Hamilton, C. and Winter, L. A. (1992) 'Opening up International Trade in Eastern Europe', *Economic Policy*, vol. 14, April, pp. 77–116.

Helm, D. and Smith, S. (1989) 'Economic Integration and the Role of the European Community', *Oxford Review of Economic Policy*, vol. 5, no. 2, pp. 1–19.

Helm, D. (1993) 'The European Internal Market: The Next Steps', *Oxford Review of Economic Policy*, vol. 9, no. 1, pp. 1–14.

Hine, R. C. (1992) 'Regionalism and Integration of the World Economy', introduction to special issue of *Journal of Common Market Studies*, vol. 30, no. 2.

Holmes, P. and Smith, A. (1992) 'The EC, the USA and Japan: The Trilateral Relationship in World Context?', in D. Dyker (ed.), *The European Economy* (London: Longman), pp. 185–210.

Jacquemin, A. (1993) 'The International Dimension of European Competition Policy', *Journal of Common Market Studies*, vol. 31, no. 1, pp. 91–101.

Jacquemin, A. and Sapir, A. (eds) (1989) *The European Internal Market; Trade and Competition* (Oxford: Oxford University Press).

Jacquemin, A. and Wright, D. (1993) 'Corporate Strategies and European Challenges post–1992', *Journal of Common Market Studies*, vol. 31, no. 4, pp. 525–37.

Kay, J. A. (1989) 'Myths and realities', in E. Davis (ed.), *1992: Myths and Realities* (London: Centre for Business Strategy, London Business School).

Kay, J. A. (1990) 'Identifying the Strategic Market', *Business Strategy Review*, Spring, pp. 2–24.

Kay, J. A. and Posner, M. V. (1989) 'Routes to Economic Integration: *1992* and the European Community', *National Institute Economic Review*, vol. 129, August, pp. 55–68.

Kay, N. (1991) 'Industrial Collaborative Activity and the Completion of the Internal Market', *Journal of Common Market Studies*, vol. 29, no. 4, pp. 347–62.

Kay, N. (1993) 'Mergers, Acquisitions and the Completion of the Internal Market', in K. S. Hughes (ed.), *European Competitiveness* (Cambridge: Cambridge University Press), pp. 161–80.

Kierzkowski, M. (1987) 'Recent Advances in International Trade Theory: A Selective Survey', *Oxford Review of Economic Policy*, vol. 3, no. 1, pp. 1–19.

Krugman, P. R. (1987a) (ed.) *Strategic Trade Policy and the New International Economics* (Cambridge, Mass.: MIT Press).

Krugman, P. (1987b) 'Is Free Trade Passè?', *Journal of Economic Perspectives*, vol. 1, no. 2, pp. 131–44.

Lawrence, R. Z. and Schultze, C. L. (1989) 'Overview', in R. Z. Lawrence and C. L. Schultze (eds), *Barriers to European Growth: A Transatlantic View* (Washington DC: Brookings Institution).

Markusen, J. and Melvin, J. (1988) *The Theory of International Trade* (New York: Harper & Row).

Mayes, D. (1990), 'The External Impact of Closer European Integration', *National Institute Economic Review*, November, pp. 73–85.

Mayes, D. (ed.) (1993) *The External Implications of European Integration* (London: Harvester-Wheatsheaf).

McGee, J. and S. Segal-Horn (1992) 'Will There Be a European Food Processing Industry?', in S. Young and J. Hamill (eds), *Europe and the Multinationals: Issues and Responses for the 1990s* (Aldershot: Edward Elgar).

Molle, W. (1990) *The Economics of European Integration: Theory, Practice, Policy* (Aldershot: Dartmouth Publishing Co.).

Neven, D., Nuttall, R. and Seabright, P. (1993) *Merger in Daylight: The Economics and Politics of European Merger Control* (London: Centre for Economic Policy Research).

O'Donnell, R. (1991) 'Identifying the Issues', in R. O'Donnell (ed.) *Economic and Monetary Union* (Dublin: Institute of European Affairs).

Padoa-Schioppa, F. (1987) *Efficiency, Stability and Equity: A Strategy for the Evolution of the Economic System of the European Community* (Oxford: Oxford University Press).

Pelkmans, J. (1982) 'The Assignment of Public Functions in Economic Integration', *Journal of Common Market Studies*, vol. 21, nos. 1 and 2, September-December.

Pelkmans, J. (1984) *Market Integration in the European Economy* (The Hague: Martinus Nijhoff).

Pelkmans, J. and Robson, P. (1987) 'The Aspirations of the White Paper', *Journal of Common Market Studies*, vol 25, no. 3, pp. 181–92.

Perez, C. (1983) 'Structural Change and Assimilation of New Technologies in the Economic and Social System', *Futures*, no. 15, pp. 357–75.

Porter, M. (1990) *The Competitive Advantage of Nations* (London: Macmillan).

Robson, P. (1987) *The Economics of International Integration*, 3rd edn (London: George Allen & Unwin).

Robson, P. and Wooton, I. (1993) 'The Transnational Enterprise and Regional Economic Integration', *Journal of Common Market Studies*, vol. 31, no. 1, pp. 71–90.

Sandholtz, W. (1993) 'Choosing Union: Monetary Politics and Maastricht', *International Organisation*, vol. 47, no. 1, Winter, pp. 1–39.

Sharp, M. (1990) 'Technology and the Dynamics of Integration', in W. Wallace (ed.), *The Dynamics of European Integration* (London: Frances Pinter), pp. 50–67.

Sharp, M. (1992) 'Changing Industrial Structures in Western Europe' in D. Dyker (ed.), *The European Economy* (London: Longman), pp. 233–53.

Streeton, P. (1992) 'Interdependence and Integration of the World Economy: The Rule of States and Firms', *Transnational Corporations*, vol. 1, no. 3, pp. 125–36.

Swann, D. (1992) *The Economics of the Common Market*, 7th edn (London: Penguin).

Thygesen, N. (1993) 'Towards Monetary Union in Europe – Reforms of the EMS in the Perspective of Monetary Union', *Journal of Common Market Studies*, vol. 31, no. 4, pp. 447–72.

Tsoukalis, L. (1993) *The New European Economy: The Politics and Economics of Integration*, 2nd edn (Oxford: Oxford University Press).

Venables, A. (1985) 'Discussion of Geroski and Jacquemin', *Economic Policy*, vol. 1, November, pp. 212–14.

Wijkman, P. M. (1990) 'Patterns of Production and Trade', in W. Wallace, *The Dynamics of European Integration* (London: Frances Pinter), pp. 89–105.

Yannopoulos, G. N. (1990) 'Foreign Direct Investment and European Integration: The Evidence from the Formative Years of the Community', *Journal of Common Market Studies*, vol. 29, no. 3.

Young, S. and Hamill, J. (eds), (1992) *Europe and the Multinations: Issues and Responses for the 1990s* (Aldershot: Edward Elgar).

Chapter 3: The Legal Environment

Bellamy, C. D. and Child, G. D. (1987) *Common Market Law of Competition* (London: Sweet & Maxwell).

Cremades, B. (1992) *Business Law in Spain* (London: Butterworth).

Gleichmann, K. (1991) *Perspectives on European Community Law* (London: European Edition).

Guery, G. (1991) *Droit des affaires* (Paris: Dunod).

Kent, P. (1992) *European Community Law* (London: M & E Handbooks).

Klunzinger, E. (1993) *Grundzuge des Handelsrechts* (Munich: Verlag Vahlen).

Lasok, D. (1986) *The Professions and Services in the EEC* (Deventer: Kluwer).

Lasok, D. (1989) *The Customs Law of the EEC*, 2nd edn (Deventer: Kluwer).

Mathysen, P. S. R. F. (1990) *A Guide to European Community Law*, 5th edn (London: Sweet & Maxwell).

Schmithoff, C. M. and Sarre, D. A. G. (1988) *Charlesworth's Mercantile Law* (London: Stevens).
Studio, Maisto and Miscali (1992) *Business Law Guide to Italy* (Wiesbaden: CCH Europe).
Weatherill, S. (1992) *Cases and Materials on EEC Law* (London: Blackstone Press).
Wyatt, D. and Dashwood, A. (1993) *European Community Law* (London: Sweet and Maxwell).

Chapter 4: Labour Markets and Industrial Relations

Auer, P. (1992) 'Continued Training for the Employed: A Europe of Diversity', in CEDEFOP, *Vocational Training 1*.
Baglioni, G. (1990) 'Industrial Relations in Europe in the 1980s', in G. Baglioni and C. Crouch (eds), *European Industrial Relations: The Challenge of Flexibility* (London: Sage).
Baglioni, G. and Crouch, C. (1990) *European Industrial Relations: The Challenge of Flexibility* (London: Sage).
Barnouin, B. (1986) *The European Labour Movement and European Integration* (London: Frances Pinter).
Commission of the EC (1989) *Summary Report on the Comparative Study of Rules Governing Working Conditions in the Member States* COM (89) 360 Final (Brussels).
Commission of the EC (1991) *Employment in Europe* (Luxembourg).
Commission of the EC (1992) *Employment in Europe* (Luxembourg).
Commission of the EC (1993) *Employment in Europe* (Luxembourg).
Crouch, C. (1993) *Industrial Relations and European State Traditions* (Oxford: Clarendon Press).
Cutler, T., Haslam, C., Williams, J. and Williams, K. (1989) *1992 – The Struggle for Europe: A Critical Evaluation of the European Community* (New York: Berg).
Derenbach, R. (1990) *Human Capital and Related Infrastructure Endowments: Investment Requirements in Problem Regions, Summary and Main Report* (Bonn), December.
Eberlie, R. F. (1990) 'The New Health and Safety Legislation of the European Community', *Industrial Relations Review*, vol. 207.
EIRR (1991) 'The EWC's Directive and Previous Participation Initiatives', *European Industrial Relations Review*, vol. 207.
Emerson, M. (1988a) 'Regulation or Deregulation of the Labour Market: Policy Regimes for the Recruitment and Dismissal of Employees in the Industrialised Countries', *European Economic Review*, vol. 32, pp. 775–817.
Emerson, M. (1988b) *What Model for Europe?* (Cambridge, Mass.: MIT Press).
Ferner, A. and Hyman, R. (eds) (1992) *Industrial Relations in the New Europe* (Oxford: Blackwell).
Gold, M. (ed.) (1993) *The Social Dimension: Employment Policy in the European Community* (London: Macmillan).
Grahl, J. and Teague, P. (1989) 'Labour Market Flexibility in West Germany, Britain and France', *West European Politics*, vol. 12, no. 2, Spring, pp. 91–111.
Hellier, J. and Redor, D. (1991) *Le travail en Europe aujourd'hui et demain* (Paris: Masson).
Hyman, R. (1991) 'European Unions: Towards 2000', *Work, Employment and Society*, vol. 4.
Kay, J. and Posner, M. (1989) 'Routes to Economic Integration: 1992 in the European Market', *National Institute Economic Review*, August, pp. 55–68.

Lane, C. (1989) *Management and Labour in Europe: The Industrial Enterprise in Germany, Britain and France* (Aldershot: Edward Elgar).

Lindley, R. (1991) 'Interactions in the Markets for Education, Training and Labour: A European Perspective on Intermediate Skills', in P. Ryan (ed.) *International Comparisons of Vocational Education and Training for Intermediate Skills* (London: Falmer).

OECD (1990) *Labour Market Policies for the 1990s* (Paris:).

OECD (1991) *Employment Outlook*, July.

OECD (1992) *Employment Outlook*, July.

OECD (1993) *Employment Outlook*, July.

Ramsay, H. (1990) '1992 – The Year of the Multinational? Corporate Behaviour, Industrial Restructuring and Labour in the Single Market', *Warwick Papers in Industrial Relations*, vol. 35.

Rhodes, M. (1991) 'The Social Dimension of the Single European Market', *European Journal of Political Research*, vol. 19, pp. 245–80.

Rhodes, M. (1992a) 'The Future of the Social Dimension: Labour Market Regulation in post–1992 Europe', *Journal of Common Market Studies*, vol. 30, no. 1, pp. 27–35.

Rhodes, M. (1992b) *Human Capital Investment, Employment and the Regional Problem: The Scope and Limits of European Community Intervention*, EPRU Working Papers, Department of Government, University of Manchester.

Steinle, W. (1988) 'Labour Markets and Social Policies', in W. Molle and R. Cappellin (eds), *Regional Impact of Community Policies in Europe* (Aldershot: Avebury).

Streeck, W. and Schmitter, P. (1991) 'From National Corporatism to Transnational Pluralism', *Politics and Society*, vol. 2, pp. 133–64.

Teague, P. (1989a) 'Constitution or Regime: The Social Dimension to the 1992 Project', *British Journal of Industrial Relations*, November, pp. 310–29.

Teague, P. (1989b) 'European Community Labour Market Harmonisation', *Journal of Public Policy*, vol. 1, pp. 1–33.

Teague, P. (1989c) *The European Community: The Social Dimension* (London: Kogan Page).

Teague, P. and Grahl, J. (1992) *Industrial Relations and European Integration* (London: Lawrence & Wishart).

Vandamme, F. (1990) 'The Reform of the EEC Structural Funds: Hopes and Limitations', *International Labour Review*, vol. 6, pp. 715–32.

Vaughan-Whitehead, D. (1990) 'Wage Bargaining in Europe', in Commission of the European Communities, *Social Europe*, vol. 2.

Chapter 5: The Financial Environment

Alexander, D. (1993) 'A European True and Fair View', *European Accounting Review*, vol. 2, pp. 59–80.

Balling, M. (1993), *Financial Management in the New Europe* (Oxford: Basil Blackwell).

Bank of England (1993a) 'Cross Border Alliances in Banking and Financial Services in the Single Market', *Bank of England Quarterly Bulletin*, vol. 33, pp. 372–8.

Bank of England (1993b) 'Financial Market Developments', *Bank of England Quarterly Bulletin*, vol. 33, pp. 469–77.

Bisignano, J. (1992) 'Banking in the European Economic Community: Structure, Competition and Public Policy', in G. G. Kaufman (ed.), *Banking Structures in Major Countries* (Dordrecht: Kluwer).

Cecchini, P. (1988) *The European Challenge 1992: The Benefits of a Single Market* (Aldershot: Wildwood House).

Cerny, P. (ed.) (1993) *Finance and World Politics* (Aldershot: Edward Elgar).

Commission of the EC (1992) *Commission Guide to VAT in 1993* (London: unpublished background report).

Commission of the EC (1993a) *Accounting Standards Setting in the EC Member States* (Luxembourg: Office for Official Publications of the European Communities).

Commission of the EC (1993b) *XXVI General Report on the Activities of the European Communities 1992* (Luxembourg: Office for Official Publications of the European Communities).

Dermine, J. (ed.) (1993) *European Banking in the 1990s*, 2nd edn (Oxford: Basil Blackwell).

Devereux, M. and Pearson, M. (1989) *Corporate Tax Harmonisation and Economic Efficiency* (London: Institute for Fiscal Studies).

Economist (1989a) *European Financial Centres, No. 1 France* (London: Economist Publications).

Economist (1989b) *European Financial Centres, No. 3 Spain* (London: Economist Publications).

Emerson, M. *et al.* (1988) *The Economics of 1992* (Oxford: Oxford University Press).

European Bank for Reconstruction and Development (EBRD) (1993) *Annual Report 1992* (London: EBRD).

Financial Times (September 1993) *Venture and Development Capital, Financial Times Survey* (London: Financial Times).

Financial Times (25 November 1993) *Germany, Financial Times Survey* (London: Financial Times).

Gammie, M. (1992) *The Rudig Committee Report: An Initial Response* (London: Institute for Fiscal Studies).

Gardener, E. P. M. and Molyneux, P. (1990), *Changes in Western European Banking* (London: Unwin Hyman).

Hegarty, J. (1993) 'Accounting Integration in Europe – Still on Track?', *Journal of Accountancy*, vol. 175, pp. 92–5.

Henderson, R. (1993) *European Finance* (London: McGraw Hill).

IASC, (1991) *International Accounting Standards 1991/2* (London: International Accounting Standards Committee).

International Monetary Fund (IMF) (1993) *International Capital Markets. Part I Exchange Rate Management and International Capital Flows* (Washington, DC: IMF).

Jacquemin, A. and Wright, D. (1993) *The European Challenges post–1992* (Aldershot: Edward Elgar).

Jeffcote, B. (1993) *The Developing European Corporate Tax System* (Basingstoke: Macmillan).

Kaufman, G. G. (ed.) (1992) *Banking Structures in Major Countries* (Dordrecht: Kluwer).

Keohane, R. O. and Hoffman, S. (eds) (1991) *The New European Community* (Boulder, Col.: Westview Press).

Lawrence, M. (1993) published comments from the IASC's 20th Anniversary Conference 'International Capital Markets and the Harmonisation of Accounting Standards', *IASC Insight*, September (London: IASC).

Mullineux, A. (ed.) (1992) *European Banking* (Oxford: Basil Blackwell).

Nobes, C. (1990) *Accounting Harmonisation in Europe: Towards 1992* (London: Financial Times Publication).

O'Brien, R. (1992) *Global Financial Integration: The End of Geography* (London: Frances Pinter/RIIA).

Official Journal of the European Communities. C19 (25 January 1993) (Luxembourg: Office for Official Publications of the European Communities).

Ohmae, K. (1990) *The Borderless World* (London: Fontana).

Robinson, A. (1993) *Benefits and Uncertainties of the EMU Process for SME's*, unpublished manuscript.

Ruding, O. (1992) *Ruding Report (Committee on the taxation of enterprises within the EC)* (Luxembourg: Office for Official Publications of the European Communities).

Rudolph, B. (1993) 'Capital Requirements for German Banks and the European Community Proposals on Banking Supervision', in J. Dermine (ed.), *European Banking in the 1990s*, 2nd edn (Oxford: Blackwell).

Smith, R. C. and Walter, I. (1990) *Global Financial Services* (New York: Harper Business).

Sandholtz, W. and Zysman, J. (1989) 'Restructuring the European Bargain', *World Politics*, vol. XLII, pp. 95–128.

Schuetze, W. P. (1992) 'An International Accounting Esperante', *IASC Insight*, December (London: IASC).

Servais, D. (1988) *The Single Financial Market* (Luxembourg: Office for Official Publications of the EC).

Steinherr, A. (ed.) (1992) *The New European Financial Market Place* (London: Longman).

Van Hulle, K. (1993) 'Harmonization of Accounting Standards in the EC. Is it the beginning or the end?', *European Accounting Review*, vol. 2, pp. 387–96.

Vipond, P. (1991) 'Financial Services and the Internal Market', in L. Hurwitz and C. Lequesne (eds), *The State of the European Community* (Harlow: Longman).

Walton, P. (1993) 'Introduction. The True and Fair View in British Accounting', *European Accounting Review*, vol. 2, pp. 49–58.

Zysman, J. (1983) *Governments, Markets and Growth* (Oxford: Martin Robertson).

Chapter 6: The Marketing Environment

Abravanel, R. and Ernst, D. (1992) 'Alliance and Acquisition Strategies for European National Champions', *McKinsey Quarterly* vol. 2, pp. 44–62.

Aron, D. (1990) 'Where are the Americans?', *Industry Week*, no. 239, 19 February, pp. 67–9.

Baden-Fuller, C. W. F. and Stopford, J. (1991) 'Globalisation Frustrated: The Case of White Goods', *Strategic Management Journal*, vol. 12, pp. 493–507.

Bartlett, C. A. and Goshal, S. (1989) *Managing Across Borders: The Transnational Solution* (Boston, Mass.: Harvard Business School Press).

Bennett, T. and Hakkio, C. S. (1989) 'Europe 1992: Implications for US firms', *Economic Review*, April, pp. 3–17.

Berger, M. (1990) 'The Paranoia Gripping Japanese Business', *International Management*, April, pp. 24–7.

Berney, K. (1990) 'Europe's Merger Mania', *International Management*, February, pp. 4–5.

Bertrand, K. (1989) 'Scrambling for 1992', *Business Marketing*, pp. 74, 49–59.

Calingaert, M. (1989) 'What Europe 1992 Means for US Business', *Business Economics*, October, pp. 30–6.

Daser, S. and Hylton, D. P. (1991) 'European Community Single Market of 1992: European Executives Discuss Trends for Global Marketing', *International Marketing Review*, vol. 8, no. 5, pp. 44–8.

Department of Trade and Industry (DTI) (1992) *The Single Market* 2nd edn (London: HMSO).

Echikson, W. (1993) 'Learning How to Sell in Europe', *Fortune*, vol. 128, no. 6, 20 September, pp. 44–5.

Euromonitor (1992) 'The European Compendium of Marketing Information'.

Euromonitor (1992) *European Marketing Data & Statistics* (London).

Eurostat (1992) *Europe in Figures*, 3rd edn (Luxembourg: Office for Official Publications of the European Communities).

Fahy, J. (1992) 'Competition in the New Europe: Perspectives from the Structural Analysis of Industries', *Association for Global Business*, Annual Proceedings, pp. 236–44.

Friberg, E. G. (1989) '1992: Moves Europeans are Making', *Harvard Business Review*, vol. 67, May-June, pp. 85–9.

Gilbert, Y. and Strebel, P. (1988) 'Developing Competitive Advantage', in J. B. Quinn, H. Mintzberg and R. M. James *The Strategy Process* (Englewood Cliffs, N.J.: Prentice Hall).

Guido, G. (1992) 'What US Marketers Should Consider in Planning a Pan-European Approach', *Journal of Consumer Marketing*, vol. 9, no. 2, pp. 29–33.

Harvard Business School (1991) *Citibank (A): European Strategy*, 9–392–021, (Boston, Mass.: Harvard Business School).

Haufbauer, G. C. (1990) 'Europe 1992: Opportunities and Challenges', *Brookings Review*, vol. 8, pp. 13–22.

Hexter, D. R. (1989) 'Europe 1992: How Will It Affect International Competition?', *Financial Executive*, September-October, pp. 20–4.

Higgins, J. M. and Santalainen, T. (1989) 'Strategies for Europe 1992', *Business Horizons*, vol. 32, July-August, pp. 54–8.

IMD (1993) *The World Paint Industry, 1992* (Lausanne: IMD).

JETRO (1992) *Handy Facts on EC-Japan Economic Relations* (Tokyo: JETRO).

Kashani, K. (1992) *Managing Global Marketing* (Boston, Mass.: PWS Kent).

Kotler, P. (1991) *Marketing Management: Analysis, Planning, Implementation and Control* (Englewood Cliffs, N.J.: Prentice Hall).

Lambkin, M. (1993) *The Irish Consumer Market* (Dublin: The Marketing Society).

Levitt, T. (1983) 'The Globalisation of Markets', *Harvard Business Review*, vol. 61, May-June, pp. 92–102.

Loomis, C. J. (1989) 'Stars of the Service 500', *Fortune*, no. 119, 5 June, pp. 83–6.

Mitchell, D. (1989) '1992: Implications for Management', *Long Range Planning* vol. 22, pp. 32–40.

Murray, J. A. and O'Driscoll, A. (1993) *Managing Marketing* (Dublin: Gill & Macmillan).

Porter, M. E. (1980) *Competitive Strategy* (New York: Free Press).

Quelch, J. A., Buzzell, R. D. and Salama, E. R. (1990) *The Marketing Challenge of 1992* (Reading, Mass.: Addison Wesley).

Reichel, J. (1984) 'How can Marketing be Successfully Standardised for the European Market?', *European Journal of Marketing*, vol. 23, no. 7, pp. 60–7.

Reisenbeck, H. and Freeling, A. (1991) 'How Global Are Global Brands?', *McKinsey Quarterly*, vol. 4, pp. 3–18.

Simpson, C. D. and Korbel, J. J. (1990) 'Getting US Companies Ready for 1992', *Journal of Accountancy*, vol. 169, pp. 60–76.

Sorenson, R. Z. and Weichmann, U. E. (1975) 'How Multinationals View Marketing Mix Standardisation', *Harvard Business Review*, vol. 53, May–June, pp. 38–56.

Thompson, I. (1990) 'Internal Market Developments, September–November 1990', *European Access*, vol. 6, pp. 15–17.

Vandemerwe, S. and L'Huillier, M. A. (1989) 'Euro Consumers in 1992', *Business Horizons*, vol. 32, no. 1, pp. 34–40.

Van der Hoop, H. (1989) 'Europhobia or Europhoria', *Distribution*, October, pp. 38–46.

Wall Street Journal (1989) *'Sticky Solutions'*, 22 September, p. 8.

Weihrich, H. (1990) 'Europe 1992: What the Future May Hold', *Academy of Management Executive*, vol. 4, no. 2, pp. 7–18.

Whitelock, J. M. (1987) 'Global Marketing and the Case for International Product Standardisation', *European Journal of Marketing*, vol. 23, no. 7, pp. 60–7.

World Bank (1987–88) *Population Report* (New York: World Bank).

Chapter 7: The Technological and Infrastructural Environment

Amin, A. and Dietrich, M. (eds) (1991) *Towards a New Europe? Structural Changes in the European Economy* (Aldershot: Edward Elgar).

Andréosso, B. and Jacobson, D. (1991) 'Le Double Processus d'Intégration Spatiale et Industrielle à la Lumière du Cas Irlandais', *Revue du Marché Commun*, no. 350, September, pp. 648–58.

Bandt, J. de (1987) 'French Industrial Policies: Successes and Failures', in Beije *et al.*, *A Competitive Future for Europe*.

Barnett, C. (1986) *The Audit of War* (London: Macmillan).

Beije, P. R. *et al.* (eds) (1987) *A Competitive Future for Europe? Towards a New European Industrial Policy* (New York: Croom Helm).

Benton, L. (1992) 'The Emergence of Industrial Districts in Spain: Industrial Restructuring and Diverging Regional Responses', in Pyke and Sengenberger, *Industrial Districts and Local Economic Regeneration*.

Best, M. (1990) *The New Competition: Institutions of Industrial Restructuring* (Cambridge: Polity Press).

Camagni, R. P. (1991) 'Regional Deindustrialization and Revitalization Processes in Italy', in Lloyd Rodwin and Hidehiko Sazanami (eds) *Industrial Change and Regional Economic Transformation: The Experience of Western Europe* (London: HarperCollins).

Cantwell, J. (1989) *Technological Innovation and Multinational Corporations* (Oxford: Basil Blackwell).

Commission of the EC (1991) *Europe 2000: Outlook for the Development of the Community's Territory* (Brussels).

Commission of the EC (1992) *Background Report 1992 Review of Telecommunications Sector*, ISEC/B4/93 (Brussels).

Chandler, A. D. Jr (1984) 'The Emergence of Managerial Capitalism', *Business History Review*, vol. 58, Winter.

Chesnais, F. (1992) 'National Systems of Innovation, Foreign Direct Investment and the Operations of Multinational Enterprises', in Lundvall (1992b) *National Systems of Innovation*.

Chesnais, F. (1993) 'The French National System of Innovation', in Nelson, *National Innnovation Systems*.

Christensen, J. L. (1992) 'The Role of Finance in National Systems of Innovation', in Lundvall (1992b) *National Systems of Innovation*.

Cole, J. and Cole, F. (1993) *The Geography of the European Community* (London and New York: Routledge).

Coriat, B. and Petit, P. (1991) 'Deindustrialization and Tertiarization: Towards a New Economic Regime?' in Amin and Dietrich, *Towards a New Europe?*

Dosi, G. (1990) 'Finance, Innovation and Industrial Change', *Journal of Economic Behavior and Organization*, vol. 13, no. 3, pp. 299–313.

Dosi, G. *et al.* (eds) (1988) *Technical Change and Economic Theory* (London: Frances Pinter).

Dunning, J. H. (1992) 'The Global Economy, Domestic, Governance Strategies and Transnational Corporations: Interactions and Policy Implications', *Transnational Corporations*, vol. 1, no. 3, pp. 7–45.

Dunning, J. H. and Cantwell, J. (1991) 'MNEs, Technology, and the Competitiveness of European Industries', in G. R. Faulhaber and G. Tamburini (eds), *European Economic Integration, The Role of Technology* (Dordrecht: Kluwer).

Freeman, C. (1988) 'Japan: A New National System of Innovation?', in Dosi *et al.*, *Technical Change and Economic Theory.*

Freeman, C., Sharp, M. and Walker, W. (eds) (1991) *Technology and the Future of Europe: Global Competition and the Environment in the 1990s* (London and New York: Frances Pinter).

Hamill, J. (1992) 'Cross-border Mergers, Acquisitions and Alliances in Europe', in Young and Hamill, *Europe and the Multinationals.*

Hansen, N. (1991) 'Factories in Danish Fields: How High-wage, Flexible Production has Succeeded in Peripheral Jutland', *International Regional Science Review*, vol. 14, no. 2, pp. 109–32.

Harbor, B. (1990) 'Defence Electronics Before and After 1992', in Locksley (1990a), *The Single European Market.*

Heertje, A. and Perlman, M. (eds) (1990) *Evolving Technology and Market Structure: Studies in Schumpeterian Economics* (Ann Arbor: University of Michigan Press).

Hobsbawm, E. J. (1987) *The Age of Empire 1875–1914* (London: Weidenfeld & Nicolson).

Holmes, P. (1990) 'Telecommunications in the Great Game of Integration', in Locksley (1990a), *The Single European Market.*

Jacobson, D. and Andréosso, B. (1988) 'Investment and Industrial Integration in Western Europe', *Administration*, vol. 36, no. 2, pp. 165–85.

Kay, N. (1990) 'The Single European Market: Industrial Collaboration and the Single European Market', in Locksley (1990a), *The Single European Market.*

Keck, O. (1993) 'The National System for Technical Innovation in Germany', in Nelson, *National Innovation Systems.*

Kristensen, P. H. (1992) 'Industrial Districts in West Jutland, Denmark', in Pyke and Sengenberger, *Industrial Districts and Local Economic Regeneration.*

Lazonick, W. (1990a) 'Organizational Integration in Three Industrial Revolutions', in Heertje and Perlman, *Evolving Technology and Market Structure.*

Lazonick, W. (1990b) *Value Creation on the Shop Floor: Organization and Technology in Capitalist Development* (Cambridge, Mass.: Harvard University Press).

Locksley, G. (ed.) (1990a) *The Single European Market and the Information and Communication Technologies* (London and New York: Belhaven Press).

Locksley, G. (1990b) 'European Integration and the Information and Communications

Technologies: The Double Transformation', in Locksley (1990a), *The Single European Market*.

Lundvall, B.-Å. (1992a) 'Introduction', in Lundvall (1992b), *National Systems of Innovation*.

Lundvall, B.-Å. (ed.) (1992b) *National Systems of Innovation: Towards a Theory of Innovation and Interactive Learning* (London: Frances Pinter).

Malerba, F. (1993) 'The National System of Innovation: Italy', in Nelson, *National Innovation Systems*.

McCloskey, D. N. (1990) *If You're So Smart* (Chicago: University of Chicago Press).

Mowery, D. C. (1990) 'The Development of Industrial Research in US Manufacturing', *American Economic Review*, vol. 80, no. 2, pp. 345–54.

Nelson, R. R. (1992) 'National Innovation Systems: A Retrospective on a Study', *Industrial and Corporate Change*, vol. 1, no. 2, pp. 347–73.

Nelson, R. R. (ed.) (1993) *National Innovation Systems: A Comparative Analysis* (Oxford: Oxford University Press).

Niosi, J., Bellon, B., Saviotti, P. and Crow, M. (1992) 'Les systèmes nationaux d'innovation: à la recherche d'un concept utilisable', *Revue d'Economie Francaise*, vol. VII, no. 1, Winter, pp. 215–50.

Odagiri, H. and Goto, A. (1993) 'The Japanese System of Innovation: Past, Present and Future', in Nelson, *National Innovation Systems*.

OECD (1988) *New Technologies in the 1990s: A Socio-economic Strategy* (Paris: OECD).

OECD (1993) *Basic Science and Technology Statistics* (Paris: OECD).

Ozaki, R. (1991) *Human Capitalism: The Japanese Enterprise System as World Model*, (Tokyo: Kodansha International).

Patel, P. and Pavitt, K. (1991) 'Europe's Technological Performance', in Freeman, Sharp and Walker, *Technology and the Future of Europe*.

Petrella, R. (1991) *Four Analyses of Globalisation of Technology and Economy*, FAST (Brussels: Commission of the EC).

Pollard, S. (1981) *The Integration of the European Economy Since 1815* (London: George Allen & Unwin).

Porter, M. E. (1990) *The Competitive Advantage of Nations* (London: Macmillan).

Pyke, F. and Sengenberger, W. (eds) (1992) *Industrial Districts and Local Economic Regeneration* (Geneva: International Institute for Labour Studies).

Roobeek, A. and Broeders, J. (1993) 'Telecommunications: Global Restructuring at Full Speed', in H. W. de Jong (ed.), *The Structure of European Industry* (Dordrecht: Kluwer).

Roscam Abbing, M. and Schakenraad, J. (1991) *Intended and Unintended Effects of Participation in ESPRIT and EUREKA for Small Countries Industrial Policies* (Maastricht: Maastricht Economic Research Institute on Innovation and Technology (MERIT)).

Rothwell, R. (1987) 'Technology Policy in Britain', in Beije *et al.*, *A Competitive Future for Europe?*

Schmitz, H. (1992) 'Industrial Districts: Model and Reality in Baden-Württemberg, Germany', in Pyke and Sengenberger, *Industrial Districts and Local Economic Regenerations*.

Sharp, M. (1990) 'Technology and Dynamics of Integration', in William Walker (ed.), *The Dynamics of European Integration* (London: Frances Pinter (for RIIA)).

Sharp, M. L. (1991a) 'Pharmaceuticals and Biotechnology: Perspectives for the European Industry', in Freeman, Sharp and Walker, *Technology and the Future of Europe*.

Sharp, M. L. (1991b) 'The Single Market and European Technology Policies', in Freeman, Sharp and Walker, *Technology and the Future of Europe*.

Vernon, R. (1966) 'International Investment and International Trade in the Product Cycle', *Quarterly Journal of Economics*, vol. 80, May, pp. 190–207.

Vernon, R. (1992) 'Transnational Corporations: Where Are They Coming From, Where Are They Headed?' *Transnational Corporations*, vol. 1, no. 2, August, pp. 7–36.

Walker, W. (1991) 'Defence', in Freeman, Sharp and Walker, *Technology and the Future*.

Walker, W. (1993) 'National Innovation Systems: Britain', in Nelson, *National Innovation Systems*.

Young, S. and Dunlop, S. (1992) 'Competitive Dynamics in the World Machine Tool Industry: Battleground UK', in Young and Hamill, *Europe and the Multinationals*.

Young, S. and Hamill, J. (eds) (1992) *Europe and the Multinationals: Issues and Responses for the 1990s* (Aldershot: Edward Elgar).

Young, S. and Hood, N. (1992) 'Transnational Corporations and Policy Dilemmas: The Problems of the Machine-Tool Industry in the United Kingdom', *Transnational Corporations*, vol. 1, no. 3, December.

Zysman, J. (1990) *Trade, Technology and National Competition*, Paper for OECD conference, Paris, June.

Index